THE
BAPTIZING
OF AMERICA

THE RELIGIOUS RIGHT'S PLANS FOR
THE REST OF US

RABBI JAMES RUDIN

THUNDER'S MOUTH PRESS
NEW YORK

THE BAPTIZING OF AMERICA
The Religious Right's Plans for the Rest of Us

Published by
Thunder's Mouth Press
An imprint of Avalon Publishing Group Inc.
245 West 17th Street, 11th Floor
New York, NY 10011

AVALON
publishing group incorporated

First printing January 2006

Library of Congress Cataloging-in-Publication Data is available.

ISBN: 1-56025-797-0
ISBN 13: 978-1-56025-797-4

9 8 7 6 5 4 3 2 1

Book design by Maria E. Torres
Printed in the United States of America
Distributed by Publishers Group West

For Marcia—With All My Love

She never doubted

She constantly believed

She always knew

That it could be done

CONTENTS

ACKNOWLEDGMENTS

Although this book is the work of a single author, it could not have been written without the inspiration, guidance, support, and cooperation of many people and institutions.

I am grateful to the Sanibel Island Library, Florida Public Library, and the New York Society Library in Manhattan for providing me with quiet writing areas and excellent research facilities. The libraries' staff members were always helpful.

Merle Price was the creative matchmaker who introduced me to Richard Curtis, my gifted literary agent, who then teamed me up with a superb editor, John Oakes of Avalon/Thunder's Mouth Press. And years ago it was Regina Ryan who started me on the long path that ultimately led to this volume.

Gerald and Deborah Strober, talented authors and lifelong friends, always encouraged me to write this book and they provided welcome encouragement and sound advice.

I have been the beneficiary of many impressive teachers, but three of them were symbolically always looking over my shoulder as I wrote this book. Reinhold Niebuhr, whose writings shaped much of my thinking about the relationship between religion and state, and between Christianity and Judaism; Harry Orlinsky, my rabbinical school professor and one of the twentieth century's greatest bible scholars; and Albert Vorspan, my mentor in American Jewish religious social action and the quest for prophetic justice.

Three remarkable Christian leaders—James Dunn, William Harter, and Marvin Wilson—have been my cherished personal friends for over thirty years. James, a Southern Baptist, has courageously maintained an unwavering commitment to the principle of church-state separation. Bill, an extraordinary Presbyterian pastor and scholar, is one of America's greatest Christian advocates for Israeli security and survival. Marvin, an outstanding evangelical intellectual, has devoted his life to teaching college students the enormous debt Christians and Christianity owe to Jews and Judaism. All three have taught me so much as have all my Christian and Jewish colleagues.

I am especially grateful to the American Jewish Committee, both its members and professional staff. Since 1968, the AJC has enabled me to work in the incredibly difficult, but always exciting vineyard of interreligious relations. It is a matchless gift and remarkable challenge I never take for granted. Since 1991 the Religion News Service has distributed my weekly newspaper column, and I thank the RNS staff and management for that unique opportunity.

I have learned a great deal from the leaders of Saint Leo University and the Center for Catholic–Jewish Studies that the University co sponsors with the American Jewish Committee. However, the views and opinions expressed in this book are my own, and do not necessarily reflect those of the AJC, RNS, SLU, or the CCJS.

Finally, the best for last. I have been blessed with the humbling experience of living with three generations of extraordinary women who are my best critics and teachers.

My wife Marcia, an amazing writer of dramas and screenplays and a former university professor of comparative religion, provided the unceasing inspiration for me to write this book. She, more than I, always believed in the project, and it was her constant love and the delicious brown-bag lunches I ate at the Sanibel and New York City libraries that sustained me.

Our daughters, Eve and Jennifer, provide daily joy and love. It is their generation of young Americans that will eventually determine the outcome of the struggle described in these pages.

However, I think I really wrote this book for Emma Mollie, our granddaughter. She was born in the first year of the twenty-first century, and I desperately want her America to maintain and preserve the historic values and principles that are currently under attack. This book is my gift to her.

CHAPTER I

TERMINOLOGY

A specter is haunting America, and it is not socialism and certainly not communism. It is the specter of Americans kneeling in submission to a particular interpretation of a religion that has become an ideology, an all-encompassing way of life. It is the specter of our nation ruled by the extreme Christian right, who would make the United States a "Christian nation" where their version of God's law supersedes all human law—including the Constitution.

That, more than any other force in the world today, is the immediate and profound threat to our republic.

In March 2005, I witnessed a physical manifestation of this specter hovering over American soil. While visiting friends in Boca Raton, Florida, my wife and I were stunned to see a skywriter flying just above us, spelling out this message: JESUS LOVES US JESUS IS THE U.S.

Although I had never seen such a message written in the sky, our friends told us this kind of thing happens quite often.

But I did not need a skywriter zooming over southern Florida to tell me that the campaign to baptize America is well under way. A committed group of Christian conservative leaders and their followers is intent on imposing their values, beliefs, and practices upon the entire American society.

Many of my colleagues and friends, both Christian and Jewish, think I am an alarmist by overstating the problem we face as a nation.

Others think I am too simplistic in my ominous analysis of the current scene and am overlooking the many historic safeguards from American history that will prevent such a catastrophe. They argue the United States is a huge country with a population nearing 300 million people. In addition, every religion known to the human family is represented in the U.S., and although about 82 percent of all Americans identify themselves as Christian, there is a large, vibrant Jewish community that in 2004 proudly celebrated its 350th anniversary in North America.

There is also a growing Islamic community, and many Hindus, Buddhists, Sikhs, Confucianists, Ba'hais, Native American spiritual groups, New Age devotees, and millions of self-defined atheists and agnostics. In addition, most Christians in the United States—Protestants, Roman Catholics, and Eastern Orthodox—either actively or passively oppose the effort to legally convert the United States into a Christian nation.

It is argued that the principle of church-state separation

has been an extraordinary feature of the United States since its creation in the late eighteenth century. Finally, many political and religious leaders reassure me that the American people's good sense and balance will always prevail and block any attempt to baptize the entire nation.

But I am not reassured that the Cross will not ultimately dominate and control the Eagle.

I am convinced that despite the large U.S. population, the religious diversity, and the Constitutional and judicial guarantees of church-state separation, the campaign to permanently transform America into a faith-based nation where one particular form of Christianity is legally dominant over all other religious communities constitutes a clear and present danger.

However, in the current complex interplay of politics and piety within contemporary America, and especially when encountering the campaign to impose Christian conservative values on the total society, it is necessary to define the involved groups and movements with precision. This is especially true regarding the various Christian denominations, church bodies, faith communities, organizations, institutions, and personalities that are currently active in the public square.

Sadly, terms that were once clearly defined are being tossed about like verbal Frisbees, and an American public already bitterly divided and confused over the appropriate role of religion in society has become even more polarized. Once-meaningful terms are currently employed to describe realities and situations far different from their original meanings. Clarity is required when confronting the forces and individuals that are leading the campaign to baptize the United States.

For example, the leaders of the current effort to change America into a Christian theocracy are often called "fundamentalists." But the term is a misnomer.

American Protestant leaders first coined the term *fundamentalism* in the early decades of the twentieth century. It was an attempt to lock in and protect core evangelical beliefs in the face of the perceived threats posed by modern culture and, especially, liberal Christian theology. Its adherents also saw fundamentalism as a necessary spiritual response to the extraordinary social upheavals created by the Industrial Revolution and the ghastly tragedy of the First World War, history's first total armed conflict.

The public articulation of the fundamentals of Christian faith was intended as a defensive measure to insulate and protect believers from the negative onslaught of critical biblical scholarship, the compelling claims of physical science (particularly evolution), and the other powerful forces of modernity deemed alien to fundamental Christian faith.

But, in fact, there are followers of every religious tradition who are fundamentalists. Most members of religious communities or spiritual fellowships hold fundamental beliefs about a Divinity; about specific texts, lands, cities, and sites considered sacred; and about charismatic teachers, revered teachings, liturgies, holidays, and rituals. All these are fundamentals of faith.

Even if we apply *fundamentalists* solely to today's Christians who seek to impose their religious beliefs and practices upon the entire American society, the term remains inadequate and incomplete. After all, many people are authentic Christian fundamentalists, but they do not participate in any movement, however broadly defined, to change the basic political, cultural, or religious structure of the United States.

Plus, there's the fact that today, the term *fundamentalists* is no longer limited to theologically conservative Christian Protestants. It is currently being used to describe Muslims, Jews, Hindus, Buddhists, and others throughout the world who affirm their own forms of spiritual certainty that are far different from the original American Protestant definition.

Another widely used term, *religious extremism*, lacks precision and is not an adequate description of the current campaign to dominate America. In today's parlance, *religious extremism* is generally associated with the physical violence and deadly terrorism carried out in the name of a particular religion. Most often, *religious extremism* is a description of anti-American, anti-Christian, and anti-Jewish Muslims who use the religion of Islam to spiritually validate their deadly political agenda.

Another convenient catchall term is *evangelicals*. In another chapter, I describe the salient characteristics of evangelical Christians, who number more than 55 million people within the United States. And indeed, evangelicals do constitute the largest group of Christians who are actively involved in politics and piety, and they lead the current effort to baptize America.

But not all evangelicals seek to permanently alter the historic communal fabric of American life. Such evangelicals may, in fact, be devout Christians, but they do not want to shatter or even weaken the long-held American principle of church-state separation, nor do they desire the legal establishment of any religion, even their own, in today's America. Like *fundamentalists*, the term *evangelicals* must be discarded as an overgeneralization.

A more accurate term is *Christian conservatives*. This describes Americans who ardently support conservative domestic and international policies for the United States. They buttress their political positions with a staunchly conservative Christian faith that provides theological justification for their views on a myriad of issues including human sexuality, abortion, capital punishment, private ownership of guns, gender roles in society, homosexuality, marriage, public education, home schooling, bioethics, faith-based religious charities that receive public funds, and the legitimacy of preemptive wars initiated by the U.S.

Sometimes the sequence is reversed: That is, a person starting with the holding of conservative political positions may then be attracted to the teachings of traditional Christianity. It is a case where theology and politics feed off one another, creating a potent combination.

President Richard Nixon's White House special counsel, Charles Colson, who served prison time for his criminal activities during the Watergate scandal in the 1970s, became a "born-again" evangelical Christian. Since his release from prison, Colson has been active in both conservative political and religious movements.

A number of other political leaders and entertainment-industry celebrities have publicly abandoned previously held secular beliefs and adopted a born-again Christian religious identity to accompany a preexisting conservative political agenda. When such a high-profile conversion takes place, the newcomer to Christianity is welcomed as a prodigal son or daughter who has, at last, "come home." One evangelical pastor explained it to me this way: "It's another notch on Jesus' conversion belt."

Christian conservatives is a better description than the other terms because it can include not only evangelical Protestants, but also Roman Catholics, Eastern Orthodox Christians, and members of progressive mainline Protestant churches not generally considered conservative or evangelical, as the words are currently understood.

In some cases, the words are reversed and the term *conservative Christians* appears in public discourse and the media. This is a less satisfying term than *Christian conservatives*, because there are many Christians who espouse a theologically conservative belief in the efficacy of prayer, the inerrancy of the bible, the centrality of Jesus in their lives, the importance of attending worship services and other practices related to their faith. But many of these self-styled conservative Christians do not subscribe to the aggressive campaign now under way to transform America into a theocracy, a country where one particular religious tradition dominates all others, and where leaders of that religion control either *de facto* or *de jure* the significant areas of American life.

The single word *extremism* is yet another term used to describe the Christian campaign to "restore a morally lost America" to its alleged former pristine spiritual moorings. But *extremism* by itself lacks both the context and the content required to convey what is actually taking place in the U.S. Like *fundamentalism*, the word *extremism* can mean contradictory things. Is it extremism when the United States strongly supports democratic institutions and rejects despotic regimes throughout the world? Is it extremism for Americans to support a Western-based declaration of human rights that is intended for all peoples on the globe? Is it extremism to assert there is only one God in the universe, to the exclusion of any other deity? Is it extremism to believe there is a code of explicit ethical behavior stemming from a single Divine Presence that is operative and binding for the entire human family?

The term *extremism* gained negative rhetorical immortality in 1964 when U.S. Senator Barry Goldwater of Arizona accepted the Republican party's nomination for the presidency in San Francisco by declaring: "I would remind you that extremism in the defense of liberty is no vice. And let me remind you also that moderation in the pursuit of justice is no virtue."

The delegates at the GOP convention wildly applauded those two sentences, but Goldwater was sharply criticized by his political opponents, including some Republicans, and by much of the media for his "reckless" remarks. Historians believe his intemperate words on extremism helped ensure Goldwater's overwhelming electoral defeat in 1964.

Because the negative fallout to his speech was so great, the Arizona senator unwittingly relegated *extremism* to the dustbin of American public discourse. No U.S. political or religious leader wants to be tarred with the extremist label.

But *extremism* was rediscovered decades after the Goldwater debacle, and it has become a handy term for defining lethal Islamic terrorists. Thus, the term *extremism*, with its problematic past and present usage, is limited and will not suffice in any serious exploration of the contemporary American domestic religious and political scene.

Clearly, different terms are needed to adequately capture the destructive power and dangerous goals of the campaign to create a Christian theocracy in the U.S. In this book, I will use the term *Christocrats* to describe both the leaders and their followers who are committed to converting America into a *Christocracy*. I will also employ *Christian conservatives* to denote those individuals who are sympathetic to the Christocratic goal but are not actively involved in the campaign to baptize America.

Interestingly, the word *Christocrat* is not new in American history. It was probably first used by Dr. Benjamin Rush (1745–1813), a prominent Philadelphia physician and one of the fifty-six signators of the Declaration of Independence. Rush was a close friend and strong supporter of Thomas Jefferson. As a faithful Christian, Rush used the term in a positive way declaring: "I have been alternately called an Aristocrat and a Democrat. I am neither. I am a Christocrat."

Rush believed religion was an important component of the American people. He supported the new Constitution, but he always expressed regret that the foundational document of the United States contained no specific mention of God. Rush was a champion of Article Six of the Constitution that forbids any religious test for elective office. Even though he was a believing Christian, Rush said there were ethical people who did not share his faith in the divinity of Jesus. He believed that candidates for public office must be judged on their merits, not their religions.

Rush opposed slavery and supported the principle of church-state separation for the newly created republic, as well as backing equal public educational opportunities for men and women.

Despite Rush's initial positive use of *Christocrat*, it has in recent years been used as a pejorative term to describe Christian zealots who are actively working to change America into a legally mandated faith-based nation, and that is how I will use Rush's unique eighteenth-century term in this book.

A Christocrat believes the American republic was once the "shining city on the hill" that has, in recent decades, lost its moral, political, cultural, and religious moorings and foundations. A Christocrat believes that a radical transformation in all areas of American national life is imperative if the United States is to fulfill its Christian "manifest destiny" and if it is to be "saved" from the relentless "secularization" of the general society.

A Christocrat distrusts the people and leaders of urban America and is threatened by demographic diversity, opting instead for the perceived spiritual and physical safety and purity of America's exploding exurban areas and traditional rural space where the residents are mainly white. A Christocrat believes that a commitment to Jesus as one's personal savior is absolutely necessary, but is not sufficient, in today's world. National, not merely individual, repentance and acceptance of Jesus as the ultimate ruler of a Christian America is imperative if the United States is to survive.

A historic act of national atonement will be the precursor to the imposition of Christocratic control over every meaningful aspect of American life.

Christocrats believe that such control is divinely ordained and biblically inspired. America requires a system of moral safeguards that will move the nation from its decadent, wanton, secular humanist ways.

A Christocrat is willing to sacrifice historic American freedoms and rights for a greater good: God's plan for the United States, as revealed to Christocratic leaders who alone have the spiritual and political credentials to define what is "Good and Godly for America." For Christocrats, the sovereignty of God and Jesus transcends national sovereignty and even the supremacy of the Constitution in the United States. People who do not share this view will be verbally tarred with two epithets: the dissenters are anti-faith and anti-Christian.

Christocrats believe it may even be necessary to destroy democracy in order to save the American people from the perils of secular humanists, economic globalization, and United Nations control of American society. Nothing less than a total change within the American nation will suffice.

Christocrats are most likely evangelical Protestants, but they can be conservative Roman Catholics, members of a mainline Protestant church, or Eastern Orthodox Christians. Most of today's Christocrats are white, but an increasing number of blacks and Hispanics also merit that term of identification. The ultimate goal of all Christocrats is the establishment of a permanent American Christocracy.

The effort to baptize our nation is intensifying, despite the fact the United States is increasingly multireligious, multicultural, and multiethnic in its rapidly growing population. This is a demographic fact that most Christocrats abhor.

A Christocratic republic would be far different than anything ever seen before in the history of the United States. Every meaningful aspect of life would be controlled and monitored by Christocratic leaders who would act as the nation's religious, political, and cultural guardians. In such an America, Republicans would become the Christocratic party that would permanently rule the country.

The Reverend Rod Parsley, a forty-eight-year-old evangelical minister, is a self-described Christocrat. A dropout from a bible college, Parsley is the leader of the World Harvest Church, a megacongregation in Columbus, Ohio. He directs a $40 million ministry that reaches fourteen hundred television stations and cable channels.

Parsley is also a political conservative who has traveled across the United States on a "Silent No More" tour, announcing his plans to be an active player on the state and national political stage.

Parsley, who has amassed great personal wealth as a result of his Christian church work, strongly affirms the position that many Christian clergy have been intimidated by the secular society and have permitted their churches to become merely social clubs.

In a 2005 Religion News Service interview, Parsley used warlike images to describe his efforts to stir Christian conservatives to action in the battle to save America. He is a foe of abortion, but supports the death penalty, calling it a necessary means "to avenge the blood of the innocent."

Parsley says he has cured cancer with prayers, but he has been unsuccessful in ridding his son of Asperger's syndrome, a form of autism. He has a license to carry a concealed weapon and is an avid hunter.

Parsley sees himself as a Christian warrior moving against "the very hordes of hell in our society . . . terrible as an army with banners." He plans a Christian-voter registration drive in Ohio that he calls an "Ohio for Jesus" effort. His candidates of choice are invariably political conservatives.

Critics contend that Parsley has crossed the line of church-state separation by endorsing specific candidates for public office. However, Parsley counters by declaring that the issue is not separation, but "the suppression of the church by the state." Those are the usual code words meaning that Christian conservatives do not yet have unlimited legal power to publicly proselytize anyone, anywhere, anytime, and anyplace in the United States.

Despite his claim of political neutrality, Parsley consistently supports conservative Republicans. He denies being a Republican or a Democrat. Instead, he calls himself a "Christocrat," the same term used by Rush; but Parsley's meaning and context are entirely different from the one used by Jefferson's political ally and personal friend.

Parsley was dissatisfied by the Supreme Court's 2005 Ten Commandments rulings in Kentucky and Texas, and his remarks hit several of the Christocratic hot buttons—criticism of liberals and secularism, and the centrality of the Ten Commandments, i.e., the bible, in the founding of America as a Christian nation.

> The first leaders of our government had no intention of creating the secular state that liberals would have us believe we live in.... The Founding Fathers called the nation to prayer.... The Ten Commandments [are] our nation's original source of law.

If Parsley is successful in his Christocratic political efforts, the once-proud Democratic party—the party founded by Jefferson, who created the phrase "the wall of separation

between church and state"—would be reduced to a per-
petual minority status through a series of carefully
crafted gerrymandering actions in the fifty states.

As a result of such redistricting, the GOP would retain
unending control of the U.S. House of Representatives
and the U.S. Senate. The model for Christocrats to emulate is the recent Republican success in eliminating seven
"safe" Democratic Congressional districts in Texas.

Several Constitutional amendments would be adopted
in a Christocracy. One would make abortion a felony for
both pregnant women and all health-care professionals
who perform the procedure. A second amendment would
prohibit same-sex marriages or any form of same-sex civil
unions. A third amendment would mandate daily bible
reading and organized prayers in all American public
schools. In practice, the overwhelming majority of scriptural passages used in schools would be verses from the
New Testament.

A fourth amendment would rescind the Constitutional
two-term limit on the president and vice president, thus
ensuring that a chief executive sympathetic to Christocrats could serve well beyond the current eight-year
period. This would be an ironic twist of history, since it was
Republicans—following Franklin Roosevelt's four elections
to the presidency between 1932 and 1944—who led the
campaign in the 1940s to adopt the current two-term limit.

The mainstream print and electronic media would be
beaten into submission and meekly reflect the Christocratic nature of what would be termed "God's America."
Underground publications, not unlike Tom Paine's
Common Sense, reminding Americans of their historical
record of religious liberty and church-state separation

would proliferate, but law enforcement authorities would vigorously search them out and prosecute publishers, editors, writers, and others who published "anti-faith trash" or distributed such material on the Internet.

The Federal Communications Commission would remain solidly in the hands of Christocrats, and it would deny broadcast licenses to radio or television stations that it deemed anti-Christian or representing secular humanist values. Motion pictures would need official government approval before they could be distributed in theaters, akin to earlier attempts—decades ago—to police the moral and sexual content of films. Such approval by Christocratic censors would require filmmakers not to "offend the religious sensibilities of the majority religion" or present any broadly defined sexually explicit content on the screen. Religious censors, appointed by the federal government, would define what is sexually explicit in films, and in the print and electronic media.

Monitoring sexual behavior, both public and private, would be at the top of the Christocratic agenda. Legal abortion would be banned in every hospital or clinic that receives public money or employs any health-care professional who received public grants or scholarships during his or her medical, nursing, or social-work education.

In addition, all manifestations of public homosexual or lesbian acts—including holding hands or kissing—would be subject to a fine and a jail sentence. Known homosexuals and lesbians would have to successfully undergo government-sponsored reeducation sessions if they applied for any public sector jobs including hospitals, schools, the military, or government service. Anti-sodomy laws would be reintroduced, and prosecutions for "deviant" sexual behavior would accelerate in a Christocratic America.

Educators who publicly support Christocratic goals, such as the elimination of scientific evolution from all curricula, would be the key decision makers in all matters relating to public schools. They would receive preferential endorsements from the government to serve on America's many school boards. Christocrats would set the educational goals and standards for a comprehensive federal education program ranging from kindergartens through graduate schools at public universities including medicine, law, journalism, and science.

Just as the words *under God* were added to the Pledge of Allegiance in the 1950s, Christocrats would demand a new personal affirmation of commitment to follow the traditional oath to support the Constitution. The added affirmation would acknowledge the sovereignty and "Kingship of God Almighty and the Lordship of Christ Jesus." Preferences in jobs, education, the civil service, and the military would be given to those individuals who made such a public commitment. Failure to publicly affirm Christocratic values would be a serious impediment in the employment and educational sectors. A strict quota system would be introduced for those who were either unable or unwilling to take the new pledge.

Achieving Christocratic goals would be a requirement for employment in the public sector. Science, history, and social-studies courses offered in public schools and universities would have to conform to biblical teachings as defined by Christocratic-controlled boards of education.

America's military academies would be thoroughly

"Christianized," a process already under way at the Air Force Academy in Colorado Springs. A series of religion courses presenting America as a Christian nation, and bible classes strongly emphasizing the New Testament, would be required for all cadets.

Academy students would be taught that they are also Christian soldiers fighting not only for the United States, but for "Team Jesus" as well. Fisher DeBerry, the Air Force Academy's football coach, has already used the latter term to describe the central role of evangelical Christianity at the Colorado Springs school.

Public libraries would be severely curtailed in both purchasing "morally undesirable" books and retaining such material on the shelves or in computer data banks.

Because most hospitals in the United States receive public funding, abortions of any kind would be forbidden in those facilities, and there would be no embryonic stem-cell research as well. The story would be similar in America's law schools. If public monies provide student scholarships, new building construction, or any other form of financial support, law schools would then be required to teach only the concept of original intent in Constitutional law, and traditional biblical teachings would form a basic part of the core curriculum.

Four religiously sponsored law schools have already instituted such a curriculum: Pat Robertson's Regent University, Jerry Falwell's Liberty University, and two ultra-conservative Catholic institutions: Ave Maria University and Saint Thomas University.

State legislatures, as well as the U.S. Congress, would adopt new statutes legally creating a Christian nation composed of fifty Christian states. A federal religion tax would be placed upon all Americans regardless of their religious identities—even if they profess no spiritual affiliation. The tax would provide funds for "faith-based" social-welfare programs directly administered by religious groups, the bulk of whom would be Christocratic institutions.

All government employees—federal, state, and local—would be required to participate in weekly bible classes in the workplace, as well as compulsory daily prayer sessions. This same rule would apply to any privately owned businesses receiving federal funds: defense contractors, construction companies, food supply organizations, and so forth.

Like the military academies, America's public space would also be Christianized with the permanent installation of the Ten Commandments, crosses, and other Christological representations within courtrooms, legislative chambers, and other governmental areas. A national identification card would be issued to every American—an internal passport—for the announced purpose of strengthening national security and making it easier for Americans to receive the appropriate pastoral care and counseling in the case of a terrorist attack or other national disaster.

However, each person's religious identity—or lack of identity—would be indicated on these required ID cards. The cards would be required in many areas and activities of American life, including air, bus, and train travel, and job and home-mortgage applications if public funding is involved. Such cards would provide Christocrats with preferential treatment in many areas of life, including home ownership, student loans, employment, and education. It would be justified as a form of "religious affirmative action" for faithful Christians who were persecuted by secular humanists in the past for their religious beliefs.

The once-prevalent principle of church-state separation would be taught in public schools as a myth that has been successfully discredited, even eradicated from American life.

Members of minority religions in America—Judaism, Islam, Buddhism, and Hinduism, and "inauthentic" Christians—would be tolerated, but younger members of these faith communities would be strongly encouraged to formally convert to the dominant evangelical Christianity. It would be made clear that a conversion would greatly enhance a person's opportunity for career advancement in all areas of American life, including the military and the civil service.

Such covert and overt religious coercion would be reminiscent of the conversion campaigns aimed at Jews in Europe, especially in Germany and Austria following the French Revolution in 1789 and the advent of the so-called Age of Enlightenment.

Prestigious cultural, academic, political, and economic positions were open only to the baptized during those years. In 1897, the famous composer and conductor Gustav Mahler (1860–1911) was baptized a Catholic so that he would be allowed to assume the leadership of the world-famous Vienna Court Opera.

Other Jews also converted to Christianity. Frequently, they saw it as their only way to enter European universities, the military officer corps, government service, and other desired professions. Heinrich Heine (1797–1856), the author of the famous "Die Lorelei," was baptized a Lutheran as a means of earning a doctorate at Göttingen University in Germany. Heine contemptuously called the baptismal certificate his "entry ticket to European culture."

In addition to Christocratic efforts to control the U.S. federal government, the campaign to baptize America has also made each of the fifty states a battleground. Nowhere is this more apparent than in Virginia, my home state, where I first encountered the religious forces now seeking to permanently change America.

CHAPTER II

CARRY ME BACK TO OL' VIRGINNIE . . .

Christian conservatives and their politically dangerous offspring, Christocrats, are not strangers to me. I know them quite well. Perhaps too well.

Three encounters with them in my home state of Virginia had a permanent negative impact on me, and decisively influenced my life as an American, a Jew, and a rabbi.

I can never forget those events, because they defined for me in a personal way the goals of today's Christocrats in America and the methods they employ to achieve them.

The first two encounters took place in Alexandria, Virginia, when I was a Jewish youngster growing up in a demographic sea of Christians, most of whom were Southern Baptists. The third encounter came much later, in 1995, at the Reverend Pat Robertson's headquarters in Virginia Beach, Virginia during the time I served as the

American Jewish Committee's national interreligious affairs director.

I was humiliated, at age eight in Virginia, for having a religious identity different from Christian conservatives. It was also in Virginia that I initially experienced the sense of rage and revenge that powers today's campaign to make America into a theocracy. And it was in Virginia that I encountered one of the most important Christian conservative leaders.

I was born in Pittsburgh, Pennsylvania, and lived there with my family until I was six years old. But in July 1941, my dentist father was called to active military duty at Fort Belvoir, Virginia. Because his call-up as an Army Reserve officer was supposed to last for only a year, my parents, brother, and I moved to nearby Alexandria for what my mother believed would be a brief twelve-month period of "camping out." That's how certain we were that our family would return to Pittsburgh during the summer of 1942.

My father had joined the U.S. Army Reserves in 1932 as his patriotic way to protest the rise of Nazi anti-Semitism in Germany. As he explained years later: "What else could an American Jew do in the 1930s? I joined the Army."

But, of course, the scheduled one-year tour of duty and the idea we were "camping out" was suddenly altered when the Japanese attacked Pearl Harbor on December 7, 1941 and America entered World War II. Indeed, my father remained on active military duty until 1947, and by that time Virginia had become our home, especially for me, the youngest member of the family. My father remained in the Army Reserve until 1957, when he officially retired from the military with the rank of lieutenant colonel.

Both my parents are buried in Arlington National Cemetery; today, the fourth generation of Virginia Rudins, the great-grandchildren of Philip and Beatrice, live in the state.

Alexandria was founded in 1749 as a port on the Potomac River, and its famous early residents included George Washington and the Lee family that produced "Lighthorse Harry," a signer of the Declaration of Independence and Revolutionary War general, and his son, Robert Edward, the top military leader of the Confederacy.

Today, Alexandria, which predates the founding of nearby Washington, D.C., by fifty years, is inextricably linked to the sprawling metropolitan area that carries the name of Alexandria's best-known resident and the nation's first president. However, in my youthful years Alexandria was a freestanding town of 30,000 people that was thoroughly "southern" in every way, including a racial segregation that affected all aspects of life: schools, libraries, housing, transportation, employment, hospitals, and public accommodations. A pervasive conservative Protestant ethos dominated Alexandria's public life, especially the city's schools.

Alexandria's political leaders of that era were part of an entrenched Democratic political establishment loyal to U.S. Senators Harry F. Byrd and A. Willis Robertson. Robertson's son, Marion Gordon or "Pat," is an ordained Southern Baptist minister who founded the Christian Coalition in 1989.

My first direct experience with Christian conservatives occurred in 1942, when I was a third-grader in Alexandria's Maury School. I didn't know it then, but that painful incident in a small red-brick school building on

Russell Road became what we now call a defining moment in my life.

On that long-ago September day, the thirty youngsters in my class eagerly began the new school year with fresh notebooks, sharpened pencils, and the usual intense curiosity about our new teacher. We did not have to wait long to discover both her authoritarian personality and her profoundly Christian religious beliefs.

Our teacher announced that she would lead the class in a ten-minute bible reading and prayer session each morning following the recital of the Pledge of Allegiance, a liturgical staple of America's civil religion even though in 1942 the two words, *under God*, had not yet been added to the Pledge. That now-contentious insertion came a decade later, in 1954.

I thought little about the bible reading and class prayers until the next morning, when our teacher asked if any Roman Catholics or Jews were in the class. I raised my hand, along with two Catholic students. Ironically, the three of us constituted ten percent of the class—the precise percentage frequently used in the now-discredited quota system that was employed for decades in the twentieth century to restrict the number of Jews per- mitted to enter medical, dental, and law schools, and other graduate programs—as well as many undergrad- uate colleges.

The next morning, a bewildered trio of third-graders was told to leave the classroom because we "were not Protestants." Being only eight years old, I didn't know exactly what being a Protestant meant, but clearly the three of us didn't qualify. The teacher ordered us to remain absolutely quiet in the hallway until the bible reading and prayers were completed. Only then would we be permitted to return to class.

It was mortifying to stand outside the classroom door as students from other grades proudly walked by, carrying morning attendance reports headed for the principal's office. They looked at us with pitying expressions. We were a trio of public outcasts, but my youthful Catholic classmates and I never complained. After all, we were eight-year-olds who dutifully followed a teacher's command.

The daily expulsions, often exceeding the announced ten minutes, continued for about two weeks until, one evening at home, I burst into tears at the family dinner table when I told my parents about the humiliation I suffered each day at school.

My parents were outraged by the teacher's religious bigotry, especially my father. He was furious and vowed to take action. His reaction reflected a lifelong energetic response whenever he detected, sensed, or experienced any form of anti-Jewish discrimination.

A few days later my father, wearing his Army officer's uniform (a requirement for all military personnel during World War II), and the parents of the two Catholic students met with Maury School's principal. The daily evictions from the classroom suddenly stopped the next day, as did the prayers and the bible readings, which I later learned were always a series of New Testament verses from the King James translation of the bible. Naturally, I was pleased to return to full-time status as a third-grader.

Not long after the end of the forced expulsions, my father recounted to me the details of the meeting. When the principal, a Southern Baptist, heard the parents' complaints, she summoned the teacher, also a Southern

Baptist, to her office, and chastised her in front of the Jewish and Catholic parents. Perhaps it was not good management technique on the principal's part, but the verbal criticism clearly worked.

According to my father, the teacher defended her actions and told her supervisor: "There are some students who are not good Baptists like us. They shouldn't be in the classroom for our prayers and bible reading."

The principal's response went something like this: "The bible readings, prayers, and sending children out into the hall must end now. After all, every Virginian knows Mr. Jefferson built a wall of separation between church and state, and that means no bible-reading is permitted in a public school, and it especially means that no teacher is allowed to disgrace children because they have a different religion."

For individuals not familiar with Virginia-speak, it must be noted that in the Old Dominion, even today, America's third president is usually called "Mr. Jefferson." This is especially true on the Charlottesville campus of the University of Virginia, an institution Jefferson founded in 1819.

Like most third-grade students in Virginia, I knew Thomas Jefferson was a U.S. president who came from our state. But when I heard about the principal's remarks, I wondered whether Jefferson had actually built some kind of brick wall of separation at his famous Monticello home, a revered historical site located near Charlottesville.

But wherever the wall was located, all I knew was that my father, the school principal, and Mr. Jefferson had happily restored me to my class. While my teacher never again expelled any students for religious reasons, Christmas and Easter were richly celebrated in the classroom.

Three months after my restoration to the class, our third-grade choir was invited to sing Christmas carols on the morning show of WRC, the Washington NBC radio station. But my mother emphatically instructed me to close my mouth when "Savior," "Christ," "Jesus," "Virgins," and all other Christological terms were sung by our excited group of eight-year-olds.

It was a good idea for both religious and musical reasons. I have never been able to successfully carry—or even drag—a tune.

I frequently recall my Maury School experience and the negative effect it had on me. While the contentious issues of church and state often take the form of academic papers, legal briefs, and learned essays on Constitutional law, I know from firsthand experience that whenever Mr. Jefferson's wall of church-state separation is breached, particularly in a public-school classroom, it has lasting, painful human consequences that severely harm the delicate psyches of youngsters.

And that's what happened to me.

Many people, including Christocratic leaders, have repeatedly told me that I have overreacted to my third-grade expulsions. One banal explanation is frequently offered: "The teacher meant no harm. That's the way it was back then."

But I reject their apologies and explanations. Each time I remember the daily expulsions, I grow more convinced that Americans of all ages and religious traditions, as well as those who have no religious affiliation, should never feel excluded from any aspect of our national life, especially within public schools. Every American must feel at home; no one is an outsider in the United States.

Besides, childhood memories, for good or ill, make indelible impressions and frequently shape adult behavior. I may not always remember what happened last week or last month, but I have never forgotten what happened to me when I was an eight-year-old growing up in Virginia.

It was only years later that I learned about Jefferson's 1802 letter to the Danbury, Connecticut Baptist Association. He wrote: "Believing with you that religion is a matter which lies solely between man and his God . . ." Jefferson praised the U.S. Constitution's First Amendment for "building a wall of separation between Church and State."

Jefferson's vivid image described his firm commitment to the principle of church-state separation that permits members of all religious groups in America, no matter their doctrine, dogma, or demographic size, and also members of no faith community, to function freely without governmental interference or control, and without coercion from any person or religious institution.

Unfortunately, there is a campaign currently under way to diminish the importance of Jefferson's words and meanings, to marginalize the significance of the wall of separation.

A typical negation comes from a 1995 speech by Pat Robertson. He called Jefferson's phrase an "impatient, offhand remark" that did not reflect his belief that "religious faith" is the foundation for political freedom.

More significant are the words of William McGurn,

President George W. Bush's chief speechwriter. In early 2005, McGurn said that too much is read into "the much venerated but almost completely misunderstood 'wall of separation' between church and state." Such attacks are certain to escalate as Christian conservatives seek to break down that historic wall.

I always recall that in 1786, fellow Virginians Patrick Henry and Jefferson, both strong supporters of American independence, sharply differed on whether citizens of the state should be taxed to support religious institutions. At the time, the bulk of such taxes would have gone to the Anglican church, the largest Christian body in the Old Dominion.

As Virginia's governor, Henry strongly supported state support of religion, and he argued that position with his well-known passion and eloquence. But two future U.S. presidents, Jefferson and James Madison, along with the Reverend John Leland, a Baptist minister, fought the proposal and worked to have the state legislature enact a Statute of Religious Freedom for Virginia. After a bitter struggle between the two patriots, each with a different view of the emerging American republic, the statute was approved in January 1786.

Among those supporting Henry's position were those who wanted Virginia and the United States to become officially and legally a "Christian" political entity. That was the existing pattern in Britain, Spain, France, and Portugal, and many believed that was the way it should be in the new republic.

Just three years after the Jefferson-Henry clash in Virginia, the French Revolution began, a revolution that violently ended the Catholic church's officially established position in that nation.

Although Jefferson's early religious instruction was also in the Anglican church in Virginia, he had a far different vision than Henry for America. He was aware that many of the first European colonists had come to America seeking religious freedom. He was also knowledgeable about the infamous Star Chamber proceedings in Britain when the established Anglican church persecuted Christian dissidents, including Methodists, Quakers, Baptists, and Congregationalists.

Roman Catholics were initially not welcomed in many of the English colonies. As a result, they sought religious refuge in Maryland. The first Jews who arrived in what later became the United States sailed to New Amsterdam from Brazil in 1654. Peter Stuyvesant, the governor of the Dutch colony, unsuccessfully attempted to expel them.

A few years earlier, Roger Williams, himself a Christian minister, was forced to flee the religiously intolerant Massachusetts Bay Colony for the safer confines of Rhode Island.

Jefferson, who opposed any form of state-sponsored or -endorsed religion, won the intense battle with Henry. Jefferson considered his authorship and adoption of the Virginia statute one of his three proudest achievements, and he had this fact inscribed on his grave along with two other notable accomplishments: the authorship of the Declaration of Independence and the founding of his state's university. Surprisingly absent from Jefferson's grave is any mention that he was the third U.S. president.

As a result of their clash, Patrick Henry and Thomas Jefferson became permanent foes.

Madison, another president from Virginia, was also a strong champion of the Constitution's First Amendment. In his *Federalist Papers,* written in 1789 to gain support for the adoption of the newly written Constitution, Madison foresaw a "multiplicity of sects" in the new nation, similar to the host of political parties that were certain to emerge in the United States.

Before the Constitution was ratified, Madison wrote a letter to fellow Virginian, James Monroe, who would years later succeed Madison as the fifth U.S. president. Madison summed up the battle against Henry's call to use public money for the furtherance of religion in Virginia:

> The Episcopal clergy are generally for it [Henry's bill]. . . . The Presbyterians [Madison's own religious faith] seem as ready to set up an establishment which would take them in as they were to pull one down which shut them out. The Baptists, however, standing firm by their avowed principle of the complete separation of church and state, declared it to be "repugnant to the spirit of the Gospel for the Legislature thus to proceed in matters of religion, that no human laws ought to be established for the purpose."

Leland was an invaluable ally of Jefferson and Madison. As an ordained Baptist minister, Leland strongly supported the principle of church-state separation. He was especially opposed to "hireling clergy," ministers who were paid by the state, and he publicly protested "religious liberty . . . anywise threatened."

Leland was even against the Sunday closings of U.S.

post offices, feeling this represented government favoritism by officially recognizing the Christian Sabbath. But today, Leland and those who share his views are out of place, a rejected minority within the Southern Baptist Convention.

There are serious systematic attempts currently under way to break down Jefferson's wall and replace it with a new church-state relationship that would create an incestuous relationship between government and religion: an American theocracy, something that Jefferson, Madison, Leland, and their colleagues greatly feared.

Nearly 220 years later, that same Virginia legislature is once again the scene of a new version of the Jefferson-Henry clash.

A George Washington High School classmate, Patsy Smith Ticer, and I served together as officers of our student government. Apparently our youthful political experiences provided her superb training because, in the early 1990s, she became Alexandria's mayor. In 1995, she was elected a Virginia state senator, representing the 30th District that includes much of that city and parts of Fairfax and Arlington counties.

Patsy is a Democrat and she told me the current legislative battles in Richmond, the Old Dominion's capital, are fierce and getting uglier each year. Both the House of Delegates and the Senate are GOP-controlled. As a result, Patsy and her colleagues are constantly battling the political allies of the Christocrats on the familiar issues of church-state separation, abortion, gay rights, religious liberty, libraries, immigrants, same-sex marriages, and civil unions.

In early 2005, the Virginia House of Delegates Privileges

and Elections Committee, with only four dissenting votes, proposed a significant change in the 1786 Virginia Statute of Religious Freedom.

Unlike Jefferson and his allies, some of today's Virginia legislators would permit religious proselytizing on all public property, including schools. The bill did not pass, but it is an indication of how strongly Christocrats want to destroy the wall of separation between church and state.

As in all such cases, the argument was made that a new law was needed because Christians are not free to express their religious beliefs and because Christianity itself is under attack in America. The sponsor of the Virginia bill, Delegate Charles W. Carrico, Sr., asserted that new legislation is required to counter "a growing bias against Christians."

Senator Ticer laments that the principle of "church-state separation has faded fast" among Virginia legislators, especially sad news in the state where Jefferson won such an important victory in 1786. My friend, the embattled state senator, told me that "the far right doesn't want anything for children" and one member of the Legislature even wanted a law passed that would make it a felony if a pregnant woman failed to report a miscarriage within twenty-four hours. She detects a strong anti-woman bias in the Republican tactics.

Patsy said Christian conservative groups play a major role in shaping the agenda and laws of Virginia. Not surprisingly, she reported that the right-wingers in Richmond have "almost dismantled *Roe v. Wade*" in the state, and the same group is seeking "to inflict their extremist values" on the total population.

She told me that as early as 1996, Mark Early, a prominent Virginia Republican legislator, angrily declared that "they" are teaching "tolerance." Senator Ticer summed up her Senate experiences in graphic language: "It's like living in a meat grinder, and it is emotionally and politically exhausting to fend off the various trash bills the far right offers." Senator Ticer's experiences are duplicated in many other statehouses as the Christocrats' campaign escalates.

My third-grade teacher is long dead, but her spiritual heirs are currently operating in thousands of classrooms and school boards throughout the country, as they continually press for required bible readings, religious instruction, and compulsory organized Christian prayers inside America's public schools. Sadly, in many cases there are no courageous Jeffersonian principals like the one who led Maury School when I was a student.

Eight years after my painful expulsion and triumphal return to the third-grade classroom, I experienced another defining event that was also a precursor to many of today's issues. It, too, had a permanent impact upon me; the kind of event few American Jews of my age experienced.

In my student days there were only two secondary schools in Alexandria: Parker-Gray for African-Americans, and George Washington High (no surprise in that name!) for whites. My GWHS senior class numbered 230, of whom only 8 were Jews.

Because Jews were a small minority in Alexandria, my public-school experience was significantly different from many other Jews of my generation. Most of them grew up in the large urban population centers of the Northeast or upper Midwest: New York City, Boston, Philadelphia, Baltimore, Chicago, Pittsburgh, Detroit, Milwaukee,

Hartford, Newark, Washington, and Cleveland. In many of those communities there were well-defined neighborhoods where Jews, many of them first-generation Americans, constituted a significant percentage of the public school student body.

Those densely populated Jewish areas included sections of Manhattan, Brooklyn, and the Bronx in New York City, Shaker Heights in Cleveland, Irving Park in Chicago, Squirrel Hill in Pittsburgh, Dorchester and Roxbury in Boston, and Wynnefield in Philadelphia.

In some of those cities, Jewish teenagers, frequently the children of immigrants, peacefully coexisted with large Irish, Polish, or Italian Catholic communities who were also recent immigrants to the United States. Unfortunately, there were many cases of young Catholics uttering anti-Semitic epithets and comments aimed at Jews. Tensions between teenage Catholics and Jews often resulted in gang fights and other forms of physical violence.

The primary source of this bigotry was the explicit and implicit anti-Jewish teachings of the Roman Catholic church that were widely promulgated prior to the Second Vatican Council's historic 1965 Nostra Aetate (In Our Time) declaration that changed Catholic teachings toward Jews and Judaism.

Several Jewish writers, notably novelist Philip Roth in his book *The Plot Against America*, have written chilling accounts of growing up in a big city in America that was filled with overt acts of anti-Semitism.

But the Jewish neighborhood in the large cities did provide young Jews with a sense of social cohesion and solidarity in a nation that still retained the social pathology of anti-Semitism, particularly in housing, employment, and education. In fact, I have met many American Jews of my generation who never developed any positive friendships with Christians during their high school years.

Mine was a totally different experience. Growing up in a small southern community where Jews and Catholics were distinct minorities provided me an intimate knowledge of Christian conservatives, especially members of America's second largest Christian group, the Southern Baptists.

This was an experience that was useful later in my professional dealings as a rabbi engaged in work with Christian conservative leaders. During the years I served in the American Jewish Committee's Interreligious Affairs Department, between 1968 and 2000, I repeatedly recalled the key elements of my youthful days in Virginia: a strong Jewish home, active involvement with a synagogue, and constant personal interaction with Christians.

In a wry reversal of the familiar fatuous claim many Christians like to make about Jews, I can honestly say, "Some of my best friends are Christians, even Christocrats."

During my junior year in high school, several of those "best friends" invited me to attend an outdoor Christian revival meeting with them. At first I declined their invitation, but finally I accepted, partly out of curiosity, but more importantly because I was at the time dating a young evangelical high-school classmate.

One Saturday night in May, four of us embarked on a strange double date, three ardent Southern Baptists and a Jew who later became a rabbi. Instead of the usual movie followed by a hamburger, fried onions, and a Coca-Cola at the neighborhood Hot Shoppe/Marriott restaurant, we drove about ten miles south of Alexandria on U.S. Route 1 to a large field near the old Hybla Valley Airport where a huge canvas tent had been erected for ten nights of Christian revival and renewal meetings.

Both the preacher and his fiery message were well known to my three friends; for them, attendance at such outdoor religious services was simply part of being a Southern Baptist in Virginia. While it was my first revival meeting, it was old stuff to the other couple and my date.

The all-white congregation of about five hundred people (I was told the "colored" conducted separate revival meetings, with their own preachers) sat on hard metal folding chairs. It was a hot night for May, and the huge number of electric light bulbs loosely strung above the congregation plus the closed tent created a high temperature that quickly produced hundreds of sweating people.

Looking back on that night, it seems clear that we were in grave physical danger, had a fire started inside the tent. It could have been a repeat of the horrific 1944 circus tent fire in Hartford that killed hundreds of people. As the evening service began, I felt uneasy both physically and religiously.

The revival meeting itself was an emotional mix of well-known Christian hymns and a sermon outlining the many sins that human beings regularly commit in their daily lives. The highlight came when the preacher fervently issued the call for people to come forward, kneel in front of the makeshift altar, and "accept Jesus into their hearts."

But strangely, the sermon didn't resonate too well with the assembled congregation that night. Perhaps most of the audience, many of them habitués of outdoor religious meetings, had come forward at a previous revival. For whatever reasons, the audience was slow to answer the preacher's call for conversion—or, in many cases, reconversion—to Jesus. My three evangelical classmates remained in their seats and did not respond to the preacher's urging to come forward.

They told me that people who attend revival meetings are often "saved," then later commit numerous "sins," and are once again "saved" at another revival service. My date called it a "Christian roller-coaster ride."

However, the atmosphere inside the revival tent dramatically changed, when the preacher began speaking about the "plagues afflicting our beloved America." I immediately perked up when I heard the word "plagues" because I was certain he would tick off the litany of woes that descended upon ancient Egypt described in the biblical book of Exodus: frogs, boils, vermin, locusts, lice, hail, blood, darkness, wild beasts, and ultimately the slaying of the first-born Egyptian males. The ten plagues are a basic part of the Jewish Passover Seder meal; just a month earlier at my family's Seder, we had recalled the traditional inventory.

Until the preacher's mention of plagues, the revival had been filled with heavily Christological references and images of Jesus that left me emotionally uninvolved. But now the preacher was talking about a more familiar religious ground. Or so I thought.

But instead of the biblical catastrophes, the revival preacher began citing the many ills he believed were infecting the America of the early 1950s. These included the existence of the organized labor movement, trade unions, the many Communists he charged were working in government (it was the McCarthy era, after all), wide-spread sexual promiscuity, the excess number of foreigners in America, and, one plague that surprised me even then, the loss of "states' rights."

The latter concept was constantly taught in our high school history classes as the true reason for the war that engulfed America between 1861 and 1865. In fact, that conflict was always referred to in school as the "War Between the States" and was rarely called the Civil War.

When he was finished, the preacher shouted out some phrases I have never forgotten: "Let's take back America! They have stolen America. It's our country, our America!" Unlike the congregation's tepid response to his earlier call to accept Jesus, this time the crowd arose from their hard metal chairs, began cheering, and then spontaneously started singing the National Anthem, followed by a rendition of "Dixie," the song most linked to the Confederacy.

I was only sixteen years old that night, but the "tent people's" sense of fury has remained with me. The preacher's heated cry that America had been stolen was no run-of-the-mill conversion sermon, nor was it the recitation of the traditional ten biblical plagues I had anticipated. Instead, it was an outburst that stunned me with its fury and its anger. Because something precious had been stolen from America and from Christians, it has to be reclaimed.

It was only decades later that I was able to fully understand and process my revival-meeting experience. Millions of Americans believe that a Protestant Christian conservative hegemony once existed in the U.S., back in the good old days. In their recollections, the United States was then a tranquil, moral nation deeply rooted to traditional Christian values: the shining city on the hill, an idyllic small-town America anchored to an old-fashioned religion that was overwhelmingly white male-centered, and evangelical Protestant.

It is a vision that offers today's Christocrats a fuzzy feel-good moment about a history that never happened that way. Those who believe that such an America actually existed suffer from historical amnesia, because the reality was far different. Cruel child labor and cheaply paid immigrant workers constituted much of the workforce needed to build and maintain an expanding economy. It was an America that actively engaged in a vicious national system of human slavery and degradation, only to be followed after the bloody Civil War by legally sanctioned racial segregation and persecution.

During those blissful years, women could not vote, and factory and railroad workers, miners, and other laborers had no recourse to collective bargaining or economic rights. There was widespread anti-Catholic and anti-Jewish bigotry that tragically led to murder in 1913 when Leo Frank, a Jew, was lynched in Atlanta for allegedly killing a young Christian girl, a crime he did not commit.

American Indians may have unwittingly provided the United States with a host of geographical place-names, but they were denied the right to vote until 1952. Many tribes were victims of a U.S. policy that systematically and forcibly moved Indians into government-built reservations that were degrading and stifling. One result of the forced confinements of the tribes was a high incidence of unemployment, alcoholism, and other maladies.

It was an America in which millions of its citizens,

including many elected public officials, were members of the racist, anti-Semitic Ku Klux Klan. And there were a host of other social, economic, and political problems in America's good old days.

But no matter. That mythical time is warmly remembered, and poignantly yearned for, by many of today's Christocrats who want to return to that era—even if it never existed.

Perceptions frequently matter more than facts. For Christian conservatives intent on taking back America, those ills, discriminations, and wretched economic conditions have been conveniently erased from their memories, if they were ever present. In place of historical reality is a hazy image of a lost young America, and a desperate craving to make America, "our America again."

To understand the current effort to baptize America, the perceived sense of traumatic loss cannot be minimized or disregarded because those feelings are the linchpin of the Christian conservatives' efforts to control every aspect of American public and private life. They suffer a sense of political bereavement, the death of a once-great Christian nation. When this mourning for a lost America is combined with religious rage and spiritual certitude, it is a powerful combination that fuels today's campaign to "take back America" and restore a Christian America.

However, both the targets and the problems have greatly changed since that long-ago Virginia revival meeting I attended. Today's Christian conservative leaders use coded language and speak of "pro-family values," "public morality," and of "secular humanist" political and religious opponents who are "out of the

American mainstream." But one thing remains the same a half-century later: the sense of profound loss. This became clear in a meeting with Pat Robertson in 1995.

As part of my professional AJC responsibilities, I arranged a meeting in Virginia Beach with Robertson and the Christian Coalition's Executive Director, Ralph Reed, who is currently a key Republican strategist. At that time he was first emerging on the national scene. Joining me at that meeting were Robert Rifkind of New York City and Jack Lapin of Houston, two top officers of the AJC, and David Harris, the AJC's executive director, based in Manhattan.

Although it took place decades after my Maury School and outdoor revival experiences, the meeting triggered the same feelings of exclusion and trepidation I had experienced as a youngster in Alexandria.

The date of our meeting was April 19, 1995.

Robertson began by reviewing his strong commitment to the State of Israel and to Jews in the former Soviet Union who were still facing anti-Semitism following the collapse of Communism. Public support for the security and survival of the Jewish state is a basic tenet of Christian conservative belief.

But our AJC leadership group, while welcoming Robertson's support, wanted to focus instead on domestic concerns. We said there was an apprehension that Christian conservative leaders perceive America as a Christian nation that merely tolerates religious groups who are not evangelical Christians.

In his response, Robertson said his primary target is not the Jewish community, but the Federal Reserve system, the Trilateral Commission, the "Rockefellers, Cecil Rhodes, Colonel House (President Woodrow

Wilson's trusted aide), and the bankers, including Paul Warburg," who, in the early twentieth century, pressed for a United States Constitutional amendment that created the federal income tax.

Robertson compared the status of "evangelical Christians" in America to that of the "Jews in Germany of the Nazi period." He said the enemies of Christian conservatives are using the same type of tactics that "Joseph Goebbels, the Nazi propaganda minister, employed to first marginalize Jews and then send them into ghettoes." I was shocked and sickened by Robertson's odious comparison with the Nazis. It was a tawdry use of the Holocaust to gain some cheap debating points.

He believes there is a "vendetta," "a religious cleansing" taking place that is aimed at Christian conservatives. "All of this began in 1962 with the Supreme Court's church-state decisions that stripped America of its moral shield." Robertson said that religious communities in many parts of the world had historically provided education for young people during the last five hundred years; but that unfortunately, in the U.S., that role was taken over by "the state." This has created a "sterile moral environment," one that must be undone.

Robertson declared that although the Christian cross was the first symbol erected by the European settlers at Cape Henry in North Carolina, he strongly advocated "no state compulsion about religion . . . I am a libertarian. I would like to dynamite Washington." The latter comment sounded like the rhetoric I heard on the *700 Club*, Robertson's TV show.

It was only after the meeting with Robertson and Reed ended and the AJC delegation headed for the flights home from the Norfolk, Virginia airport that we heard the first news reports that the Alfred P. Murrah Federal Building in Oklahoma City had been, in fact, been blown up and 168 people killed. It was an eerie moment, coming less than an hour after Robertson's ominous "joke" about blowing up Washington, D.C.

Robertson has built a large Christian-based media empire and is one of America's most prominent evangelical leaders. In his book *The New Millennium*, published in 1990, Robertson wrote: "In essence, the destiny of this nation is in the hands of the Christians."

Another well-known Christian conservative leader, Beverly LaHaye, chair of Concerned Women of America, has written: ". . . America is a nation based on biblical principles. . . . Christian values dominate our government. Politicians who do not use the bible to guide their public and private lives do not belong in government."

Both Robertson and LaHaye represent the growing number of religious and political leaders who seek to covert the U.S. into a legally sanctioned Christian nation, a theocracy. But their demand is nothing new. Because the country's Founders forgot to create a Christian republic, Christian nation advocates unsuccessfully tried to pass a Constitutional amendment in the 1860s and 1870s, and they failed again in the 1950s. However, it is an issue that will not go away.

At its June 2004 convention, the Texas Republican party approved a platform plank that called the United States "a Christian nation." The Lone Star GOP also denounced the "myth of the separation of church and state." During the 2004 presidential election, Cardinal Justin Rigali of Philadelphia termed the historic American principle of church-state separation a "misinterpretation of the Constitution."

In confronting today's Christocrats and their aggressive campaign to baptize America, I am constantly drawn back to Virginia, and to Jefferson, Madison, Henry, Leland, Robertson, the Maury School teacher and principal, and the revival tent preacher.

Which set of Virginians will emerge victorious in this epic battle? The outcome is very much in question, but there is no doubt at all that a war is currently under way that will determine the future not only of Virginia, but of the other forty-nine states as well.

CHAPTER III

HARSH DOMINIONISM: THE CHRISTOCRATS' GOAL FOR AMERICA

In their campaign to gain control over all aspects of American life, Christocrats constantly reassure the public that they are simply supporting "traditional moral standards," "biblical principles," or "mainstream values." They also assert their belief that "God's law" is superior to any "human law," including the U.S. Constitution. Such religious rhetoric, a staple of the Christocrats, provides a theological justification for their political efforts. It also shields their true intentions.

Having staked out their position on the supremacy of "God's law," only Christocrats have the power to determine precisely what God desires for the United States.

Critics who dispute this monopoly of divine knowledge are quickly branded as "anti-faith" or "anti-Christian." When the coercive or aggressive tactics of Christocrats are criticized, the immediate response is that any questioning of either their righteous motives or goals is an attempt to suppress religious liberty or stifle freedom of conscience.

Christocrats continuously exploit this win-win situation to achieve political success and silence their critics. They are then free to pursue their baptizing-of-America campaign under the protective umbrella of "bringing God back into the secular public square." If their methods, motives, or modes of operation are challenged or questioned, they lash out at critics, calling them "opponents of the First Amendment" who are preventing Americans from exercising their Constitutionally guaranteed religious freedoms.

This tactic of constant personal attacks frequently succeeds in wearing down or even quashing critics and opponents, especially when the denigration is aimed at people who do not affirm clearly defined religious identities and beliefs.

Because such rhetoric is constantly repeated, many Americans nod in silent, passive agreement with much of the Christocratic agenda. After all, who among us does not endorse public morality, family values, or ethical behavior from our fellow citizens and from political leaders? Who among us does not yearn for a simpler halcyon-like America that is tranquil and faithful to moral values and teachings?

But such fluffy Christocratic language deliberately obscures a harsh religious ideology that provides the philosophic and theological fire and fuel for the movement to baptize America. Many Christocratic followers, the proverbial men and women in the church pews, are frequently unaware of the potent ideology that calls for the dismantling of the American democracy and especially its extraordinary number of personal freedoms, and its replacement by an authoritarian Christian commonwealth that strictly carries out "Old Testament" laws and regulations.

In an irony, Judaism, in its rich post-biblical rabbinical tradition, consciously moved away from a literal interpretation of harsh biblical regulations. The Talmud and centuries of careful interpretation significantly softened so-called "Old Testament law." But that set of ancient biblical laws is precisely the legislation many Christian conservatives want to impose upon the entire American society.

Anti-Semites usually condemn Judaism, calling it a static religion of oppressive law that is unbending and without mercy. Christianity is portrayed as a religion that has spiritually replaced a repressive Judaism with "love," "compassion," and "grace."

Yet Christocrats who yearn for an America based solely on "Old Testament law" strongly support the full implementation of all the harsh legislation contained in the Hebrew bible, while Jews long ago systematically reinterpreted those verses to make them adhere to a standard of mercy and compassion.

The ominous belief system that powers much of Christocratic thinking bears two unwieldy names: *Dominionism* and *Christian Reconstructionism*. Although they are somewhat different movements, their goals, methods, and principles are similar and both must be explored in any analysis of the current Christocratic movement in America.

While Christian Reconstructionism is a more extreme form of Dominionism, all Christian Reconstructionists are

Dominionists, but not all Dominionists are Reconstructionists. And, of course, the Christian Reconstructionist movement is totally different from the Jewish religious movement founded by Rabbi Mordecai M. Kaplan (1881–1983) that is also called Reconstructionism.

Dominionism is a strident form of evangelical Protestant Christianity that seeks total "dominion" over the United States, its people, and ultimately the entire world. Francis A. Schaeffer (1912–1984), a Philadelphia-born Protestant theologian of German background, is credited with creating the theory of Dominionism in the 1970s and 1980s while living in Switzerland. His books and films have attracted extraordinary attention from Christian conservatives, both clergy and lay.

Closely connected to Dominionism is Christian Reconstructionism, whose theological-political parent was a New York City–born religious thinker from an Armenian background, John J. Rushdoony (1916–2001).

Even now, both Schaeffer and Rushdoony are little known to the American public, but their radical writings form the intellectual and religious foundation for much of today's Christocratic movement.

A central tenet of Dominionism is the conviction that God ordained the United States to be a Christian nation based solely on biblical laws and principles. To achieve this seemingly unattainable goal, the democratic traditions, laws and policies of the American republic, especially individual freedoms, must first be destroyed and then permanently replaced with a Christian theocracy anchored to strict "Old Testament law." The secular U.S. Constitution, superseded by biblical law, will be rendered inoperative and discarded.

The use of "Old Testament law" is always troubling and represents a form of subtle religious anti-Judaism. Christianity retained the Hebrew bible and pejoratively labeled it the "Old Testament." The adjective old indicated that it was only preparation for the "New Testament." The adjective *new* conveys freshness and a sense of replacement of the *old*.

In this old/new description, a clear dichotomy frequently prevails regarding the religion and the God of Israel: The "Jewish God" is a divine figure of stern wrath and jealousy, while the "Christian God" is a comforting parent filled with grace. The "Old" Testament was fulfilled by the "New" Testament. The "New Israel" (the church) replaced the "Old Israel" (the Jews); liberating "Christian grace" supplanted suffocating "Jewish law," the loving "people of Jesus" superseded the deceitful "people of Judas."

While Schaeffer's writings and films initially attracted the attention of only a small coterie of Christian conservatives, we can see the result of Schaeffer's ideas today within much of the Christocratic movement.

Marvin Olasky, a journalism professor at the University of Texas and a Christian conservative author, has written that the "major figure behind the election and re-election of George W. Bush . . . [is] a theologian most Americans have never heard of: Francis Schaeffer."

Olasky argues it was Schaeffer who "concluded that if Christians stayed aloof from political and cultural debates, Western civilization would go down the drain." Schaeffer's death in 1984 was "at a time when some hard-line Christian separatists still looked down on political involvement as cavorting with Satan. . . ."

Interestingly, in his writings, Schaeffer did not call for a Christian theocracy in America. That view is, however, the central core of Rushdoony's Recon theology. Schaeffer was somewhat fearful of Christian acts of "civil disobedience" in the U.S. because "there are so many kooky people around."

But many of Schaeffer's Dominionist followers believe civil disobedience, especially focused on the abortion issue, is a necessary tactic to gain control of America until the Second Coming of Jesus and the final triumph of God's Kingdom on earth. Because the commandment to achieve Christian control of the entire world comes "from God," any tactic or strategy hastening that goal is not only acceptable, but divinely sanctioned. Divine ends, even violent ones, justify harsh means.

Many critics charge that Timothy McVeigh and Eric Rudolph were deeply influenced by the teachings of Dominionism and Christian Reconstructionism. McVeigh's 1995 bombing of the Murrah Federal Building in Oklahoma City can be religiously justified as a necessary attack upon an evil "secular" American government facility.

Rudolph's murderous attacks upon abortion clinics can also be defended as a legitimate act of authentic Christian resistance to an evil that must, at all costs, be punished.

Dominionists argue the Second Coming of Jesus cannot take place until they have gained control of every human government and all sectors of society. They are not interested, indeed are not permitted, to enter into alliances or coalitions with any other groups; only Dominionists are endowed with the divine power to control the globe.

Dominionists are called the faithful "regents" of Jesus. It is no accident that the Robertson's Virginia Beach Christian educational institution is called "Regent University."

A biblical source for both the movement's name and its central purpose is this verse in Genesis 1:26:

> And God said, Let us make man in our image, after our likeness: let them have dominion over the fish of the sea, and over the fowl of the air, and over the cattle, and over all the earth, and over every creeping thing that creeps upon the earth.

The traditional Jewish interpretation of the verse is that God grants to humans an awesome responsibility: stewardship of the earth and permission to use animals in agriculture, travel, and other similar endeavors, as well as for sources of food and clothing. But with that "dominion" also comes the ethical imperative to respect all of nature, all animals and fish, and for humans, as faithful custodians of the environment, to use that "dominion" with compassion.

Dominion in Judaism does not mean superiority or control; rather, it is the sacred commitment of caring for the planet's well-being. In exchange, humans are permitted to draw upon the resources of nature for their existence.

But Schaeffer and his devoted followers turn the Genesis verse on its head and interpret the biblical words as a direct commandment from God to control and dominate not only the animals of the planet, but the political institutions of the earth itself and its diverse human population. Dominionism teaches that Christians are obligated by God to conquer the world and force all peoples to accept the biblical laws of the "Old Testament." Naturally, the Dominionists, God's elite, will occupy the upper leadership positions in the new religious order they will establish.

Governments of nations based on human laws are temporary, flawed instruments that must be replaced by a Christian ruling authority based on biblical principles; a dominion that will apply God's stern rigorous laws upon the world's population. Associate Supreme Court Justice Antonin Scalia declared in a recent speech:

> that government . . . derives its moral authority from God. Government is the "minister of God" with powers to "revenge," to "execute wrath," including even wrath by the sword. . . .

Such language excites Christocrats, who see Scalia's words as a legal green light to move forward with gaining "dominion" over all governments and then using "the sword" to punish opponents who are classified as wrongdoers.

There is always the lurking question as to whether Dominionists are using religion as a socially acceptable cover, or as justification for their real goal: achieving absolute political power. In the twentieth century, totalitarian political regimes—Nazi Germany, Soviet Russia, and Communist China—attempted to crush all religions in their domains in order to gain and then exercise total political power.

For Hitler, Stalin, and Mao, the free expression of religion was a constant threat to their brutal regimes. Authentic religions had to be eliminated and replaced by puppet spiritual authorities who were totally controlled by the state.

The Nazis created the odious Deutsche Kristen, whose clergy placed the swastika upon their ecclesiastical robes and offered up the Nazi salute at religious services. Stalin, a former Eastern Orthodox Christian seminarian, created state-controlled Orthodox churches in the Soviet Union that were part of the Communist party apparatus. Mao attempted to crush manifestations of traditional Chinese religions.

But in the early years of the twenty-first century, we are witnessing an important role reversal. Today's totalitarian Islamic and Christocratic forces, both acting in the name of religion, seek to destroy all existing political systems, despotic or democratic, and replace them with their own religion-soaked political regimes that will be utterly subservient to the spiritual authorities. Governments are only the vessels needed to control societies and, when necessary, to punish disobedient sinners.

Dominionism and its theological soul mate, Christian Reconstructionism, provide the kind of dual strategy that is the signature mode of operation for Christocrats. That is, they must attack the hated secular institutions of American society without mercy or compromise, especially the government, until all institutions of political authority, education, science, medicine, law, and culture crumble and are destroyed. Dominionists and/or Christocrats will infiltrate the despised sectors of society to hasten the total destruction of all societal structures.

In 1991, Robertson offered this specific strategy:

> Rule the world for God.
> Give the impression that you are there to work for
> the party, not push an ideology.

Hide your strength.

Don't flaunt your Christianity.

Christians need to take leadership positions. Party officers control political parties and so it is very important that mature Christians have a majority of leadership positions whenever possible, God willing.

In 1982, two years before his death, Schaeffer appeared on Robertson's TV program, *The 700 Club*. His remarks on that show were a blueprint for Christocrats and an eerie forecast of what is currently taking place in America:

Today we live in a humanist society. They control the schools. They control public television. They control the media in general. . . . The courts are not subject to the will of the people through elections or re-elections. . . . All the great changes [in church-state matters] have come through the courts. . . . The government as a whole, but especially the courts, have become the vehicle to force this view on the total population, even if the total population doesn't hold this view.

Three years later, on April 29, 1985, Billy Graham was a guest on *The 700 Club*. Graham told Robertson and the program's audience,

The time has come when evangelicals are going to have to think about getting organized corporately. . . . I'm for evangelicals running for public office and winning if possible and getting control

of the Congress, getting control of the bureaucracy, getting control of the executive branch of
government. I think if we leave it to the other side
we're going to be lost. I would like to see every
true believer involved in politics in some way,
shape, or form.

In later years, Graham moved away from discussing politics in public or taking stands on contemporary issues and
concerns. In his 2005 New York City Crusade, an ailing
Graham eschewed any political statements at both his press
conference that I attended and at his three public appearances that attracted nearly a quarter of a million people.

But in the late 1960s and early 1970s, Graham was a
close confidant and adviser to Richard Nixon, and it was
in 1972 that he uttered his now famous anti-Jewish statements during a private White House conversation with
the president.

Unknown to the evangelist, Nixon secretly taped the
exchange, and when Graham's remarks were made
public in 2002, he apologized to the Jewish community.
On the eve of his 2005 visit to New York City, Graham
reached out again to Jews and apologized once more,
saying he would "crawl on his hands and knees" seeking
forgiveness for his anti-Jewish remarks.

George Grant, an ardent Dominionist, was the executive director of the Blue Ridge Ministries and the author
of *The Changing Guard: Biblical Principles for Political
Action.* Grant echoes the Dominionist ideology.

He believes Christians have a sacred task to gain control of America for Jesus Christ, and have dominion over
all sectors of society. Grant wants dominion, not merely

an influential voice as part of a democratic coalition that governs the United States.

In February 2005 following President Bush's second-term victory, a jubilant group of Christian conservative leaders met at the Reverend D. James Kennedy's Coral Ridge Presbyterian Church in Ft. Lauderdale, Florida. Kennedy, like many other prominent evangelical pastors, leads a multi-million-dollar mega-church.

Jane Lampman, a *Christian Science Monitor* journalist, reported that in the material given to conference partici-pants, Kennedy made plain the ultimate goals of the Christocratic movement. Perhaps to leave no doubt in anyone's mind, Kennedy specifically used *dominion*, the key operating verb of the entire campaign to baptize America:

> As the vice regents of God, we are to bring His truth and His will to bear on every sphere of our world and our society. We are to exercise godly dominion and influence over our neighborhoods, our schools, our government . . . our entertainment media, our news media, our scientific endeavors— in short, over every aspect and institution of human society.

Describing the same meeting, Bob Mosner of *Rolling Stone* wrote that in the conference's opening ceremony, the attendees recited an oath that reflects Christocratic hopes and dreams for all America:

> I pledge allegiance to the Christian flag, and to the Savior for whose kingdom it stands, One

Savior, crucified, risen and coming again, with life and liberty for all who believe.

The oath's last two words speak volumes about the Christocratic movement's demand for purity of religious belief, ideological conformity, and spiritual submission and obedience.

But the U.S., while the home country for many Dominionists, is only the start of their campaign of conquest. The target is global control of families, instruments of governance, schools, the judiciary—all for God and Christ.

Schaeffer and the Dominionists whom he influenced clearly understand lessons from history that illustrate how to gain and hold on to total power within a society. The Dominionist message must be constantly asserted with strength, conviction, and no ambiguity or ambivalence. Repeating the same clear message over and over again ultimately impacts people. This tactic confirms Nazi propaganda minister Joseph Goebbels's belief that if a "big lie" is repeated often and loud enough, the public will accept it as true.

Everything the Dominionists do must appear to be "Godly," and the positions and policies of the "secular humanists" must appear as "anti-God." Making that distinction is central to the Dominionist ideology.

Every opponent in any sector of society must be reduced to political or religious impotence, and all adversaries must be completely eliminated from positions of authority.

A key component of Dominionism is constantly maintaining the appearance of power, certainty, and inevitability of success. To achieve a divine end any means—including cruelty, deception, and brute force—is justified.

Dominionists can even excuse horrific behavior from fellow believers because of a Christian doctrine that affirms: "Once saved, always saved." This means that spiritual salvation is not linked to or contingent upon ethical behavior of a "saved" person. The religious importance of doing "good works" is mentioned in the New Testament book of James (2:14–26), but James's teaching that "faith without works is dead" does not apply to Dominionists and to Christocrats, their spiritual offspring.

What counts is "faith," not "good works," in their mission of gaining "dominion." More importantly, the execution of harsh laws, even lethal actions, does not matter, because "once saved, always saved."

Dominionists stress the importance of infiltrating and controlling two key targets within American society: a major political party, and the nation's churches. In the spring of 2005, Christian conservatives, while not all of them Dominionists, held the majority of positions in 36 percent of all GOP state committees, about eighteen states out of fifty. In addition, they had large and growing minorities in over 80 percent of the other thirty-two states.

That kind of presence guarantees control of Republican platform committees and nominating conventions, and supplies a pool of ideologically-committed candidates for elective office.

Moderate Republicans like former U.S. Senator John C. Danforth of Missouri have expressed alarm that Christian conservatives dominate the GOP. In a *New York Times* Op-Ed in March 2005, Danforth wrote that the Republican party, by moving so aggressively in opposing embryonic stem-cell research and by using the federal government to

intrude into the Terri Schiavo case in Florida, "has gone
so far in adopting a sectarian agenda that it has become
the political extension of a religious movement."

In the same month that Danforth's Op-Ed appeared,
Republican Representative Christopher Shays, a Republican from Connecticut, expressed his horror: "This
Republican party of Lincoln has become a party of theocracy." But Representative Tom DeLay of Texas, the GOP's
House Majority Leader, has a wholly different perspective, one that resonates with Dominionism:

> He [God] is using me all the time, everywhere to
> stand up for a biblical world view in everything
> I do and everywhere I am. He is training me.

While the basic beliefs of Dominionism are harsh enough
as first developed by Schaeffer and then later embellished
by his followers, Christian Reconstructionism is even
more extreme in its stated goals for the United States. The
movement merits close attention because its philosophy
provides for its followers the necessary religious validation to fight the war that is currently raging within the
United States. In addition, the venomous ideology of
Christian Recon highly motivates the Christocratic shock
troops—voters, militants, protestors, activists, demon-
strators, and domestic terrorists—who are intent on
destroying the American government, then seizing all
levers of political power in the United States and controlling every room in the American national house.

When I describe the basic tenets and stated goals of
Recon to both Jews and Christians, they are usually dismis-
sive of the movement and its doctrines. It is a dismaying

experience to be repeatedly told I am "overreacting" to the wild views of a fringe group. But tragically, people of good-will throughout history, including the twentieth century, have been either unwilling or unable to accept the fact that fanatical leaders who spew forth hateful philosophy, ide-ology, and goals, along with the methods to achieve them, mean precisely what they write and say. Americans who fail to take seriously Christian Reconstructionism fall into the same trap as earlier generations of well-intentioned people who failed to grasp the enormity and danger of the evil political movements they were confronting.

Christian Recon is powered by Rushdoony's eight-hundred-page book, *The Institutes of Biblical Law,* that was published in 1973. The title and format of this book is based upon John Calvin's (1509–1564) magnum opus, *Institutes of the Christian Religion,* published in Switzer-land in 1560. Although Rushdoony died in 2001, he remains the driving force of Christian Reconstructionism. Before his death, he established the Chalcedon Founda-tion, which has continued his menacing campaign to destroy American political and religious freedom. Chal-cedon is the name of the church council that took place in Turkey in October 451 A.D.

To read *The Institutes of Biblical Law* is to enter a new and fearful world of religious thought, where Jewish and Christian teachings of compassion, mercy, and love are transformed into cruelty, violence, and brutality. Because Rushdoony uses traditional religious vocabu-lary in his book and cites the Hebrew bible, the "Old Testament," as the source of his authority, many readers have been confused by the true goals of Christian Reconstructionism.

However, one person not confused by Rushdoony's writings is Dr. Bruce Prescott of the Interfaith Alliance Forum on Religious Extremism; he is a Presbyterian minister. As a Christian, Prescott has provided a clear analysis of Christian Reconstructionism.

Rushdoony strongly opposed the U.S. Constitution's First Amendment. In his *Institutes*, Rushdoony leaves no doubt about the future status of those who do not share his views:

> In the name of toleration, the believer is asked to associate on a common level of total acceptance with the atheist, the pervert, the criminal, and the adherents of other religions.

Earlier in his massive tome, Rushdoony wrote: "The only true order is founded on biblical Law. All law is religious in nature, and every non-biblical law-order represents an anti-Christian religion." Nor does Rushdoony shy away from using force to achieve the goals of Christian Reconstructionism: "Every law-order is in a state of war against the enemies of that order, and all law is a form of warfare."

In his study of Rushdoony's movement, Prescott lists the six "barest essentials" of Recon:

> 1) Make the ten commandments the law of the land 2) reduce the role of government to the defense of property rights 3) require "tithes" to ecclesiastical agencies to provide welfare services 4) close prisons—reinstitute slavery as a form of punishment and require capital punishment for all of ancient Israel's capital offenses—including

apostasy, blasphemy, incorrigibility in children, murder, rape, Sabbath breaking, sodomy, and witchcraft 5) close public schools—make parents totally responsible for the education of their children 6) strengthen patriarchially ordered families.

Prescott adds:

> With the exception of the call to close prisons, significant steps toward the kind of reforms that they [Christian Reconstructionists] envision are already being made in our society. What they have been able to accomplish has been done by their allying themselves with the Republican party and the conservative Christians and working through the political process. . . . Reconstructionists realize that sooner or later, there is bound to be a backlash against the kind of society they intend to create . . . when that happens, I believe that some, if given the opportunity, will be willing to take up arms and wage another civil war . . . that is [for them] morally and theologically justified. . . .

Prescott wrote his sobering analysis in 2002. I believe the situation has become even more perilous since then.

CHAPTER IV

THERE'S A WAR GOING ON, IN CASE YOU HAVEN'T NOTICED

While America is currently fighting a global war against international terrorism, there is an equally important war currently going on within the United States. It is the most significant internal struggle since the Civil War, when Americans fought fellow Americans in the 1860s. Like that war, the outcome of today's conflict will decisively determine the future of the American republic.

Christocrats are waging an all-out campaign to baptize America. It is a struggle that will decide whether the United States remains a spiritually vigorous country but without an officially established religion, or whether America will become "Christianized," a land in which the religious beliefs and practices of Christian conservatives become the dominant faith: a legally mandated American theocracy exercising control over all aspects of our country's public and private life.

This war will decide whether the U.S. follows the path of many other nations where religion and state have been inextricably ensnared, with disastrous results. The stakes for Americans are that high.

In the current war, Christocrats seek permanent control of the major political, cultural, educational, medical, judicial, economic, media, and legal institutions of the United States. Some Americans mistakenly believe that the campaign to baptize America began with George W. Bush's victory in the 2000 presidential election. But the battle actually started much earlier, and it will continue after Bush leaves the White House.

In the early 1970s a group of evangelical Protestant leaders led by the late Carl Henry, a prominent Christian theologian and Baptist seminary faculty member, conducted a summit conference of like-minded colleagues in an Arlington, Virginia motel near the Key Bridge that spans the Potomac River. The meeting was to plan a Christian conversion campaign intended to "call America to Christ."

The organizers believed that if millions of individuals converted to evangelical Christianity, the entire country would be morally transformed. The effort was dubbed "Key '73," and although it failed in its proclaimed goal, it was one of the first nationwide attempts to make evangelical Christianity the dominant religion in the United States.

Unlike today's Christocratic campaign, Key '73 was a personal faith-centered operation that had little overt political content. It focused on gaining individual conversions to Christianity.

But seven years later, the combination of conservative

politics and conservative religion was first unveiled. That was when the Reverend Jerry Falwell, a Southern Baptist pastor from Lynchburg, Virginia, established an organization he called the "Moral Majority," whose stated purpose was making Christian conservative values the dominant force in American political life. The name, "Moral Majority," was a brilliant public relations strategy, since it made all other Americans who were not members of Falwell's group de facto members of the "Immoral Minority."

Until 1980, Falwell was best known as the pastor of the Thomas Road Baptist Church, a large SBC church in Lynchburg. But his bluntly stated views on many issues, including anti-homosexuality, a call for organized and mandated prayers in public schools, and support for the security and survival of Israel, made him an attractive media personality on television and radio talk shows. As a result of his many media appearances, Falwell became a recognized religious "talking head," beloved and believed by his fans, and despised and distrusted by his critics.

Falwell's political goal in 1980 was the electoral defeat of President Jimmy Carter, a fellow Southern Baptist who was perceived as politically weak and a person who lacked a sufficient commitment to traditional Christian values. Indeed, the U.S. presidential campaign that year marked the emergence of the growing political power of Christian conservatives. Falwell and his "Moral Majority" energized a group of voters who later came to be called the "base" of the Republican party.

The 1980 presidential election was notable in an important way. Carter acted as an impotent incumbent, self-imprisoned in the White House as a result of the Iranian hostage crisis in Tehran. He conveyed a depressing sense of moral rectitude; some termed it excessive self-righteousness, and Carter maintained a dour personal piety that contrasted greatly with the sunny optimistic personality of his GOP opponent, former California Governor Ronald Reagan.

Carter was also perceived as a detail-loving micro-manager, while the ebullient Reagan stressed only a few major goals without revealing too many specifics: tax cuts, smaller government, strong national defense, and a pride in all things American. Reagan was a divorced film star who was once the president of a trade union in Hollywood, the Screen Actors Guild. In addition, until the election of 1980 he never exhibited much interest in publicly identifying as a church member, much less as an evangelical Christian.

U.S. Representative John Anderson, a Republican from Illinois, also ran for president that year as an independent candidate; like Carter, he, too, was an active Christian. Anderson was a lay leader in the Evangelical Free Church of America, a smaller group than the Southern Baptist Convention, but a denomination that also stressed conservative theological positions.

At first glance, it would have appeared that Carter and Anderson together would win most of the Christian conservative vote. The president was even a Sunday School teacher in a Southern Baptist church, and Anderson was a prominent member of an evangelical denomination.

But surprisingly, it was the divorced movie star who gained most of the Christian conservative vote and, with it, the presidency. Clearly, perceived social values counted far more than active church membership. Reagan's public positions on abortion, gun ownership, and other issues were more congruent with the Christian conservative agenda than those of the overtly "Christian" Carter or Anderson.

For Falwell and his colleagues, Reagan's 1980 victory gained them public credibility and, more importantly, access to the White House. Falwell's triumph was a significant milestone in the new American Civil War.

The battle to baptize America that began decades ago has already lasted much longer than the four terrible years of the first Civil War, and today's struggle has no end in sight. I have personally participated in some of the battles of that long-running war as the American Jewish Committee's interreligious affairs director.

Following my tour of active duty as a United States Air Force chaplain in Japan and Korea, and after serving congregations in Kansas City, Missouri, and Champaign-Urbana, Illinois, I joined the AJC's interreligious affairs department in 1968. In the following years, I worked closely with the various Christian communities: Protestants, Roman Catholics, and Eastern Orthodox. During that period, I devoted much of my time to working on a series of cooperative programs with Christian conservatives, a growing force in American life.

The AJC was the appropriate place for such efforts. It was founded in 1906 as a direct reaction to the lethal anti-Jewish pogroms that were then taking place in Czarist Russia. To achieve its goals, the AJC has always worked closely with the political and religious leaders of the United States. In addition to protecting Jewish rights and lives around the world and, after 1948, building support for the state of Israel, one of the AJC's primary mandates has been combating religious anti-Semitism and building positive relations with all branches of Christianity.

I quickly learned the Christian conservative political agenda is fueled by equally conservative theological beliefs; the two are inextricably linked. I also discovered that while most Christian conservatives are white evangelical Protestants, the group also includes conservative Catholics, African-American Protestants, Eastern Orthodox Christians, and members of various religio-political organizations conveniently lumped together and called the Religious Right.

The most important Religious Right group is the Virginia Beach-based Christian Coalition (CC), founded by Robertson in September 1989. The organization's first executive director was Ralph Reed.

The Coalition's announced mission is to provide "a means toward helping to give Christians a voice in their government again." The key word is *again*, since Robertson and Christian Coalition members believe "their America" was once a morally based republic that has been taken from them by a combination of "secular humanists," "activist judges," and others.

The CC grew out of Robertson's failed 1988 bid to gain the GOP presidential nomination. Left with a large list of supporters, Robertson established the CC and appointed Reed its first executive director, a post he held until 1997.

Robertson described the Christian Coalition's mission and strategy in the seventeen-minute 1990 CC video, *America at a Crossroads*. Robertson said:

Christians founded this nation, they built this
nation, and for three hundred years they governed
this nation. We can govern again. That is why I
founded the Christian Coalition. . . . The mission
of the Christian Coalition is simple: to mobilize
Christians one precinct at a time, one community
at a time, one state at a time, until once again we
are the head and not the tail, at the top rather than
the bottom, of our political system.

Another significant leader of the Religious Right is the
Reverend Dr. James C. Dobson's Focus on the Family
(FOF) organization, which is headquartered in Colorado
Springs, Colorado.

In its Guiding Principles, FOF, a strongly Christian
group, supports church, family, and government as the
three "basic institutions" of society, and it opposes "the
humanist notions of today's theorists."

In recent years, Dobson has become a highly visible
supporter of conservative politics and the Republican
party, and a foe of such GOP moderates as Senator Arlen
Specter of Pennsylvania. Immediately following the 2004
election, Dobson unsuccessfully attempted to block
Specter from assuming the chairmanship of the Senate's
Judiciary Committee. In recent years, Dobson has shed
much of his earlier persona as a family-oriented psychol-
ogist, and is today considered one of the top three Christian conservative leaders in the U.S. He speaks out
frequently on political, religious, and cultural issues.

As a result of my interreligious work, I met and gained
an understanding of the leading Christian conservative
personalities, including Graham, Falwell, and Robertson.

I also observed the composition, beliefs, strategies, and programs of the many theologically conservative church bodies and organizations in the U.S.

For most of my years with the American Jewish Committee, I was an optimist, an American rabbi who believed that the encounter between Judaism and Christianity offered enormous, even extraordinary, possibilities for reversing the lachrymose history that has existed between those two ancient faith communities and for replacing that history with human bridges of mutual respect and understanding.

I also believed that the unique American experiment in religious liberty and freedom of individual conscience, based on the rights guaranteed by the First Amendment of the Constitution, was our nation's hallmark and a model for the rest of the world to emulate. I believe that all those goals are still within our reach.

Until recently, I viewed Christian conservatives as simply one more faith community, albeit a large one, in a religiously pluralistic America that today numbers over five thousand separate religious groups.

But during the past few years, I have witnessed a new and angry militancy among Christian conservatives, and particularly among Christocrats. It is a stridency that has moved far beyond the fiery sermons and the loudly sung hymns that are so much a part of their spiritual lives. Something new has erupted within America: Christocrats have mounted a campaign aimed at imposing their values on the total society, and it is a campaign they intend to win.

I am convinced they seek to control what takes place in every room of the American mansion: the bedroom, the hospital and operating room, the news and press room, the library room, the courtroom, the schoolroom, the public room, and the workroom—the major facets of American society. It is a new and ominous chapter in a very old story.

Since the founding of our nation, there has been a continuous struggle to maintain a legal separation of church and state, of government and religion. Because of that extraordinary effort, both institutions, religion and state, have remained robust but independent entities within the total American society.

America's two-centuries-plus experiment in legally separating religion and state—few other countries in the world have been so successful for so long in this difficult undertaking—has prevented entanglements between the two, and made certain that neither of these two powerful bodies dominates or controls the other.

The church-state battle was already well under way with the founding of the American republic in the late 18th century, and it has continued unabated ever since. But today's battles are much more turbulent than in the past. The well-organized Christian conservative movement, both its leaders and their supporters who seek to baptize America, are politically stronger, more energized, and better financed than ever before in American history.

In a bizarre twist of self-perception, Christian conservatives, though numbering in the tens of millions within the United States, are today driven by a sense of rage and revenge that is aimed at an amorphous and handy target: an all-pervasive "secular humanist" society that, it is charged, scorns traditional spiritual values and provides the major anti-religious culture cues in the U.S., especially "abortion on demand," a "homosexual lifestyle," and publicly accepted pornography.

Christian conservatives are convinced that they are America's underdogs, a mocked minority, and a beleaguered community that is reviled by a "liberal, Godless" contemporary society. A widely believed Christian conservative mantra asserts: "We are in America, but not *of* America."

But this view of a besieged minority constantly under attack conceals the reality that Christian conservatives actively participate in, and influence, all aspects of contemporary American society. It is, in fact, a highly active and talented community that includes a full complement of educated men and women who have gained professional positions of authority and leadership within the private and public spheres.

Many of today's Christian conservatives that I know publicly affirm and act on their religious identity with a pride—critics would say with an arrogance—that was lacking in recent years. Yet, to the surprise of most Americans, many Christian conservatives still believe they are hated outsiders in America.

Sure-footed and supremely confident in their own political beliefs and religious certitude as never before, Christocrats are committed to a systematic campaign to shape American society in their own religio-political image.

It was once fashionable, even comforting, to dismiss such people by labeling them "rednecks," "crackers," or "Elmer Gantrys." As a rabbi who has heard anti-Semitic descriptions of Jews, I always recognized that such pejorative descriptions were never accurate and reflected an ignorance of an important sector of the American population. Christian conservatives have used such bigoted stereotypes and caricatures as a rallying cry, and they now seek revenge for a century of perceived ridicule and defamation. Their goal is the political and cultural emasculation of the hated "secular humanists," the perceived source of anti-Christian rhetoric.

Christocrats believe that the public's continuing encounters with current American culture, especially the news media, universities, and the entertainment industry—all "ultra-liberal"—mock traditional Christian beliefs, weaken family lives, impact negatively upon moral values, and deplete America's moral strength. The best way to preserve the Christian conservative "way of life" is to gain control of the key institutions that mold American society.

Only when such a decisive victory is achieved can the traditional Christian community be preserved and the larger American community be "saved," not merely "saved" in Christian theological terms, but "saved" politically and culturally from the evils of a "Godless" secular society.

All Christocrats share the belief that America has lost its moral compass as a nation. The imposition of desperately needed moral values can occur only when a Christian theocracy espousing traditional beliefs and practices is legally established. Nothing less will solve the problems of a secular-soaked nation that has lost its way, stumbled into sinfulness, and debased traditional Christian values.

It is a dire diagnosis that requires a radical Christian cure: an American nation legally anchored to a Christocratic political agenda, and a conservative Christian theology.

Christocratic leaders constantly invoke "divine authority" as the justification of their policies and platforms. "God's law," as they and they alone define it, transcends and supersedes any human legislation, even the cherished U.S. Constitution. Acting as the exclusive source for defining divine authority in all temporal matters provides Christocrats with a sense of absolute religious and political certainty that intimidates much of the media and silences weak-kneed critics who are afraid to speak out lest they be tarred with the chilling epithet of "secular humanist."

Christocrats relentlessly characterize their political and religious opponents as sinful or ungodly. By constantly using the powerful rhetoric of "family values," "public morality," and "sanctity of life" to describe their platform, they have energized voters and gained a *de facto* veto power, if not effective control, over the Republican party in the United States. They believe a "Christian America" will embody the exclusivist theological beliefs necessary to solve society's acute problems.

But if this is true, why didn't America's Founders create a "Christian America" back in the eighteenth century when they had every opportunity to do so? Was it an oversight, an accident, or a deliberate effort to keep religion and/or Christianity out of the nation's two most important documents?

The Declaration of Independence in 1776 makes no mention of "God," "Jesus," or "Christianity." The Constitution drafted in 1787 has several references to a Divinity, but, again, there is an absence of specific religious and/or Christian references.

The struggle to achieve Christian conservative

domination comes at a moment in history when many Americans still falsely, even naïvely, believe that the church-state issue was definitively settled long ago, when the Bill of Rights—including the First Amendment —was incorporated into the Constitution.

But despite the Bill of Rights and more than 220 years of national history, the appropriate role of religion in a religiously pluralistic America has never been fully resolved. Strong coercive forces of Christian piety, emboldened by a series of recent electoral victories, are now demanding full control over every aspect of public and private American life.

Yet most Americans are only vaguely aware of the effort currently under way to convert the United States into a legally sanctioned "Christian nation."

Such people mistakenly view the church-state battle as simply a series of arcane court cases involving efforts to require prayers and bible-reading in public schools, the elimination of the teaching of evolution in schools, or attempts to erect a Christian crèche in front of a City Hall during the December holiday season. They are convinced that the relationship between church and state is a remote, abstract principle that does not touch their daily lives.

But they are wrong. The emergence of a politically charged Christocratic movement has grave implications for the general American society.

As the battle to baptize America intensifies, several significant points need to be emphasized.

There is, of course, no objection to full participation by Christians—along with every other religious community —in the American political process. Separation of church and state does not mean the separation of religion and politics, and many of America's religious groups have long been active in the public square as they attempt to enact or block specific legislation they deem important to themselves and their members.

Indeed, the religious communities of America were central players in the campaign to achieve American political independence from Great Britain. Presbyterian minister John Witherspoon of New Jersey signed the Declaration of Independence, and Rabbi Gershom Mendes Seixas of New York City was an active supporter of the movement to break free from Great Britain. Seixas was one of the clergymen present at President George Washington's first inauguration in 1789.

Leaders of the American religious communities were a prophetic force in the abolitionist movement. Some notable examples are Reform Rabbi David Einhorn; Presbyterian minister Lyman Beecher; his daughter Harriet Beecher Stowe, who wrote *Uncle Tom's Cabin;* and William Lloyd Garrison.

However, it must be admitted that some Christian clergy and rabbis, especially those living in the South, used bible verses to theologically justify human slavery prior to the Civil War.

The adoption of a Constitutional amendment prohibiting the manufacture of alcoholic beverages in the U.S. during the 1920s and 1930s was the result of a concerted effort by some Protestant churches and their leaders, especially members of the Methodist-based Women's Christian Temperance Union (WCTU).

In more recent times, many faith communities and their leaders have been in the forefront on such key issues as support for environmentalism and civil and human rights, as well as opposition to the Vietnam War, capital punishment, ownership of guns, and a host of other concerns. Religious leaders are found on all sides of abortion and gay rights concerns.

Religious groups have rarely been absent from American political life, but they have always perceived themselves and have been seen by others as one of the many players in the noisy and competitive public square.

In one way, Christocrats emulate other religious groups by using a stream of selective biblical quotes to buttress their political positions. But they go further and prayerfully wrap themselves in the American flag and proclaim an exclusivist, non-pluralistic vision of America. Instead of being just another public advocate in the crowded public square, they seek no political or religious accommodation when they demonize their opponents. It is God's way or no way.

In advancing their agenda items, Christocrats frequently do not seek coalitional partners or temporary allies, who may share differing religious beliefs. Instead, they loudly claim that they are the sole legitimate interpreters of American values, and that their agenda alone is from and of God, with no compromise possible.

That agenda includes strong opposition to the Equal Rights Amendment, embryonic stem-cell research, legal abortion, any prohibition or infringement on the right to own firearms, "secular humanism," assisted suicides for the terminally ill, government aid to artists or artistic groups that are "obscene, profane, or in other ways subvert 'family values,'" and fierce opposition to any "special rights" for gays and lesbians, including same-sex marriages or civil unions.

Christocrats generally support term limits for elective offices (except for certain favored political leaders), financial vouchers using public funds for parents of private- and parochial-school students, capital punishment, student-led prayer and bible-reading in public schools, an abstinence-based sex-education curriculum, the teaching of the so-called scientific creationism or the so-called intelligent design in public-school science classes, and severely limiting immigration into the United States.

Since Americans are more, not less, diverse in their religious identities, the attempt by the Christian conservative community to create a constricted "Christian America" flies directly in the face of demographic facts.

The 2004 election of George W. Bush to a second term as president confirmed the extraordinary power of conservative religious issues in determining the campaign's outcome. Audio tapes released in 2005 of Bush's 1998 private conversations with Douglas Wead of Texas reveal the political importance of the Christian conservative community and the strong shadow it was already casting over the 2000 race for the White House.

Bush, then governor of Texas and preparing for a presidential campaign, told Wead: "There are some code words. There are some proper ways to say things, and some improper ways. . . ."

Those code words, key issues for Christian conservatives, can be lumped together as the "Three Gs" of God, guns, and gays; but they also include attacks on popular culture, and support for unrestricted expressions and symbols of Christian faith in the shared communal square, especially in public schools and courtrooms. Those values, often transmitted in "code words," were the major concerns of nearly one quarter of the voters in 2004, trumping jobs, health care, education, the war in Iraq, the energy crisis, and even terrorism as key election issues.

Political observers, many of them stunned by the high priority that voters placed on religious issues, emphasized that white Christian conservative voters supported Bush over Senator John Kerry, the 2004 Democratic presidential nominee, by a four-to-one margin. But the same observers often overlooked the fact that Bush, a United Methodist born-again Protestant Christian, also received 52 percent of the Roman Catholic vote, 60 percent of the Hispanic evangelical ballots, a quarter of Jewish votes, and, surprisingly, 16 percent of black evangelicals. There were also millions of Bush voters who identify as Christians, but are not conservative or evangelical in their theology or religious practices.

However, it is the white Christian conservative community, especially members of the evangelical community, that supplies the religious and political ideology, along with the foot-soldiers, a.k.a. voters, who fuel the current religious war. One key initiative on the agenda is the active promotion of religion in all phases of public life, opening "faith-based" Christian action cadres in the 435 Congressional districts, and working for the appointment of "constitutionally and theologically" sound judges to the Supreme Court and all other judicial positions.

But evangelicals, while a major component of the Christian conservative community, are erroneously equated with the Religious Right, fundamentalists, extremists, Pentecostals, and charismatics. Each of these groups has a specific identity and history.

In her 1994 American Jewish Committee study, *The Political Activity of the Religious Right in the 1990s,* Rabbi Lori Forman wrote:

> The Religious Right is made up primarily of Christian evangelicals and fundamentalists. . . . In the early 1920s a subgroup came to be known as fundamentalists . . . those determined to wage an aggressive war against theological and cultural modernism. . . . Fundamentalists entered the political arena relatively recently. For years they followed a policy of strict separation from . . . the world of politics. This was based on their conviction that the world was sinful and not worthy of their involvement, since Jesus' Kingdom would soon arrive. . . . In the 1970s, politicians of the secular New Right reached out to the fundamentalist and evangelical churches . . . to expand their political base. . . . Today . . . the fundamentalists have overwhelmingly abandoned their old distrust of politics. . . . This trend is likely to continue.

The largest numbers of those foot soldiers, the politically motivated Christocratic "Warriors for Christ" are found within the white evangelical Protestant community. But who are they? What do they believe?

CHAPTER V

WHO ARE THE EVANGELICAL CHRISTIANS, AND WHY HAVE SO MANY ENLISTED TO FIGHT IN TODAY'S RELIGIOUS WAR?

Some Americans mistakenly believe today's Christocratic movement is composed solely of Protestant fundamentalists or religious extremists. While the majority of Christocrats are, in fact, white evangelical Protestants, the movement also includes theologically conservative Catholics and African-Americans.

The Catholics who have joined the movement to baptize America are frequently rebelling against the reforms adopted by the world's bishops between 1962 and 1965 at the Second Vatican Council in Rome.

Critics of the Council's actions—and they are highly vocal—charge that those reforms have significantly weakened traditional Catholic teachings and spiritual faithfulness, especially in North America and Europe. They claim that the use of the vernacular in worship services instead of Latin, the once unifying language of the

Mass, as well as other changes in liturgy and Catholic doctrine, has created large numbers of "cafeteria Catholics" in the U.S. who pick and choose which tenets of the church to follow.

The specifics of American Catholic religious behavior and observance were widely discussed in the media following the April 2005 death of Pope John Paul II. While Catholics in the U.S. adored the Pope, they frequently did not follow his conservative teachings regarding birth control, abortion, and several other issues.

As a result of the Protestant Reformation, evangelicals have historically viewed Roman Catholicism and its followers with suspicion and opposition. Some evangelicals even perceived the Catholic Church as the embodiment of the dreaded anti-Christ, and they rejected the dogmas, liturgy, and papal authority of Catholicism.

Anti-Catholicism was an important factor in the 1928 U.S. presidential election when New York Governor Alfred E. Smith, a Roman Catholic, ran unsuccessfully against Herbert Hoover. John F. Kennedy, America's only Catholic president, also faced some anti-Catholicism, particularly from several prominent Protestant ministers, including the late Dr. Norman Vincent Peale, the author of the best-selling self-help book *The Power of Positive Thinking*.

But in recent years, evangelicals and conservative Catholics have for the first time formed coalitions based on shared values and beliefs. In 2004, such a coalition was clearly at work in the joint evangelical-Catholic promotion and support of Mel Gibson's controversial film *The Passion of the Christ*. The popular movie star personally financed and directed the film, and Gibson also wrote much of the screenplay.

Gibson, who calls himself a "traditionalist" Catholic, rejects many of the Vatican II reforms and believes that the years of Pope Pius XII (1939–1958) represent the last authentic pontificate. Art and film experts noted that *The Passion of the Christ* features classic medieval Catholic depictions of Jesus' death, along with special cinematic reverence for Mary. Such graphic imagery in religious art and the adoration of Mary have long been anathema to evangelicals, but that did not prevent them from strongly supporting and promoting the *Passion* film.

Many Jewish and Christian leaders, including myself, charged that the film transmitted toxic anti-Jewish images and stereotypes that placed the responsibility for Jesus' death not on the Roman occupation authorities of the time, who alone had the power to inflict capital punishment, but upon the venal bloodthirsty Jewish community of ancient Judea.

But despite the vigorous criticisms, evangelical Protestants saw in both Gibson and his film a return to traditional Christological values, and they used the movie as a cinematic battering ram for use against liberal churches. A month before the film's general release in February 2004, I attended a screening of *The Passion of the Christ* in a large Protestant church in Winter Park, Florida, that attracted nearly four thousand evangelical pastors and lay leaders. The enthusiastic audience was urged to use the film in campaigns to convert people to Christianity. The Gibson movie was called the "greatest evangelistic tool in 2,000 years."

An example of the evangelical embrace of Gibson's film was in evidence during Christian Holy Week in 2005, a year after the movie's initial release date. Two southwest

Florida Protestant congregations, the Cape Coral Community Church and the First Presbyterian Church in Bonita Springs, featured *The Passion of the Christ* during their Good Friday services. The film is now considered a part of the sacred ritual for an increasing number of mostly white churches.

A much smaller number of Christocrats is found in African-American churches. Not surprisingly, leaders of those churches have for decades advocated a progressive social-justice agenda calling for improvement in civil rights, welfare, housing, education, employment, and medical care; but those same leaders are often theologically conservative on the issues of abortion, same-sex marriages, "public morality," and "family values."

Because of the "split personality" prevalent among many African-American church leaders, some pastors have been attracted to the Christocrat movement. However, their number is much smaller than the white evangelicals who supply the largest number of "warriors and voters for Christ."

But any understanding of the Christian conservative attempt to control American life requires a detailed definition and description of white evangelical Protestants.

Most Christian conservatives are evangelicals, but not every evangelical is part of the Christocratic campaign. The term *evangelical* comes from the Greek word *evangelion,* meaning "good news." By this definition, all Christians and their churches are evangelical, that is, they seek to spread the "good news" of the Gospels to the entire world.

But within the United States, the term *evangelical* is generally associated with Protestant Christians who believe that the bible—the Hebrew Scriptures and the New Testament—is the sole authority for religious belief and practice. The Assemblies of God, a major evangelical church body, proclaims: "The bible is an all-sufficient rule for faith and practice." Among evangelicals, this affirmation of biblical truth is termed *inerrancy*, since they have faith that the Holy Scriptures are without error and literally true.

Most evangelicals have had a personal conversion experience, either instantaneous or one that evolved over a period of time. This religious phenomenon is usually called being "born again," and it involves the acceptance of Jesus as one's personal Savior and Messiah. A third striking feature of evangelicals is the need to evangelize either collectively or individually: "Go ye therefore, and teach all nations, baptizing them . . ." (Matthew 28:16–20). This is called the "Great Commission," and it remains a source of intra-Christian debate regarding how this commandment should be actually implemented.

During the past thirty years, many "mainline" or "progressive" Protestants have muted or abandoned direct missionary activities, particularly those aimed at Jews. The teachings of American theologian Reinhold Niebuhr (1892–1971) have influenced several generations of mainline Protestants. In his 1958 book *Pious and Secular America,* Niebuhr condemned Christian efforts to convert Jews, declaring that such missionary activity was spiritually incompatible with Christianity, as well as being theologically insulting to Jews and Judaism.

But in recent years some evangelicals have intensified their campaign to bring their particular brand of Christianity to Jews. In 1996, delegates to the annual meeting of the Southern Baptist Convention in New Orleans adopted a resolution calling for increased "evangelization" efforts directed to the Jewish community. But evangelist Billy Graham, himself a Southern Baptist, publicly criticized the SBC's action. Years earlier, during the Key '73 evangelistic campaign, Graham, citing verses from the New Testament Book of Romans (chapters 9–11), declared:

> I believe God has always had a special relationship with the Jewish people. . . . In my evangelistic efforts, I have never felt called to single out Jews as Jews. . . . Just as Judaism frowns on proselytizing that is coercive or that seeks to commit men against their will, so do I.

It is estimated that over 55 million Americans consider themselves evangelicals, and they live in all sections of the United States. Evangelicals are members of many different churches; and almost every major Protestant denomination has within it an active evangelical component that presses for a renewal of "traditional Christian beliefs and practices."

For example, a leading mainline denomination, the United Methodist Church, "continues its strong evangelical heritage. Within each congregation is a vital center of biblical study and evangelism—a blending of personal piety and discipleship."

An evangelical scholar, Thomas A. Askew, has noted that:

> evangelical Christianity has never been a religious organization, nor primarily a theological

system, nor even a containable movement. It is a mood, a perspective, an approach grounded in biblical theology, but reaching into the motifs of religious experience. . . . The evangelical faith has roots that reach back to European Reformation theology . . . as well as to the Puritan tradition.

The Southern Baptist Convention (SBC) is the largest evangelical denomination in the United States, with more than 16,400,000 members and thirty-seven thousand churches. While the Roman Catholic Church has more members, the SBC has more individual congregations. The SBC maintains a major publishing house in Nashville, Tennessee, and sponsors seminaries in Kentucky, Texas, North Carolina, California, Missouri, and Louisiana. The SBC also has many denominational offices in the Atlanta metropolitan area.

Because of its exclusivist theology, the SBC is not a member of either the ecumenical World Council of Churches (WCC), based in Geneva, Switzerland, or the National Council of Churches (NCC) in New York City, a consortium of thirty-three Protestant and Eastern Orthodox Christian bodies. During the past three decades, the SBC has experienced a series of well-publicized intrachurch conflicts pitting theological conservatives against moderates. The conservatives emerged victorious in the various bitter struggles for control of the denomination's seminaries, its publishing facilities, and the SBC bureaucracy. One moderate SBC leader who was intimately involved in the battles has said: "It was a fight for control of the SBC's body and soul, and the religious conservatives have clearly won."

The well-known television commentator Bill Moyers, himself an SBC minister, has denounced the conservative takeover of his denomination. In 1999, he said:

> The Lenin of the SBC—the man who plotted and perpetrated the takeover—had determined that reactionaries would be named to run every one of the denomination's seminaries, colleges, boards, and agencies. But he had more than religious power in mind. . . . In the past 20 years reactionary Baptists forged an alliance to take over a major political party and promote an agenda of state—sanctioned prayer, public subsidies, and government privileges. Their first, and most successful, strategy was to seize control of the Southern Baptist Convention, whose pews they envisioned as precincts of power. The cabal that took over the Southern Baptist Convention could only succeed by a supreme act of ecclesiastical arrogance.

Bitter internal Baptist battles are nothing new. In the middle of the nineteenth century, the Baptists in America split into two distinct denominations over the volatile issue of slavery: the SBC, and the American Baptists Churches (ABC). The separated Baptist branches have never been reunited—unlike the Presbyterians, who also broke into two denominations because of the slavery issue. The two wings of the Presbyterian came back together in 1983.

The second-largest Baptist group is the ABC, or "northern Baptists," with about 1,600 thousand members.

Its denominational offices are in Valley Forge, Pennsylvania. Unlike the far larger SBC, American Baptists are members of the WCC and the NCC. Today there are over twenty separate denominations of Baptists in the United States.

A fast-growing evangelical body is the Assemblies of God (AG), which was established in 1914 and is headquartered in Springfield, Missouri. In 1970, the Assemblies listed 625,000 members, but the current figure is 2.2 million, a remarkable 42 percent increase. The AG is theologically even more conservative than the SBC, and Assembly of God members encourage glossolalia (speaking in tongues). Glossolalia is considered a "physical sign" of one's faith. Members of the Assemblies of God are a key component of the Republican party's electoral base.

Just how important are they? The day after the 2004 Democratic National Convention ended, President Bush flew to Springfield to officially inaugurate his reelection campaign. In his speech that day, he sent a clear two-sentence message that every evangelical in America understood: "They [the GOP's political and cultural opponents] somehow believe the heart and soul of America can be found in Hollywood. The heart and soul of America is found right here in Springfield, Missouri."

Although smaller in membership, the Evangelical Free Church of America, based in Minneapolis, Minnesota, is another center of evangelical Christianity that has experienced strong membership growth since 1970.

The increased growth of evangelical churches has come at a time when the six largest mainline (i.e., non-evangelical) Protestant bodies—the Episcopal Church, the Presbyterian Church (USA), the United Methodist Church, the Evangelical Lutheran Church in America, the United Church of Christ (Congregationalists), and the ABC—have all suffered significant membership losses. The decline in their numbers, along with the high median age of mainline Protestants, has weakened the "Big Six's" ability to counter the aggressive religio-political campaign of the evangelical churches.

The noted church historian Martin E. Marty of the University of Chicago has described the recent rise of the evangelicals as "the most significant religious trend in the United States."

Historically, evangelical Christianity was, in fact, the mainstream of American Protestantism until the 1890s, when the mainline, or more liberal, churches eclipsed it in social status, membership, and influence in the larger society. The Methodist circuit riders and the itinerant Baptist lay preachers are part of American history, and it is no accident that the largest number of churches in the South and Southwest still reflect the presence of early Methodist and Baptist preachers.

But the combination of modern biblical scholarship, rational thinking stemming from the Enlightenment, and the rise of a social-justice component within progressive Protestant churches gave strength to those denominations and helped them gain dominance over evangelicals. For the first seventy years of the twentieth century, mainline churches and several well-known divinity schools—Harvard, Yale, and Union Theological Seminary in New York City—were the primary "addresses" for American Protestantism.

The defeat of the Confederacy in the Civil War was also

a key factor in the rise of mainline church bodies. Not only was the American South politically discredited, economically devastated, and physically occupied by federal troops, but the region's conservative evangelical religious tradition was devalued as well. As a result, evangelical churches, especially in the South, became objects of ridicule in the North, and members of those churches were perceived as religiously backward, even theologically illiterate.

Evangelicals were further shunted aside and scorned by their more liberal Protestant brothers and sisters following the famous 1925 Scopes "Monkey" Trial in Tennessee that pitted the evangelical lay leader and three-time Democratic presidential candidate William Jennings Bryan against the religiously liberal Clarence Darrow as contending lawyers. The success of the popular play and film *Inherit the Wind* in the 1950s artistically confirmed liberal religion's decisive victory over evangelism, and, with it, evolution's triumph over the biblical account of creation. But that victory existed only on the stage and the silver screen, not in real life.

The successful 1976 presidential campaign of Georgia Governor Jimmy Carter, a Southern Baptist Sunday School teacher and former missionary, and the founding of the Moral Majority four years later by another Southern Baptist, the Reverend Jerry Falwell, placed evangelicals on the center of the American political stage. Until then, most evangelicals had focused their energies on "getting right with Jesus"—that is, establishing a personal relationship with God.

For them, politics was a distasteful, albeit necessary, business to be carried out by others. Evangelical churches—and there are thousands of them scattered throughout the South and Southwest—were until recently primarily places for Sunday-morning services and Wednesday-night bible classes. The church was often the social center of a community, but it did not serve as a political clubhouse or a site of electoral instruction and indoctrination. That came later with Republican electoral victories in the South and an aggressive successful Religious Right campaign to maximize the evangelical vote.

The once commonly accepted evangelical principle of separating church life from political involvement stemmed from two sources. Baptists who fled to the thirteen original British colonies in America were victims of religious persecution in Great Britain. It was a campaign of vilification carried out by the Church of England, whose leaders also defamed Methodist leaders John and Charles Wesley and other "dissident" Christian leaders.

Bitter memories of a state-supported Church of England that carried with it the full power of the British Crown, including Star Chamber proceedings against members of Baptist and Methodist churches, remained a key part of the southern Protestant tradition for several centuries.

Because of their painful experiences at the hands of the British Crown and the Church of England, Baptists have historically been strongly committed to separation of church and state, religious liberty, and freedom of conscience. However, recent positions adopted by the SBC have weakened and even abandoned the historic Southern Baptist stand on church-state separation.

The turning point came at the SBC's 1982 national meeting, when the "messengers," or delegates, adopted a resolution supporting the adoption of a Constitutional amendment mandating prayers in America's public schools. No one doubted that the majority of such classroom and assembly prayers would be Christian in tone and substance.

The Reagan administration had proposed the amendment, but in 1984, two years after the SBC action, the attempt to constitutionally require school prayer failed to receive the necessary two thirds, or sixty-seven votes, in the U.S. Senate.

Until 1982, the SBC had been among the strongest Christian supporters of church-state separation, but since then the denomination has taken positions contesting that historical principle. Critics charge that Southern Baptist leaders and their Christocratic followers have abandoned a cherished and historically significant part of their spiritual tradition.

The New Testament verse to "render unto Caesar what is Caesar's"(Mark 12:17) was a religious leitmotif of evangelical Christianity until the late 1970s. Voting in elections was important, but more significant than any earthly political regime was the Kingdom of God, Christian belief in the world to come, and a relationship to Jesus. It was a duality of separated interests and outlook that remained constant for many years.

However, evangelicals did vote in elections, and until recently their vote, especially in the South, went in large numbers to Democratic candidates. This voting pattern was the result of the harsh Republican-led Reconstructionist efforts following the Civil War and the success of the FDR-initiated New Deal in the 1930s and 1940s that provided government-sponsored economic aid to America's poorest regions, especially the South.

Evangelicals frequently elected political leaders who supported racial segregation and the anti-black Jim Crow laws enacted following the Civil War. That voting pattern has dramatically changed in recent years, and it is now the Republican party that wins most of the evangelical votes.

For nearly three centuries, evangelical Christianity has remained a significant spiritual expression for millions of Americans, particularly those residing in the South and Southwest. While it went underground for nearly seven decades during the twentieth century in the face of theologically progressive Protestant churches, an often-ridiculed evangelical Christianity reemerged as a strong and highly visible movement in the 1970s.

Carter's election as U.S. president in 1976, and the enormous popularity of evangelist Billy Graham, provided two important confirmations that a religious and political sea change had taken place in America.

David F. Wells, an evangelical scholar, graphically describes those changes:

> liberal Protestants [the National Council of Churches and its mainline church membership] had always taken it for granted that . . . there was a divine mandate securing for them their role as custodians of the culture. In the early 1970s this notion was unceremoniously abandoned. . . .

But despite their large numbers and growing political influence, most evangelicals still perceive their brand of Christianity as being under constant siege and themselves as objects of derision. The two arch-adversaries of evangelicals, "secular humanists" and "new-age globalization," are considered alien threats to traditional values.

The powerful forces of modernity have stirred up a sense of fear and anger among evangelicals and created a cadre of Christocrats, dedicated Christian warriors intent on defending themselves and their faith from perceived hostile attacks. It is that revenge-filled group of Christians that is actively working to undermine more than 220 years of American history by imposing their religious values upon the general society. That history, based upon freedom of religion in all its forms and the legal principle of church-state separation, is under severe attack.

The SBC defined its chief enemies in the starkest terms at the denomination's 2000 meeting in Orlando, Florida: "The New Age globalism advocates a one-world government, a one-world religion, and a one-world economy. . . ." Secular humanism is "the belief that no religion can or does possess objective truth and that all religions are of equal worth. . . ."

A year earlier, SBC delegates meeting in Atlanta adopted a resolution, On Public Discourse and the Free Exercise of Religion. The resolution singled out for sharp criticism "the media, the entertainment industry, the courts, the political system, and the system of public education." The SBC said those institutions fostered "a climate of growing and pervasive hostility toward religion. . . ."

In reaction to such positions, the Cooperative Baptist Fellowship (CBF) was established by SBC moderates in the 1990s, and approximately two thousand congregations are affiliated with the new group. The CBF is open to programs with other Christian church groups and the Jewish community, and it continues to strongly affirm traditional Baptist positions on church-state separation and religious liberty.

Another moderate Baptist group, the Alliance of Baptists, was formed in 1987 and is headquartered in Washington, D.C. Some among its sixty thousand members continue their affiliations with the SBC. The Alliance describes itself as seeking "to build bridges of reconciliation in a world that desperately needs to be brought closer together."

As part of that effort, the Alliance adopted a resolution in March 1995 confessing past sins against Jews and Judaism, denouncing all forms of anti-Semitism, and urging Baptists to engage in dialogue with Jews. But both the Alliance and the Cooperative Baptist Fellowship are minority voices within the overall Baptist community.

The Christocrats, led by white evangelicals who seek to baptize America, must answer some critical questions: What is the status—legally, politically, and religiously— in a "Christian nation" for non-Christian Americans including Jews, Muslims, Hindus, Buddhists, agnostics and atheists? In such an America, what is the status of Christians who do not share the religious and political beliefs of Christian conservatives?

One disturbing answer has come from Brandon, Florida, a small city located near Tampa. In early 2005, Rabbi Robert A. Goodman wrote: "Living in Brandon almost gives credence that the United States is a Christian nation. There are upwards of twenty-five Baptist churches in our community, with a smattering of mainstream Protestant denominations. . . . When I went to join the local min-isterial association, I quickly discovered that its bylaws stated that one had be an ordained Christian minister in order to be a member . . . to include a rabbi (a possibility the Association members had never thought about) would have decimated the organization because at least half of the members did not want me there. . . . I withdrew my request to join. A few months later . . . a liberal minister and I started the Brandon Area Interfaith Coalition. . . ."

Despite their membership growth and political success in various elections, evangelicals, like other religious groups in America, are now confronting the difficult issues of accommodation to the modern world, a world of both religious and political pluralism. Seeking to impose a religio-political Christian theocracy upon America is one defensive reaction to the difficulties posed by a complex society.

Most evangelicals in the United States have not fully processed the stunning electoral victories attributed to them. Nor have they abandoned their traditional "us against them" fortress mentality, which has defined them for many years.

Nor has the evangelical community come to terms with the gifts and problems of the modern world: rapid scientific advances, especially in bioethics; growing secularism; independent religious scholarship; economic globalization; the population growth of immigrants within the U.S.; and a host of other issues.

Will the 55 million evangelicals in America opt for mutual respect and understanding and live in harmony with members of other faith communities that include liberal Protestants, Vatican II Catholics, Jews, Muslims, Hindus, and Buddhists? Or will the ultimate evangelical response to modernity and pluralism be the Christocrats' current campaign to dominate American life by imposing their values, norms, and beliefs upon the total American population?

But as the majority of the evangelical community sorts out these concerns and ultimately makes up its collective mind, other evangelicals—Christocrats, inwardly fearful, but outwardly arrogant; inwardly fearful of modernity, but outwardly masters of their domain—have embarked on a high-stakes campaign to baptize America. Christocrats believe that their efforts alone will preserve traditional spiritual values in the United States.

But to accomplish their goal, the Christocrats may first weaken and then rescind religious liberty and personal freedom, two of the greatest achievements of American democracy. It is a case of destroying the republic in order to save it.

It is a strategy that holds special peril for one religious community that strongly opposes the Christocrats' goal: American Jews.

CHAPTER VI

CHRISTIAN CONSERVATIVES AND THE JEWISH COMMUNITY: DOMESTIC ADVERSARIES? INTERNATIONAL PARTNERS?

As the Christocrats move forward in their efforts to baptize America, the ambivalent relationship between evangelical Protestants, including Southern Baptists, and the Jewish community becomes an important factor, because these two groups are major players on the American religious and political stage. Indeed, the clash between most American Jews and assertive Christian conservatives is one of the central features of the campaign to baptize America.

How do Christian conservatives, who are bent on imposing their beliefs on the United States, relate to Jews, who are overwhelmingly opposed to any attempts to Christianize America? How do Jews, for whom Israel's survival is so important, relate to evangelicals, who are the strongest Christian supporters of the state of Israel?

Jews fear that if the United States ever became a

Christian America, their hard-won political freedom and religious liberty would be in grave danger. Jews, with their keen historical antennae, feel in their bone marrow and guts that such an America would give rise to publicly sanctioned anti-Semitism, something that has happened throughout their history in other religion-based societies and nations, but not in the United States.

Indeed, Jews first arrived in what is now the U.S. in 1654 to escape religious persecution. A group of twenty-three Jews reached the Dutch colony of New Amsterdam in that year after fleeing their homes in Recife, Brazil, when the long arm of the Catholic Inquisition had crossed the Atlantic Ocean and reached that Portuguese colony.

While New Amsterdam was more hospitable to Jews than Recife, the newcomers still encountered anti-Jewish policies and actions from some of the colony's leaders, most notably Governor Peter Stuyvesant, who did not want the newcomers to remain.

The situation improved somewhat when the Jewish members of the Amsterdam-based Dutch East Trading Company, the colony's parent body in Holland, intervened on behalf of their coreligionists. Still, when the Jewish refugees from the dreaded Inquisition organized the first synagogue in what was to become the U.S., they pessimistically named it Shearith Yisrael, "the Remnant of Israel." They had no way of knowing that they would forever be honored as the founders of the largest Diaspora Jewish community in history.

The American Jewish community's opposition to the Christocrats cannot be fully understood without an awareness of the unique relationship that exists between religion and state in the U.S., the strong commitment of Jews to the principle of church-state separation, and the Christian conservative perceptions of Jews, Judaism, and the modern state of Israel.

One of the teachers in my Alexandria, Virginia synagogue school was an American history buff. In addition to our Hebrew prayers, he had his young Jewish students memorize Article Six of the U.S. Constitution, part of which reads: "no religious test shall ever be required as a Qualification to any office or public Trust in the United States."

And naturally he emphasized the Constitution's First Amendment, a part of the Bill of Rights:

> Congress shall make no law respecting an establishment of religion, or prohibiting the free exercise thereof; or abridging the freedom of speech, or of the press, or the right of the people peacefully to assemble, and to petition the Government for a redress of grievances.

This special American emphasis on religious liberty that my teacher loved is embedded within the Constitution. It is particularly impressive when one remembers there were perhaps only five thousand Jews in the newly formed United States in 1787 out of a total population of 3 million, led by white Protestant Christian males. The rest were women, Native Americans, and, of course, black slaves, all groups without any voting or political power when the U.S. was created.

Thomas Jefferson, George Washington, James Madison, and their colleagues, the nation's other Founding Fathers, could easily have designated Christianity as the official "established" religion of America, but they consciously chose not to do so. Their action had far-reaching and positive implications for the emerging American Jewish community and for all other non-Christian religions in the United States.

That is one reason Jews strongly oppose the current efforts to transform America into a "Christian nation." Under the law and because of the American historical experience, no religious group, no matter its size, can become the favored or "established" church, and all faith communities in the U.S. are free to mount independent campaigns to win the hearts, souls, and purses of the American people.

To put the matter in modern business terms: Jews and millions of other Americans believe that from the very beginning of the American republic, religion was a "deregulated" enterprise, free of government support or control.

While the Recife twenty-three were Sephardic (Spanish–Portuguese) Jews, the overwhelming majority of today's American Jewish community is of Ashkenazic (Central and East European) background. Jews from Germany and the old Austro–Hungarian Empire followed the early Sephardic immigration, and began arriving in the U.S. in large numbers after the failed 1848 political revolutions in Europe.

But the largest Jewish immigration to the U.S. took place between 1881, following the imposition of harsh anti-Semitic laws by the Russian czar, and 1924, when America adopted a highly restrictive immigration policy that discriminated against immigrants from southern and eastern Europe. Many demographers and historians estimate that nearly 70 percent of today's American Jews trace their family roots to Poland or Czarist Russia.

In more recent years, especially after the 1979 Islamic takeover of Iran and the collapse in 1990 of the former Soviet Union, increased Jewish immigration to the United States has come from those two areas of the world.

As a result, Jews in America, whether those descended from the earliest arrivals or those who came in recent years from Iran and the former USSR, all share a collective memory of the dangers that exist for them when the state controls the religious life of its people or when a religious group controls the state. The results for minority religious communities in those situations were usually disastrous.

Jews have stored in their collective memory banks the remembrance of persecution and discrimination when a state and a particular religion or Soviet-style atheism were legally linked or deeply intertwined. For many Jews, the principle of church-state separation is a civic icon, a heat shield, offering legal protection from religious zealots.

Historically, the largest American Jewish population centers were located in the Northeast and the Upper Midwest. Most of the post-1881 Jewish newcomers to America were economically poor and lacked knowledge of the English language. They settled with other immigrant groups in the large urban centers of the United States, cities that also attracted millions of other Europeans— many of whom were Roman Catholics from Italy, Ireland, and Poland or Eastern Orthodox Christians from Romania, the Balkans, and Russia.

During the same period, American evangelicals, mainly the descendants of the earlier Protestant immigrants from Great Britain and other western European countries lived as the religious majority in the South and Southwest where only small Jewish communities existed prior to the late nineteenth century's mass migration. As a result of these distinctive immigration and demographic patterns, the formative American experiences for Jews and evangelicals took place in dissimilar regions of the nation.

During World War II, more than six hundred thousand Jews served in the U.S. armed forces, where they came into direct contact with many evangelicals who were also in the American military. But even this shared wartime experience, some of it in overseas combat situations, did not substantively change the negative misperceptions the two groups had of one another.

Neil Simon's comedy *Biloxi Blues* and Irwin Shaw's novel *The Young Lions* capture part of the American Jewish experience during World War II.

Jews and evangelicals, different in religious beliefs and separated by geography, were like two ships in the night that did not encounter one another as vibrant religious groups until recently. As a result, mutual ignorance, pejorative caricatures and ugly nicknames emerged within both groups. The negative terms "redneck," "cracker," "Elmer Gantry," and "bigot" were often used by Jews and others to describe members of Christian conservative churches in the South; in return, pernicious epithets including "Christ-killer," "scribes and Pharisees," "Shylocks," and "Jewing someone down" were fired off by evangelicals. It was frequently assumed the two communities were natural adversaries because of the geographical, religious and sociological distances that existed between them.

It was not until 1969 and the early 1970s that several major academic interreligious conferences were first convened in an attempt to overcome the centuries of mutual suspicion and ignorance. The evangelical–Jewish encounter was the "third wave" of American interreligious history, and in many ways it remains the most tenuous because of the current campaign to baptize America, clearly an effort that leaves Jews fearful and angry.

The liberal or mainline Protestant churches were the first to enter into significant dialogues with Jews following World War II, and the Roman Catholic Church followed them in 1965 when the world's Catholic bishops, meeting at the Second Vatican Council, adopted the Nostra Aetate declaration that rejected the infamous deicide or "Christ-killer" charge that had historically been used against Jews. Nostra Aetate also condemned anti-Semitism and called for "mutual respect and knowledge" between Catholics and Jews.

The initial modern encounters between Jews and Southern Baptists and other evangelicals had a promising beginning. One of the first Southern Baptist-Jewish national conferences took place in 1969 in Louisville, Kentucky, and the first evangelical-Jewish meeting was in New York City in 1975. I was directly involved in those pioneering meetings that the American Jewish Committee cosponsored with various Christian partners. Numerous other national and regional meetings have followed since then.

At the time of those groundbreaking dialogues, I wrote that a "dam of pent-up interest, curiosity and excitement had burst" between Jews and Southern Baptists and other evangelicals. All the major topics that separated and united the two groups were discussed, debated, and deliberated.

They included the meaning of Messiah in both traditions, Jesus the Jew, biblical theology, the meaning of modern Israel and Jerusalem for Christian conservatives and Jews, conversion, witness, mission, and the negative images each group had of the other.

The conferences also focused on the plight of Jews and Christian believers in the Soviet Union, the quest for human rights, the roots of religious anti-Semitism, the Holocaust, church and synagogue polity, the principle of church-state separation, and the role of religion in American society.

Interestingly, in those years there was near Christian-Jewish unanimity on the last two topics; sadly, that is no longer true.

Of course, evangelicals and Jews differed on key matters of faith and religious belief. How could it be otherwise when people of faith meet in open dialogue? However, they also discovered those areas of mutual interest and agreement that need to be reemphasized today as the two communities edge farther apart over the role of religion in American society.

The areas of agreement included a similar congregational polity and structure that emphasizes the importance of independent churches and synagogues without the presence of a clerical hierarchy. Both Jews and evangelicals, including Southern Baptists, share a reverence for the integrity and authenticity of the Hebrew bible, the foundation of Jewish and Christian spiritual values. The two faith communities have a joint commitment to the security and survival of both the people and the state of Israel.

The evangelical commitment to Israel creates some of the ambivalence in the Jewish relationship to that large part of the Christian community. Yet it is not too difficult to understand the powerful feelings so many evangelicals have about Israel.

Evangelicals who are committed to Israel's security and survival have many reasons for that commitment. However, there are two distinct Christian conservative understandings of the rebirth of Jewish sovereignty in the land of Israel that account for their unwavering support of modern Israel.

One approach is rooted in the many biblical verses that speak of a Jewish restoration in the land of the bible. For theologically conservative Christians, Israel is God's elect (Deuteronomy 7:6–8), the state of Israel is a fulfillment of prophecy (Isaiah 43:5–6, Ezekiel 37), Israel occupies a special place in God's kingdom (Ezekiel 36:30, 33–38, Amos 9:1–15, Zech. 8:22–23, Romans 9:11), and Israel has a God-ordained right to the land (Deuteronomy 28–30, Acts 7:5).

Millions of evangelicals, including those pressing for a "Christian America," share this belief. For such individuals, including Christocrats, Israel plays a unique role in their lives because it presages the Second Coming of Jesus to Jerusalem. Without an Israel, an ingathering of Jewish exiles, this major event in Christian eschatology cannot take place.

That is why some evangelicals are dismayed at any Israeli withdrawal or disengagement from any area of the biblical "Holy Land." That is also why the strong Christian conservative support of Israel is not linked to Middle East realpolitik or America's growing thirst for Arab oil.

Many Jews are uncomfortable with such a strong Christological basis for supporting modern Israel. As one of my rabbinical school professors put it: "We Jews are actors in someone else's divine script. We are not independent players on God's stage of religious history."

One thing, however, is beyond dispute: The strongest Christian support for Israel's security and survival comes from evangelicals, who seem able to reconcile their campaign to baptize America with a profound concern for Israel.

There is also a second major Christian conservative response to Israel. Like the first, it, too, is highly supportive, but not directly linked to biblical prophecy texts or end-time beliefs. Christians and Christianity in every part of the world anchor this position on the twin concepts of justice and morality for the Jewish people who have been brutally victimized for twenty centuries.

The Holocaust took place in Europe, and was carried out by men and women who overwhelmingly were baptized Christians. Many evangelicals now perceive the horrific mass murders of the Holocaust not as punishment because the Jews "rejected" Jesus, but rather as the culmination of negative Christian teachings and practices all aimed at Jews and Judaism.

This response argues that the creation of the state of Israel can in no way atone for past Christian sins against the Jewish people, nor can it wipe the slate of history clean for Christianity. Solidarity with Israel, however, is one concrete and compassionate way to begin the Christian process of eradicating anti-Semitism and of building a respectful relationship with the Jewish people who have been wronged by Christians for so long. Modern Israel represents the Jewish right to self-determination and national identity.

But it would be a mistake to view evangelical support as monolithic.

In 2003 and 2004, the Pew Forum on Religion and Public Life conducted surveys of evangelicals, who make up about 26 percent of the total U.S. population.

Only 35 percent of all Americans polled believed the U.S. should support Israel over the Palestinians, but 52 percent of white evangelicals agreed with the statement. The more traditional evangelicals, Pentecostals and charismatics, were much stronger in expressing support for Israel; 64 percent agreed, and only 18 percent disagreed, lower than the rank-and-file evangelical response of 25 percent.

On the theological question of whether Israel fulfills New Testament prophecy about the Second Coming of Jesus, 63 percent, nearly two of every three of the more traditional evangelicals, answered in the affirmative, while only 36 percent of all Americans agreed with the eschatological importance of Israel.

Recently, the National Association of Evangelicals (NAE), an umbrella group of various organizations and fifty-two denominations representing 30 million members, began exploring the possibility of adopting a unified evangelical statement on the Middle East that would encompass the Israeli–Arab/Palestinian conflict.

This marks a departure for the NAE, which has in the past avoided such a comprehensive statement. But achieving that goal will not be easy since, despite a popular misconception, there are a host of views on Israel and the role it plays in evangelical thinking.

Some evangelicals believe that the modern state of Israel is a necessary precondition for the Second Coming of Jesus. Other evangelicals reject that view and believe the existence of Israel makes no difference in their belief system.

That is because the Christian Church, and specifically evangelicals, is the "New Israel" that has replaced the "Old Israel," both the modern state and the Jewish people who live in the Diaspora outside of Israel. For such evangelicals, they, not the Jews, represent the authentic "spiritual Israel" that has little or no relevance to the state in the Middle East that achieved its independence in 1948.

Putting all those views into one statement will be difficult, and it will be even more difficult to gain general acceptance of such a document.

But Gary Bauer, a Christian conservative and a former Republican presidential contender, was fully confident that any NAE statement on the Middle East would be strongly supportive of Israel's survival and security. While Bauer is not a member of the NAE, he is certain that evangelicals "are not confused about who the good guys are in the Middle East and who the bad guys are."

In those heady years of national scholarly conferences that took place after the Six-Day War of 1967, the SBC and evangelicals and the Jewish community also discovered they shared another abiding commitment, besides Israel. Both communities expressed strong support for the historical principle of separation of church and state in the U.S. But the SBC position on this critical issue has dramatically eroded in recent years. The early meetings also revealed a mutual involvement in the struggle to achieve human rights and religious liberty throughout the world.

Scholars from both communities noted that when Baptists and Jews first came to America they were suspicious and even fearful of attempts to link any one specific religious group with the state.

Southern Baptists and Jews instinctively know that they thrive best when there is a clear and legal separation of religion and state: when religion, all religion, is permitted to express itself in a voluntary setting, free of state interference and control. But, sadly, if religion and politics become intertwined both will suffer greatly. While not all evangelicals share these views, they do represent the spiritual beliefs of millions of people.

But it is the ardent evangelical support of Israel that draws the most public attention, and sometimes blinds Jewish perceptions about the Christocratic attempt to dominate America.

Kay Arthur is a popular Christian writer. One of her books, *Israel, My Beloved,* is set in the seventh century before the birth of Jesus. Arthur reflected the beliefs of many evangelicals when she publicly declared that, forced to choose between the United States and Israel, it would be no contest for her: "I would stand with Israel as a daughter of the King of Kings, stand according to the word of God." At the outbreak of the 1982 Middle East war, Jerry Falwell declared that God would smite any nation that raises its hand against Israel, even the United States.

Because the leadership of several mainline churches—the Presbyterians, the United Church of Christ, and the United Methodists—has been highly critical of many

Israeli policies and sometimes even of Israel's right to exist as an independent nation, most American Jews and Israelis have welcomed the evangelicals' strong support of the Jewish state. It is widely known that the largest numbers of American Christians who visit Israel each year come from evangelical churches, and their members can be counted upon to petition U.S. and United Nations officials regarding the pressing needs and concerns of Israel. A number of non-missionary evangelical organizations are located in Israel as a tangible sign of Christian support.

Unfortunately, some evangelicals in the U.S. and Israel are active in campaigns to convert Jews to Christianity. These activities further exacerbate relations between Christian conservatives and Jews.

Hebrew Christian groups, such as Jews for Jesus, have sometimes been successful in gaining important support, both financial and moral, from evangelical churches.

Clearly, on some issues, such as vigorous public support for Israel, evangelicals and Jews stand together. But on other key issues, it is the mainline churches that often act in coalition with the American Jewish community.

But one must be careful not to draw the dividing lines too sharply on such complex issues. Not all evangelicals are strong supporters of Israel and not all evangelicals seek the conversion of Jews to Christianity. And not all mainline church leaders are harsh critics of Israel, and there are conversionist elements within some of those liberal Protestant churches as well.

The old assumptions are changing as Jews recognize the sharp differences within the total Protestant community. This was especially apparent in the spring of 1984, when the complex relationships Jews hold with Protestants was on public display for all to see in the U.S. Congress.

A U.S. Senate subcommittee conducted hearings on President Reagan's proposed Constitutional amendment that would mandate organized prayer and bible reading in America's public schools. In their testimony before the subcommittee, representatives of six major Jewish organizations opposed the amendment joining forces with thirteen mainline Protestant groups.

The negative Jewish reaction to bible reading and classroom prayer was hardly surprising since the majority of American Jews believe any mandated prayers or bible readings are likely to be Christian with most of the verses from the New Testament. The theologically and politically liberal National Council of Churches, representing, in 1984, thirty-two Protestant and Eastern Orthodox Church bodies and 40 million members, also spoke against the amendment. This position was consistent with the NCC's long-held support of church-state separation.

In that same year, Jerry Falwell and his Moral Majority organization were riding the crest of public popularity and political power. At the Senate hearings, the Moral Majority's founder voiced strong support for bible-reading and prayer in public-school classrooms. Like most evangelicals, he believed "God was absent" from our schools and, he believed, with the introduction of daily prayers and Scriptural verses in classrooms, the moral life of America would dramatically improve.

At the conclusion of the hearings, a Senate staff member remarked to me: "Well, nothing new here . . . the predictable coalition of Jews and liberal Protestants are against the amendment, while the Christian conservatives led by Falwell are strongly for the proposal. Just a case of business as usual. . . ."

The amendment received sixty Senate votes, seven short of the two-thirds necessary for the adoption of any Constitutional amendment. The staffer was correct: The historic coalition of liberal Protestants and most American Jewish groups had gained another significant victory in the ongoing battle to maintain the separation of church and state.

But six weeks later, it was not "business as usual." A House of Representatives subcommittee conducted hearings on a bill that would move the American Embassy in Israel from Tel Aviv, where it had been located since Israel's independence in 1948, to Jerusalem, Israel's capital city.

Some of the same Christian and Jewish organizations that had testified earlier on the public-school Constitutional amendment also appeared at this hearing, but this time with a great difference in the lineup. Jewish representatives spoke in favor of the proposed embassy move, arguing that with the exception of the Defense Ministry, all the major Israeli government institutions were in Jerusalem.

But the NCC's Middle East affairs director argued against moving America's embassy to the Holy City. He cautioned the Congressional subcommittee that such a move would offend Islamic sensibilities and weaken our nation's relations with the Arab world.

Once again, Falwell appeared in Washington to testify before Congress, and this time he joined with the Jewish organizations in supporting the proposed transfer of the Embassy. The same Senate staffer mentioned above told me after the hearings: "The NCC and the Moral Majority are usually in different camps, opposing one another. But now the Jews seem to be the 'swing' vote on certain issues. Sometimes they're with the liberal Christians on church-state matters, and sometimes they are with the Moral Majority and the evangelicals on issues related to Israel."

That situation has not significantly changed in the years since 1984. Many Jews and evangelicals are convinced that liberal Protestants, especially the leaders of the mainline Protestant churches, have "sold out" Israel because of their one-sided concern for the Palestinians who are considered the underdog in the Middle East conflict.

In response, liberal Protestants warn the American Jewish community that the strong evangelical support for Israel masks the Christian conservatives' true intention: the conversion of Jews to Christianity. Liberal Protestants charge that evangelicals may love Israel, but they perceive Judaism as a spiritually exhausted faith that long ago served its purpose as a preparation for Jesus and the rise of Christianity.

Liberal Christians further contend that evangelicals stand on opposite sides from the Jewish community on key domestic social-justice issues, especially questions related to church-state separation.

As the bitter debate inside the Protestant community escalates—progressives versus evangelicals—the American Jewish community is frequently asked to choose sides. The result is what boxers call a "split decision." Some Jews eagerly accept evangelical support for Israel and conveniently look the other way at conversion campaigns and the attempted imposition of a Christocratic agenda on the country. For such Jews, Israel's survival and security trump all other concerns.

Other Jews remain aware of the evangelicals' domestic goals and express suspicions about working with that Christian community on any issue, even Israel.

They believe American Jews are not a one-issue community, but are, in fact, committed to a host of important concerns, both international and domestic. Their attitude is to work with the entire Christian community—cooperating when appropriate, and differing when necessary. This strategy is difficult to follow, but it is the one that accurately reflects today's American Jews: opposed to any breach in the church-state wall of separation, committed to Israel's survival and security, and supportive of social-justice issues in the U.S.

Because of these complexities, I am reminded of the quotation attributed to the late French president, Charles de Gaulle: "France has no permanent friends, it has only permanent interests." When *the Jewish people* is substituted for *France*, the phrase offers an accurate picture of the contemporary American Jewish community.

But Jewish suspicion of evangelicals still remains, despite the evangelicals' public support of Israel and the many academic conferences that have brought leaders of the two faith communities closer together.

A 2004 American Jewish Committee survey of American Jewish opinion was revealing. A quarter of the Jews polled believe that most, or at least many, of the evangelicals in the United States are anti-Semitic. Only Muslims scored higher in this negative category. Although Orthodox Jews often share similar positions with evangelicals on such issues as opposition to abortion and support of public financial aid to religiously sponsored schools, it is the Orthodox Jewish community, more than any other segment of the American Jewish community, that senses a high amount of anti-Semitism among evangelicals.

Other ethnic or religious groups fared far better in the AJC poll: Jews expressed a lower degree of anti-Semitism among Hispanics, Asians, blacks, Catholics, and Mormons than they sense among evangelicals.

As with other religious groups, evangelicals themselves are not of one voice on all questions and issues. For example, the late William S. LaSor was a leading evangelical theologian, but he rejected attempts to convert Jews. LaSor declared:

> Just as I refuse to believe that God has rejected his people [the Jews] (Romans 11:1) and that there is no longer any place for Israel in God's redemptive work or in the messianic hope, so I refuse to believe that we who were once not his people, and who have become his people only through his grace, can learn nothing from those who from of old have been his people.

It is as if many evangelicals publicly hold up two different posters at the same time. One poster proudly embraces the modern state of Israel as the necessary factor in hastening the return of Jesus to earth: "No Israel, no Second Coming." But campaigns to move Jews away from their ancient faith and the "Old Covenant" to Judaism's successor, Christianity, and the "New Covenant" continue.

The uneasy Jewish–evangelical relationship is, in many ways, the mirror image of the Jewish–mainline Protestant engagement. Many liberal Protestants oppose attempts to impose a Christocratic theocracy upon America. In that, they are united with American Jews. In addition, mainline churches and much of the American Jewish community have formed coalitions in support of many domestic issues: the Equal Rights Amendment, pro-choice abortion protection, opposition to bible-reading and prayers in public schools, gun control, opposition to anti-Semitism and racism, equal rights for gays and lesbians, and a myriad of other issues. Many liberal Christians have abandoned missionary activities aimed at Jews.

But some of the liberal Protestant leaders in such coalitions also espouse anti-Israel positions that anger their Jewish partners. Again, it is a case of two conflicting posters being hoisted by the same persons or the same church bodies: One affirms the integrity of the Jewish religion, and the second denounces Israel as a harsh oppressor of the Palestinians.

To complicate matters even more, several mainline churches, notably the Presbyterian Church in the U.S.A. (PCUSA), voted in 2004 to explore divesting their holdings from any business or corporation doing business in Israel unless it can be shown that such companies are engaged in solely peaceful activities. Calls for divestment have further strained relations between the American Jewish community and the involved mainline churches.

But interreligious relations are not a kind of quid pro quo game in which American Jews conveniently overlook the disturbing political agendas of their evangelical dialog partners because of support for Israel. Nor do Jews overlook the anti-Israel positions of several mainline Protestant church bodies, even though they may be coalitional partners on domestic issues.

For many Jews, it is tempting to welcome evangelical support for the Jewish state while never questioning the Christian conservatives' campaign to radically and permanently change American society. But that would be a major mistake.

Despite the fact that so many Jews suspect the presence of anti-Semitism within the Christian conservative community, Rabbi Forman points out:

> It is difficult to point to any explicit anti-Semitic statements in its [the Religious Right's] carefully worded rhetoric . . . but Pat Robertson [a prominent Religious Right leader] blames liberal Jews in America for their "ongoing attempt to undermine the public strength of Christianity."

Still, the suspicion remains that an always-latent anti-Semitism will emerge if the Christocrats succeed in their efforts to change America into a faith-based "Christian nation." But many evangelicals have their own set of questions about Jews as well. They wonder why American Jews remain staunchly liberal in their voting patterns, particularly in U.S. presidential campaigns.

Some evangelicals understand the historical source of this liberalism: the memory of Jewish suffering in Europe under the yoke of reactionary despots and tyrannical religious authorities. But after more than a century of American freedom and openness, evangelicals are often baffled by the American Jewish apprehension of a vigorous religious presence in the American public square.

Evangelicals constantly reassure Jews that such a presence will not erode the fundamental religious freedoms that are America's unique hallmark as a nation. However, most Jews remain unconvinced.

Evangelicals also wonder why many American Jews, who are deeply committed to a Jewish state in the Middle East, are often ardent supporters of secularism in the U.S. But even when Jews describe their families' painful European experiences when religious leaders, notably members of the Christian clergy, represented the anti-Semitic interests of an entrenched aristocracy, evangelicals are quick to point out that "America is different."

Jews remain highly skeptical that a "Christian America" would be that different from the grim realities their ancestors faced in a Europe saturated with a religious anti-Semitism that was the result of an "unholy" embrace between church and state that trampled on religious liberty and freedom of conscience.

The definition each community attaches to the term *religious pluralism* graphically illustrates the radical differences between evangelicals and much of the American Jewish community.

For most Jews, cultural and religious pluralism is a positive term. Indeed, it was coined by a rabbi's son, Professor Horace Kallen (1882–1974), in the early twentieth century. Kallen, who was my wife's teacher at the New School in New York City, recognized that the culture of the United States has many values, beliefs, and facets.

Kallen wrote that pluralism allows "for some degree of cultural diversity within the confines of a unified [American] national experience." Kallen believed that every ethnic, religious, and racial group is important, with each one making a significant contribution to the total American society. Taken together, cultural and religious pluralism can be compared to a lustrous tapestry that reflects the extraordinary diversity that exists among the American people.

But no one "strand" of the national tapestry is more important or dominant than any other. If any of the many strands pulls apart from the others, the entire tapestry or society can become undone, resulting in civil strife, religious wars, and other forms of national disruption.

For decades, the American Jewish community has warmly affirmed Kallen's concept of pluralism, seeing in it another shield of protection from an aggressive majority religious group that may seek dominance or control of the United States. While pluralism began as an academic sociological term, some Jewish and Christian leaders seek to develop a "theology of pluralism" that would anchor the empirical fact of religious diversity to a firm spiritual base.

However, in my interreligious work I have discovered that many Christian conservatives dislike, even fear, the concept of pluralism because it affirms the religious legitimacy and authenticity of all religious faiths. Many Christocrats see the term *pluralism* simply as a way to describe America's religious diversity, and nothing more. The meaning of pluralism in America remains a divisive issue, despite Kallen's original positive use of the term.

During the spring of 2005, following the Israeli government's approval of the withdrawal of eight thousand Jews from settlements in Gaza, a unique, but not surprising, "pluralistic" coalition became active in the United States to protest the pullout.

New York Assembly member Dov Hikind, a Democrat from Brooklyn and an Orthodox Jew, joined forces with the Reverend James Vineyard of Oklahoma City, who raised over $600,000 to publicly express his opposition to the Gaza withdrawal. Vineyard's campaign included placing newspaper ads and leading other evangelical pastors on study missions to Israel.

As with other evangelicals, Vineyard believes Gaza is part of the biblical Israel described in the book of Genesis. God gave the entire land of Israel to the patriarch Abraham and his descendants as an eternal gift. That land must remain forever in Jewish hands so as to hasten the Second Coming of Jesus to Jerusalem.

Echoing the 1982 Falwell statement at the time of the Lebanon war, the Oklahoma Christian leader said:

> The judgment of God will fall on America if this [the Gaza withdrawal] goes through.

CHAPTER VII

THE BATTLE OF CAMP DAVID: A VICTORY IN 1991, BUT COULD IT BE WON TODAY?

Back in 1991, I was personally involved in a battle that focused on this nagging question: Is the United States a Christian nation? But despite its importance, the fight took place far from the public view, in a high-profile location with one of America's best-known addresses: Camp David, Maryland.

The important issues raised at the presidential retreat in the Catoctin Mountains were a preview, a foretaste of what is currently taking place throughout the country. But now, years later, I wonder if the Battle of Camp David would have turned out the same way in today's highly polarized political and religious climate.

April 21, 1991 was a cold and rainy Sunday. Despite the depressing weather, my wife and I were excited because we were among the 150 guests invited to join President George H. W. Bush in the formal dedication service of the newly constructed interfaith chapel at Camp David, the presidential retreat.

Although the chapel dedication took place more than ten years before the 9/11 terrorist attacks, security was extremely tight as our car approached the entrance to Camp David. Metal detectors swept over every vehicle, including the area underneath each auto and truck. Car trunks, personal packages, and purses were examined, and armed guards checked and rechecked our names on a master list.

While the lengthy security procedure was taking place, I thought back to the day two years earlier when my friend Bishop James Mathews of the United Methodist Church had invited me to join the Camp David Chapel Committee, composed of clergy and lay people.

Since the days of FDR, American chief executives have used the camp near Thurmont, Maryland as a secluded wooded retreat, free of the White House press corps and the general public. Originally built as a public works project in the 1930s during the New Deal, Camp David had been a Boy Scout campsite before April 1942, when Roosevelt chose it as a presidential escape from the brutal Washington summer heat.

FDR mischievously called it "Shangri-La" to make it sound remote and mysterious, although it is only seventy-four miles from the capital. The more prosaic President Dwight D. Eisenhower named the camp in honor of his grandson, David.

Surprisingly, in 1989, there was no permanent chapel at Camp David. Over the years, beginning with FDR in the 1940s, religious services had been held in the camp's kitchen or bowling alley.

The lack of a chapel building at Camp David upset Kenneth Plummer, a devoted United Methodist layman, from nearby Chambersburg, Pennsylvania. In the late 1980s, Plummer began a personal campaign to build a permanent chapel. As a teenager, Plummer had participated in Boy Scout outings at the camp, and as an adult his construction company had transformed the site into America's presidential retreat.

With the White House's official permission and encouragement, Plummer started his campaign by asking his fellow Methodist, Bishop Mathews, to assist him in putting together a working group of religious, civic, political, and business leaders to build what came to be known as "The Camp David Interfaith Chapel."

Besides Mathews, the fifteen-member "blue ribbon" chapel committee included Archbishop Iakovos, the Greek Orthodox primate of North and South America, Episcopal Bishop Theodore Eastman of Maryland, Cardinal James Hickey of Washington, D.C., Methodist Bishop Fenton May, and former U.S. Senator J. Glenn Beall, Jr. (R-Maryland). I was the only Jewish member of the group.

Our committee's task was to raise private funds to construct a building that would be used for worship, study, and meditation by presidents, their families, Camp David's military support staff, and visiting world leaders.

We were successful in our efforts, and the chapel was completed in the spring of 1991; on that gloomy Sunday, our committee was officially turning the facility over to the United States government as "a gift to the American people." The government would then be responsible for the building's maintenance.

At the time of my appointment, I was the American Jewish Committee's national interreligious affairs director with more than twenty years of experience in Christian–Jewish relations with an emphasis on church-state matters and U.S. religious history.

In addition to raising money, our committee was also responsible for the chapel's architectural plans and the artistic designs of the eight stained-glass windows of the new building.

When I accepted Mathews's invitation, I had no idea that the committee's internal debate over the proposed window designs would become one of the most difficult and significant fights of my life. I call the chapel window dispute the "Battle of Camp David" because it raised issues central to American life that have extraordinary relevance today as Christocrats seek to dominate our national life.

Even though the Battle took place out of public sight at a highly secret and secure location, a place 99.9999 percent of Americans will never visit, it reflected the tension between those who see America as a Christian nation and those who believe our nation has no established religion, but instead provides Constitutional guarantees of freedom of religion and conscience for all its citizens.

These issues began with America's Founding Fathers in the late eighteenth century and have never been fully resolved or permanently settled. What is the proper relationship between religion, especially Christianity, and the state in our national political life? Should Christianity, the majority faith community, and its adherents receive preferential treatment?

Before joining the AJC staff in 1968, I had served as a

United States Air Force chaplain in Japan and Korea, where the Christian clergy and I shared the same chapel building and support staff. I understood firsthand what an interfaith chapel was and how it operated.

My years in the Air Force when I worked closely with priests, ministers, and pastors made a deep impression upon me. I believed that military interreligious cooperation was a model to emulate in civilian life.

As a Camp David Chapel Committee member, I had the distinct sense of representing not only the American Jewish community, but I also felt an obligation to promote the mutual understanding between Christians and Jews that I had experienced in the Air Force. I also believed that I was defending the Constitution's First Amendment, which guarantees freedom of religion and the historical church-state legacy of Jefferson, Madison, Mason, and Leland.

The committee work was both exhilarating and discouraging. It was exciting for a rabbi to participate in a history-making project at the world-famous Camp David. But it was disheartening because some committee members, despite the chapel's official interfaith name and announced purpose, insisted that we were building a Christian church and not an edifice of sacred space where all Americans would be comfortable, as well as the camp's international visitors.

The Battle of Camp David began when a highly patriotic and deeply religious Hungarian Christian émigré artist, Rudolph Sandon, and his wife Helen, of Little Valley, New York, presented their plans for the windows.

When the designs were first laid out, I found them totally unacceptable, but remained silent with my criticisms. There were "oohs" and "aahs" from committee members since it was clear that the Sandons were skilled artists.

However, I was dismayed by the initial drawings. Six of the eight windows contained the denominational logos of major Protestant bodies, including the Presbyterian Church, the United Methodist Church, the Episcopal Church, and the United Church of Christ. The seventh window featured a Christian cross representing Roman Catholicism, and the eighth window included symbols of Judaism, Islam, and Hinduism. The Sandons' original plan also called for a large presidential seal.

I was eager to hear the reactions of my Christian colleagues. Unfortunately, their responses were disappointing, once the initial artistic praise subsided. It seemed that everyone was satisfied with the dominant Christian themes for the chapel windows. Everyone but me.

I waited in vain for a committee member to raise some of the issues that were churning within me. But as person after person lauded the window designs, I realized that any objections would have to come from me.

When my turn came to speak, I carefully presented my critique. I made it clear that my objections to the window designs were not aimed at the Sandons or their artistic skills. In fact, the Sandons remained the chapel's primary artists, and ultimately the final window designs were theirs.

I clearly recognized that the Sandons' plans expressed a basic view held by many committee members. That is, the Camp David Chapel should contain specific Christian symbols reflecting the majority religious population of the United States, with one window allotted to Jews, Muslims, and Hindus. There was nothing for Buddhists,

Shintoists, and followers of American Indian religious traditions.

And in the six "Protestant" windows, the artists went far beyond the mere use of the cross or other recognizable Christian symbols.

Incredibly, they planned to create stained-glass versions of the specific logo designs of six major Protestant church bodies; designs that usually appear on denominational stationery and in various church publications. If the original designs had been accepted, the chapel windows would have reflected the corporate images of Protestant Christianity.

I said that even if one shared the Sandons' view of Christian triumphalism and dominance in the United States, their math was poor. One of every four Americans is a Roman Catholic; by that reckoning, Catholics "rated" two of the eight Camp David windows. Three quarters of the windows were allocated to a half-dozen Protestant churches whose total membership was nowhere near 75 percent of the total U.S. population.

But, of course, my strong objections to the initial window plans were not based on demography or the number of people identified with a specific faith community, no matter how large. I was outraged by the arrogant belief that Christianity, and indeed, only a part of that faith community, merited stained glass windows at Camp David's interfaith chapel. I especially objected to the not-so-subtle message that only Christianity and Christians deserved to be highlighted in the chapel windows of the presidential retreat. The implication would be obvious to any visitor to Camp David: Only Christianity and Christians truly merited the term *American*.

I felt strongly that the chapel should contain no permanent symbols or artistic representations of any particular faith. The key word was *permanent*. I knew from Air Force experience that the Christian baptismal fount, the crucifix, the Torah scroll, and the Holy Ark that houses Judaism's sacred scrolls, the Menorah, and other religious objects were not a permanent part of the military chapels I had used in Japan and Korea. Rather, in a spirit of mutual respect and understanding, the specific objects required for liturgy and religious ritual were brought into the chapel area for use during a Christian or Jewish worship service and then returned to well-maintained storage areas.

Since this arrangement worked well in "ordinary" USAF chapels overseas, I felt it was even more important that such procedures be followed at the presidential retreat chapel. I stressed to my committee colleagues that U.S. presidents and their families will come and go, but the religiously diverse American people, the true owners of Camp David, will always remain. Even though few of them may actually visit the place, Camp David belongs to all Americans, and, I argued, the proposed chapel must reflect this fact.

I protested that the proposed designs ran counter to the spirit of American history and the Bill of Rights: i.e., there must be no *de jure* "establishment" of any single religion in America. Unfortunately, the proposed windows singled out *de facto* one faith community of America for permanent validation, and they minimized or excluded other faiths including Judaism, Islam, Buddhism, Hinduism, and American Indian spirituality.

Devoting seven of the eight windows to artistic

representations of Christianity was a disservice to American traditions, values, and jurisprudence. I said it would be a serious error and a misreading of our nation's history if Camp David, of all places, did not reflect our long-standing national commitment to religious freedom and spiritual diversity.

I continued my litany of objections by pointing out that every religion known to the human family was represented in the United States, and that extraordinary demographical reality will not change. I added that because leaders from other nations, many of them not Christians, are frequently guests at Camp David, it was imperative their unique religious sensibilities be respected.

I reminded my chapel committee colleagues that Israeli Prime Minister Menachem Begin, an Orthodox Jew, and Egyptian President Anwar Sadat, a devout Muslim, had hammered out a peace agreement between their two countries at Camp David in 1978. In previous years, Soviet leaders had had high-level meetings with U.S. officials at the camp, aimed at easing Cold War tensions.

We now know that some USSR diplomats, while outwardly professing atheism and Communist dialectic materialism, secretly practiced Eastern Orthodox Christianity, a faith community that was omitted from the original chapel window designs.

Finally, I urged that the original plans for the windows be scrapped and redesigned to express universal religious values common to all peoples. I told committee members that I had no problem with the presidential seal and the famous words from the Constitution: "We the People. . . ." It was, after all, the chapel for the American presidential retreat.

Because of my strong objections to the Christian symbols and themes in the Sandons' window designs, what had started as a polite aesthetic debate soon became a robust debate.

I noted that the key issue, which is hotly debated today, is whether the United States is, in fact, a "Christian nation," or whether it is a religiously diverse country with no one "established" faith.

Until the Battle of Camp David, I had falsely, perhaps naïvely, believed that both issues had been definitively settled. Settled, I thought, more than two hundred years earlier by the adoption of the Bill of Rights containing the Constitution's First Amendment, which guarantees religious freedom and prohibits the official "establishment" of any religion by our government. Settled, I had mistakenly thought, in the early 1800s by President Jefferson's historic letter to members of a Danbury, Connecticut, Baptist church, asserting that a "wall of separation" exists between religion and state. Settled, too, by the many legal decisions, including U.S. Supreme Court cases, that legally upheld the principle of church-state separation.

But the Camp David fight over the artwork of the chapel windows proved that I was wrong. I learned that nothing is ever really settled when it involves the interplay between God and the United States, between religion and state, and between the American Eagle and the Christian Cross. It remains a neuralgic concern that never goes away, a divisive political and religious issue.

In recent years, the Republican party has vigorously worked to expropriate the traditional values of God and religion and make them a political monopoly:

"GOP=God's Own Party" is the text of some Republican bumper stickers. In April 2005, one prominent Republican leader, Senator William Frist of Tennessee, appeared on a television program that labeled Democrats who opposed President Bush's nominees for the federal bench as "people against faith." The pejorative language of Frist and others was designed to stick in voters' minds and win future elections for the GOP.

Because the issue is raw and the Democrats are so defensive, it was neither surprising nor accidental that Senator John Kerry received his greatest ovation at the 2004 Democratic National Convention in Boston when he declared: "I don't want to claim that God is on our side. As Abraham Lincoln told us, I want to pray humbly that we are on God's side."

But despite the Constitution, Jefferson, Lincoln, and the many decisions of various courts, each generation of Americans has been forced to redefine the issues of religion and state and the relationship between politics and piety. The Camp David Chapel debate between 1989 and 1991 was my turn.

The fight over what artistic representations would appear on eight two-inch-thick stained-glass windows was a microcosm of today's political fights over such potent terms as *Christian nation* and *mainstream America.*

Camp David was the perfect arena for such a vigorous debate. I believed then, and I believe even more strongly today, that what finally appeared on the Camp David Chapel windows reveals a great deal about who we are as Americans and how we perceive ourselves.

I would like to say that my words of criticism immediately swayed the views of the other committee members.

They did not. The Sandons were visibly upset with my remarks. Although I had been careful not to criticize their artistic creativity, I had struck them in an even more vulnerable spot: their religious zeal and strong Christian identity.

At first, the committee members were reluctant to abandon the carefully prepared designs that the Sandons had submitted for approval. Initially, there was resistance to my key points: that the Camp David Chapel, especially its permanent artwork, must represent the spiritual beliefs, strivings, and ideals of all Americans; and that the chapel must also reflect universal values even though various religious groups will use it for worship services, study, meditation, and rites of passage like weddings and funerals.

The issues that I raised were discussed at a series of committee meetings that took place over several months. Slowly, the tide turned, and interestingly, the Christian clergy on the committee were among the first to support my call to scrap the original window plans.

They clearly understood the need for the Camp David Chapel to be more inclusive in its design and construction. But it required more time and extensive debate to convince the lay people on the committee to request new stained-glass designs from the artists.

As we debated the issue, each of the committee members realized the significance and long-term importance of their decisions. Our animated discussions became an unanticipated seminar on church-state issues, religious diversity within the United States, and religion's role in American society.

We knew we were making critical decisions that would last for decades to come. At one point during the discussions, I told my colleagues that I recognized how difficult it was for people of goodwill to give up previously held beliefs and replace them with something different. But throughout the debate, I remained confident that I stood on principled American historical and religious ground.

In the end, the Camp David Chapel Committee did request seven new window designs from the Sandons. Instead of Protestant church logos and other uniquely Christian symbols, the artists came back to us with radically revised plans. The new windows featured visual representations of the sea and an anchor, a mountain, a globe, an open book, a tree of knowledge, a sheaf of wheat, seven flames, a dove, and a lamp with a flame. I was satisfied with the designs, and the committee unanimously approved the new submission.

After the final vote was concluded, many committee colleagues thanked me both publicly and privately for my efforts to make the chapel inclusive and welcoming. Some members admitted that it was their first encounter with an assertive advocate of religious pluralism.

The Battle of Camp David is long over. In retrospect, some people may view it as an insignificant debate, a minor skirmish over colored pieces of glass in a building few Americans will ever visit.

I do not agree.

During the hours of debate at Camp David, I believed that I was fighting for a basic, even a sacred principle of American life. In a country of nearly 300 million people, no one faith community or religion can ever claim that it is legally, historically, or artistically America's religion. The concept of religious diversity buttressed by

Constitutional guarantees of religious freedom is as old as the republic and as fresh as today's headlines.

While I was personally involved in many other inter-religious confrontations and issues during my years with the American Jewish Committee, I consider the Battle of Camp David a high point of my entire career.

Once the issue of the windows was decided, the committee moved quickly and adopted a chapel dedication liturgy reflecting the religious pluralism for which I had fought.

In addition to Chapel Committee members and their families, the guest list at the dedication included prominent clergy and national, state, and local public officials, including two United States Senators, Howell Heflin (D-Alabama) and John Danforth (R-Missouri)—the latter is an ordained Episcopal priest.

Other guests were U.S. military chaplains and members of President Bush's family: First Lady Barbara Bush, their son George W. Bush, his wife Laura, and some of the president's grandchildren.

The dedication itself began with an 8:30 A.M. breakfast attended by the president, who spent an uninterrupted hour with us. He was wearing a red cashmere sweater and black cowboy books embossed with the Texas Lone Star. As he chatted easily with our group, I noticed he consistently dropped the final *g* from all his gerunds. It was strange to hear, since Bush, the son of a Republican senator from Connecticut, was born, raised, and educated in New England. Clearly, President Bush had attempted to copy the speaking style of Texas, his adopted state.

Because the president was so casual and at ease during our breakfast, my wife jokingly whispered to me that the man sitting next to us was probably an actor impersonating the president, while the real George Bush was attending to the nation's business elsewhere. But, of course, it really was the American president.

Once the breakfast was over, Marcia and I walked around the grounds. Camp David's buildings are far from luxurious. In fact, the entire area resembles a well-maintained slightly upscale summer camp. Perhaps its simplicity is why presidents have used Camp David as a respite, a place where they can walk, jog, or ride a bicycle in total security and privacy.

The formal chapel ceremony began at 11:00 A.M. with our carefully crafted interreligious liturgy. My task during the service was to read an English-language selection from the Hebrew bible, or what Christians call the "Old Testament." I chose some verses from the prophet Isaiah.

During the service I glanced at the eight stained-glass windows that dominate the beautiful chapel. The building's rich oak wood and the rugged stone blend perfectly into the building's rustic mountain setting. But my mind and my eyes constantly wandered back to the windows as I relived the Battle of Camp David.

Like most of the participants who attended the dedication service in 1991, today's visitors to Camp David will never know the intense struggle surrounding the choice of symbols that were used in the stained-glass windows. That is true even when they read the official brochure describing the chapel.

While I did not write the text, I take personal pride in the brochure's words: "The building's response to its site is expressed through the choice of materials and with the more obvious symbolism of the 'tree like' shapes of the exposed laminated wood columns and window designs. . . . All symbols were selected and designed to be open to various understandings by persons of differing faith traditions. . . . For example, the mountains may be seen as the land God created or Mount Sinai, or Mount Moriah, or Mount Calvary."

I particularly like the words "designed to be open to various understandings by persons of differing faith traditions. . . ." That is what the fight was all about.

I like to think those earlier Virginians—Jefferson, Madison, and Leland—would have been pleased with my efforts at Camp David. At least I hope so.

It is likely that if the Camp David Chapel was being built today, several clearly identified Christocrats would be members of the committee. They would surely press for the inclusion of specific Christian symbols on the chapel windows. They would not be satisfied with the somewhat bland Protestant denominational logos and symbols that were first proposed. The Christocrats would certainly object to the windows' final abstract designs.

Instead, they would likely demand a stained-glass portrait of Jesus, several Christian crosses, some angels, perhaps a representation of the Last Supper, the New Testament, and John the Baptist's encounter with Jesus at the Jordan River. Who knows what else they would want on the windows, as well as inside the building?

Christocrats would want the chapel at the presidential retreat to make clear to all visitors that America is, in fact, a Christian nation.

It is said that in love and politics, timing is everything

and back in 1989–1991, the fierce campaign to baptize America had not yet gained the strength that it has now achieved.

But that was then, and this is now.

CHAPTER VIII

THE BEDROOM

An old maxim asserts that there are only three topics in life truly worth discussing: sex, politics, and religion. In recent years, the Christocrats have melded these three supercharged issues and placed them at the top of their domestic agenda, forming an explosive mixture that threatens to permanently transform our nation.

Christocrats want to impose their beliefs upon the entire American society, not by simply witnessing to their beliefs about sexual behavior within their families and personal lives and inspiring others to follow their example; instead, they aim for total control of the levers of political power in the United States.

But it is always sex that gets the biggest play and attention from Christocrats. Seemingly obsessed by what takes place in America's bedrooms, they especially seek to punish homosexuals and lesbians who exhibit "deviant" sexual orientations. Punishment may include Christocratic support of a proposed Constitutional amendment that would define marriage as solely between a man and a woman, thus prohibiting same-sex marriages and perhaps same-sex civil unions throughout the country.

Sometimes the public rebukes against homosexuals involve church membership. In 1997 the Reverend William Merrell, the Southern Baptist Convention's vice-president for convention relations, said:

> It is a fundamental contradiction to say "gay minister." . . . The teachings of Scripture are plain; that one is called to live a life that is in keeping with the principles the Lord has given us. Homosexuality is a fundamental denial of those principles.

Merrell believes that SBC ministers who are homosexuals should be removed, and gay and lesbian people must renounce their sexual behavior if they want to be church members.

Not surprisingly, Christian conservatives voiced loud criticism of the 2003 ordination of the Reverend Gene Robinson, an openly gay minister, as the Episcopal Bishop of New Hampshire. Christocrats and the followers also strongly oppose the U.S. military's "don't ask, don't tell" policy on gays serving in the armed forces.

Southern Baptist leaders and other Christian conservatives urge gay men and women to change their sexual orientation by devout prayer and spiritual counseling. The SBC's publication *Critical Issues: Homosexuality* declares that homosexuality is not caused by genetic or hormonal factors—physiological causes—but rather it is the result of an unhealthy or painful relationship of a child with one's parents.

Even though Christian conservatives like to say "We hate the sin, but love the sinner," their goal is to legally ban homosexuals from the military, teaching posts, and other high-profile positions. Christocratic punishment may take a legal form by refusing to support legislation specifically aimed to protect the rights of gays and lesbians. The argument used is that existing laws already provide such protections; but gays, lesbians, and their religious and political supporters assert that such laws are insufficient in a society where homosexuals are the victims of unique discrimination and other prejudicial acts.

Christocrats strongly oppose any "gay rights" or special anti-discrimination legislation that would legally provide sexual orientation the same "protected" category as race, religion, gender, national origin, ethnic group, physical disability, and age.

The Christocratic demand for legislation to ban or penalize homosexual behavior has accelerated since the 1970s. For decades, Christian conservatives, especially white evangelical Protestants, conveniently kept sex, politics, and religion isolated from one another by creating three neatly separate compartments in their lives. They voted for political candidates, but they believed that casting ballots in various elections was merely a necessary requirement of governance and citizenship: acts without any spiritual overtones or meaning.

While many southerners benefited greatly from the economic gains of President Franklin Roosevelt's New

Deal, most evangelicals of that region did not perceive government or its elected leaders as viable or appropriate instruments to carry forward Christianity's core teachings.

Until the 1970s, evangelicals did not see government as the agent authorized to punish gays and lesbians for their sexual behavior. Nor did most Christian conservatives look to a political party to fulfill their deepest spiritual beliefs.

For the first seventy years of the twentieth century, evangelicals were mainly content to "render unto Caesar what is Caesar's, and to God what is God's." In practical terms, this meant the government did what the Constitution mandated it to do, and evangelicals did what their personal faith commanded them to do, including the support of aggressive campaigns seeking the conversion of others to their brand of Christianity. In those years, religion and politics operated in parallel universes.

Evangelicals were generally in favor of organized prayer and bible-reading in public schools, although the Southern Baptist Convention historically championed strict separation of church and state. They also opposed sexually explicit material, "smut" or "porn," in books, movies, magazines, and television. These issues were lumped together as "family values," and it is instructive to note that Pat Robertson's TV network was originally called The Family Channel.

But the quest for personal salvation, even while living in the midst of grinding economic poverty, had far more appeal and value among evangelicals than supporting a political party's platform or believing the promises of gifted often-glib politicians. It was unusual to link an individual congregation or Protestant denomination to the public policies of either the Democrats or the Republicans. That potent and dangerous connection came later when numerous Southern Baptists, members of the Assemblies of God, and other Christian conservatives enthusiastically endorsed the GOP's policies and platform, especially as they related to homosexuals and abortion.

But for many evangelicals, making God the central factor in one's life was more important than believing that a political party could deliver God's promises to the faithful and punish homosexual "sinners."

It is an old story that was confirmed in a 2005 *New York Times* survey that focused on class structure in the United States. Increased personal wealth and income inevitably diminishes the importance of God for an individual. Seventy-nine percent of Americans earning less than $30,000 a year believe that having faith in God is important in their lives. The percentage remains fairly constant until a person's annual income goes above the fabled $100,000 barrier. Only 61 percent of 100K earners feel that God is important to them, and for those earning more than $150,000 a year the figure drops even more, to 54 percent.

But among America's high-income groups today, there is a highly educated affluent cadre of Christocrats who influence and lead like-minded Christians with lower incomes and class standing. It is a serious mistake to assume that all Christocrats are "lower-class" zealots.

It is also an error to believe that as evangelicals and other Christian conservatives climb the economic ladder and live out the "American Dream," they will abandon their more traditional forms of religion and move into theologically less-demanding mainline churches or will eschew Christian belief and commitment entirely. In that sense, today's evangelicals are going against the accepted conventional sociological wisdom that as people acquire more money, they become less and less "religious."

Until recently, most Christian conservatives viewed a person's sexual orientation, in particular, and human sexuality, in general, as highly private matters. Celebrated American writers including William Faulkner, Margaret Mitchell, and Tennessee Williams created a series of southern characters, both men and women, who were filled with repressed sexual drives that churned and bubbled just beneath the carefully preserved thin veneer of social respectability and family propriety. But both the fictional characters and real-life evangelical readers never expected governmental agencies to intervene in or control their sexual behavior, whether heterosexual or homosexual.

Many people, including Christocrats, mistakenly believe that the Christian concept of original sin relates to sexual matters. That is often a reason for their extraordinary fixation on sexual matters.

However, some prominent Christian theologians teach that the sin of Adam and Eve's disobeying of God's command in the Garden of Eden has nothing do with sex. A divine voice tells them not to eat of the fruit of the tree of knowledge of good and evil. They do so anyway and then recognize their own nakedness. Original sin for Christians is not a sexual one, but one linked to faith and belief.

For generations of evangelical Christians, religion was perceived as a family and church activity. Local congregations, centers of conservative religious beliefs and practices, were communities of faith that exhibited only limited interest in the political issues of the day and what went on in the nation's bedrooms. The focus was on "getting right with the Lord."

As a high school student in Virginia, I was keenly interested in the political events of the time, including the emerging battle for civil rights, the growing dangers of nuclear proliferation, and the horrific mass murders of Nazism during World War II that later became known as the Holocaust. Some of my high school classmates shared these concerns, but many others were content with the political and social status quo and focused much time and attention on their spiritual well-being by attending evangelical churches.

In addition, when members of conservative churches did, in fact, venture forth and endorse specific policies or programs in the American political arena, those initiatives were frequently defeated and the evangelical supporters publicly humiliated. The successful drive led by Christian conservatives to enact a Constitutional amendment prohibiting the manufacture and use of alcoholic beverages in the United States was a disaster. Adopted in 1920, the amendment was repealed thirteen years later, to the delight of most Americans.

For many years after the repeal of the hated amendment, millions of Americans blamed evangelicals for Prohibition's catastrophic results that included the growth of organized crime and widespread tolerance for breaking the law by secretly visiting speakeasies or by manufacturing banned alcoholic beverages.

Evangelical opposition to legalized gambling, while passionate and well organized, often resulted in a series of electoral failures. State sponsored lotteries and casinos, already prevalent in many areas of the U.S. with large evangelical populations, are currently increasing in number. Worst of all, strong white evangelical support for the harsh racial segregation laws that were enacted after the abolition of slavery identified such Christians as bigots in the eyes of many other Americans.

Faced with such animosity and ridicule, Christian conservatives of an earlier era retreated into the comfortable bosom of their local church fellowship rather than battle unsuccessfully for lost and unpopular causes in the public arena. As a result of political defeats, many Christian conservatives abandoned active participation in major public-policy questions, and turned inward, seemingly immune to the outside forces that were influencing and changing American life. It was also the time of liberal Protestant dominance in American life, the seven-decade era of mainline church hegemony that began to end in the 1970s.

During those years critics charged that evangelicals seemed more interested in the welfare of their own souls than the earthy physical needs of society or the sexual behavior of their fellow citizens. Even today, when Christocrats are aggressively pressing for legal restrictions against homosexuals, lesbians, and same-sex unions, critics claim such anti-gay policies deliberately minimize the urgent religious demands of combating political oppression throughout the world, and confronting the persistent challenge of economic poverty, inadequate education, limited employment, environmental waste, and substandard housing that exist in contemporary America.

By expending extraordinary amounts of political and religious capital on opposing homosexuals and same-sex marriages, Christocrats, it is charged, ignore the crushing social-justice needs of our time. Despite the criticisms,

homosexual behavior and same-sex unions of any kind
remain prime targets for today's Christocrats.

Their fierce opposition to homosexual behavior, both
public and private, is primarily based upon six sets of
verses, three from the Hebrew bible and three from the
New Testament.

> Do not lie with a man as one lies with a woman;
> that is detestable. (Leviticus 18:22).

> If a man lies with a man as one lies with a
> woman, both of them have done what is
> detestable. They must be put to death; their
> blood will be upon their heads. (Leviticus 20:13).

> Before they had gone to bed, all the men from
> every part of the city of Sodom—both young and
> old—surrounded the house. They called to Lot,
> "Where are the men who came to you tonight?
> Bring them out to us so that we can have sex with
> them." (Genesis 19:4–5).

> Do not be deceived: Neither the sexually immoral
> nor idolaters nor adulterers nor male prostitutes
> nor homosexual offenders nor thieves nor the
> greedy nor drunkards nor slanderers nor
> swindlers will inherit the kingdom of God.
> (1 Corinthians 6:9–10).

> . . . the law is not made for a righteous person,
> but for the lawless and insubordinate, for the
> ungodly and for sinners, for the unholy and

> profane, for murderers of fathers and mur-
> derers of mothers, for manslayers, for fornica-
> tors, for sodomites, for kidnappers, for liars,
> for perjurers, and if there is any other thing
> that is contrary to sound doctrine. (1 Timothy
> 1:9–10).

> . . . the men, giving up natural intercourse with
> women, were consumed with passion for one
> another. Men committed shameless acts with men
> and received in their own persons the due penalty
> for their error. (Romans 1:26–27).

Christocrats cite these verses as definitive proof texts that must be the foundation of all civil and criminal legislation about homosexuals in today's society. They derive from these verses the belief that not only is homosexuality "detestable," but gays must be punished and receive their "due penalty for their error" with "their blood upon their heads."

Since Christocrats believe in the bible's inerrancy, scriptural passages, and especially those dealing with homosexuality, are not subject to debate or conflicting interpretations. The texts are without error and they mean exactly what the words say, even in translation from the Hebrew or Greek.

Christocrats revere the bible as the eternal source of religious certitude that is immune to any questioning, doubt, ambivalence, or ambiguity. The bible provides divine comfort for Christocrats without raising troubling questions, spiritual security without encouraging sincere probing doubt; and scripture is a powerful weapon of faith for use against all perceived enemies, including "secular humanists," "globalists," and "liberal Christians and Jews."

However, inerrancy—that is, taking a biblical text at face value without employing any linguistic or historical analysis—is itself a particular form of scriptural interpretation. It is unfair to charge that only "progressives" or "liberals" interpret the bible, and it is inaccurate for Christocrats to claim that their understanding of the bible is the only true one.

Inerrancy is similar to the Constitutional "original intent" theory that many Christocrats and conservative political leaders currently affirm. They believe that the text of the U.S. Constitution, as originally drafted in Philadelphia in 1787, means exactly what it says, and must be understood precisely as it was written. But, as with the bible, that is not as easy as it sounds.

Everyone agrees that the Constitution's text, like the bible's words, cannot be changed. What matters is how the words in both documents are interpreted and implemented in today's America.

The Constitution was written in candlelight by human beings, albeit gifted ones, for a new nation of less than 5 million people. But today Americans live in a space-age high-tech nation with a highly diverse population nearing 300 million. In addition, close to thirty Constitutional amendments have been adopted since 1787, and there are hundreds of court decisions that have interpreted and reinterpreted the original document.

Nevertheless, many conservative legal scholars and political leaders are part of a growing campaign to restore the "original intent" of the Constitution to

American life. They grieve that the original meaning, as they define it, of the eighteenth-century document is currently in "exile" and must be restored to its full grandeur and power, shorn of the many restrictions and supposed misinterpretations that have been placed upon it.

But Christocrats go even further with the bible than they do with the U.S. Constitution. Since they believe that scriptures are the literal word of God and are not the product of even divinely inspired human beings, no amendments or court decisions are possible or required for such a sacred text. It is as it is written.

But inerrancy runs completely counter to both the historic Jewish understanding of the bible and to the teachings of most Christians. Jews, Roman Catholics, Eastern Orthodox Christians, and many Protestants have a long tradition of biblical commentary and analysis. They believe that scholarly interpretations amplify and enrich the biblical verses and provide spiritual understanding and religious strength for their faith communities.

They also believe that knowledge of the ancient Middle East, its languages, literature, legal system, and geography can provide valuable insights into the biblical text. Modern scholars also employ archeology and anthropology as they delve deeper and deeper into the meanings of the bible's books.

For Jews, the huge number of rabbinic commentaries, compiled over many centuries and in many lands, is co-equal in importance and sanctity with the written text of the bible. Jews believe that God, acting in history at Mt. Sinai, revealed to Moses and the ancient Israelites both the Hebrew bible and the vast array of interpretations that followed.

The unique combination of written and oral teachings has prevented the bible from becoming a sacred book frozen in time and rendered irrelevant to its readers. Jews believe that interpretations, commentaries, questions, doubts, and debates are imperative if the bible is to remain a living document.

Roman Catholics also have a rich tradition of biblical scholarship whose purpose is to deepen an individual's understanding of the bible. The teaching power of the Catholic Church, the *magisterium,* is as binding for believers as the written biblical text itself. When reading scriptures, Catholics must bring with them more than a pious reverence for the printed text. That reverence is necessary, but not sufficient. The Catholic scholastic tradition of biblical interpretation must also be part of an authentic understanding of the bible.

The Catechism of the Catholic Church, published in 1994 with the imprimatur of Cardinal Joseph Ratzinger, now Pope Benedict XVI, contains this instruction:

> To interpret Scripture correctly, the reader must be attentive to what the human authors truly wanted to affirm and to what God wanted to reveal to us by their words.
>
> In order to discover the sacred authors' intention, the reader must take into account the conditions of their time and culture, the literary genres in use at the time, and the modes of feeling, speaking, and narrating then current. (Paragraphs 109–110).

Protestant biblical scholarship has also provided significant new insights and teachings based upon scholarly interpretation. An example of that tradition is the meaning Boston University Divinity School Professor J. Paul Sampley, a United Methodist, gives to the biblical verses about homosexuality. His commentary flies in the face of Christocratic inerrancy.

In the 2002 edition of the *New Interpreters' Bible*, Sampley tackles the well-known verses of First Corinthians (6:9–10) cited above:

> If one knows nothing of the cultural practices and prejudices of Paul's time, one can more easily take these ancient terms from that context and make of them what one wishes. In Greek and Roman times, what we would call heterosexual married males (and one can suppose the same was true for their female counterparts) might frequently keep a boy (or in the case of wives, a girl) for their pleasure. Sometimes the kept person was a slave, who by definition would have no choice, but there were also boys who solicited sex with elders for pay.
>
> For the most part these relationships caught no special attention. Around Paul's time, however, certain prominent moralists had begun to note the more extreme, exploitative cases and to object to them. All of those instances consider abuses; none of those texts concerns itself with relationships in which there is no exploitation.

Because of the long Jewish and Christian traditions of offering biblical interpretations and commentaries, it is not surprising that the literal Christocratic understanding of verses dealing with homosexuality and many other issues has been severely questioned and criticized.

The English-language version of *The Catechism of the Catholic Church* is 803 pages in length, but homosexuality is mentioned in only a scant three paragraphs: 2357–2359. Those paragraphs cite the verses from Genesis, Romans, Timothy, and Corinthians mentioned above.

But completely lacking in *The Catechism* is any mention of punishment for homosexuals, certainly not the harsh penalties prescribed in the Hebrew bible and the New Testament that are constantly cited by Christocrats. While the Catholic Church cannot "approve" of homosexual behavior, it does demand "respect, compassion, and sensitivity" for gays.

> Homosexuality . . . has taken a great variety of forms through the centuries and in different cultures. Its psychological genesis remains largely unexplained. . . . [Catholic] tradition has always declared that "homosexual acts are intrinsically disordered." . . . Under no circumstances can they be approved. . . . The number of men and women who have deep-seated homosexual tendencies is not negligible . . . for most of them it is a trial. They must be accepted with respect, compassion, and sensitivity. Every sign of unjust discrimination . . . should be avoided. . . . Homosexual persons are called to chastity. . . . They can and should gradually and resolutely approach Christian perfection.

I constantly hear Christocrats demanding that homosexuals in America be punished "according to the teachings of the bible." But if such demands were actually carried out, it would mean that gays would "be put to death" with "blood upon their heads," all of them suffering their "due penalty." That was the justification used in the brutal 2003 murder in Colorado of Matthew Shepard, a gay man who was first beaten by anti-gay Christians and then dragged to his death.

Boston College Professor Alan Wolfe believes that the same-sex marriage issue "could be the final battle of the culture wars." I disagree.

The fight over same-sex marriage and civil unions is simply the first of many battles the Christocrats are fighting across a broad social, religious, political, and cultural front. Even if they are defeated in one battle, they will renew their efforts in another. Instead of the "final battle," we are witnessing a kind of trench warfare in which the gains for the Christocrats are measured by a myriad of court cases, judicial-nominee fights, political elections, rallies, demonstrations, prayer vigils, and a host of other small "victories" that the Christocrats believe will bring them eventual control, not only of the extended battle-front, but of America itself.

In late June 2005, the Reverend John H. Thomas, the president of the United Church of Christ, a mainline progressive Protestant body with 1.3 million members and fifty-seven hundred congregations, publicly supported same-sex marriage. Speaking in Atlanta on the eve of his denomination's national meeting, Thomas said:

> [The UCC] should affirm the rights of gay, lesbian, and transgender persons . . . [to have marriages] equal in name, privileges, and responsibilities to

married heterosexual couples. I believe our local
churches, as they are able, should move forward
the development of marriage-equality policies.

During the same week that Thomas was speaking in support of gay marriages, the Spanish Congress of Deputies
in Madrid voted 187–147 to approve a bill giving homosexual couples in that country the same marital rights as
heterosexual couples, including the legal right to adopt
children.

The action joins Spain with Holland and Belgium, two
other nations that legally recognize gay marriages. Most
of the other western European nations provide civil
unions for gay couples.

The Spanish action and the avalanche of anti-gay marriage votes in the United States is a historic irony. Spain is,
of course, the land of the religious Inquisition with its tor-
tures and public executions. Spain, more recently, is also
the nation that endured the long fascist regime of Francisco Franco, which was closely allied with a conservative
Roman Catholic Church.

Yet Spain is moving in one direction on gay marriages
while the United States, which has never suffered an
Inquisition or a fascist dictatorship, is rapidly moving in
the other direction. Spain votes for homosexual freedoms
while the United States seeks to limit those same freedoms with restrictions and punishments.

But how should people who revere the bible and its
profound teachings respond to the Christocrats' cry for
biblical literalness regarding punishment of gays and
others? Are people who cherish the bible forced to jettison
the scriptures and their extraordinary truths because they

reject the cruel language used against homosexuals and other groups of people?

Of course not.

The first thing is not to surrender authentic biblical interpretation to the Christocrats. If they are the only people able to define the bible's meaning for the general American society, Christocrats will have gained an enormous victory in their effort to baptize America. Christocrats love to quote the bible literally and point to it as the ultimate authority on all issues of life. Once they have convinced the public that they, and they alone, correctly interpret the bible, they are then able to label their opponents as "anti-bible" or "secular." It is a clever, insidious tactic that has, unfortunately, worked too long and too well, and always in the Christocrats' favor.

As mentioned above, for centuries Jewish and much of Christian biblical teaching has provided commentaries and interpretations that mitigate such extreme language and the requirement to carry out harsh penalties.

The case of the rebellious son is the quintessential example of how gifted and faithful interpreters of the bible retained a seemingly harsh text while calling for mercy and compassion. It represents an important and authentic religious response to the public vindictiveness expressed by many Christocrats. Because the case of the rebellious son is not related to homosexuality, this particular interpretation offers a method of biblical understanding that can be applied throughout scripture.

Deuteronomy 21:18–21 seems cruel, especially when the prescribed punishment is directed at a young boy:

If a man has a wayward and defiant son, who does not heed his father or mother and does not obey them even after they discipline him, his father and mother shall take hold of him and bring him out to the elders of his town at the public place of his community. They shall say to the elders of his town, "This son of ours is disloyal and defiant; he does not heed us. He is a glutton and a drunkard." Thereupon the men of his town shall stone him to death. Thus you will sweep out evil from your midst: all Israel will hear and be afraid.

Despite the call for capital punishment in the text, there is no record of a rebellious or defiant son ever being executed in biblical Israel. One ancient rabbi said, "It never happened and it never will happen!"

The Talmud, Judaism's oral tradition, sharply reduced the possibility of the death penalty ever being used against a son. A rebellious son must be at least thirteen years old, but not more than thirteen years and six months in age. Beyond that narrow window, the son is then defined as a "man," a completely different legal category from a "son."

In such cases, parents can condone their son's "offense" and withdraw any complaint. But if parents still press charges, a court of three judges must adjudicate whether the son is in fact rebellious, disloyal, and defiant.

The Jewish interpreters of the text also taught that capital punishment is similar to the rite of sacrifices that were carried out when the Holy Temple stood in Jerusalem. For them it was: "No Temple, no capital punishment."

The entire teaching of the rabbis in the Talmud was

aimed at the abolition of capital punishment, whether for a rebellious son, an adulteress, a homosexual, or any other person the bible teaches is liable for execution.

Ultimately, the rabbinic interpreters of these verses noted that the text must be taught only for the purposes of "education and deterrence." Because reverence for one's parents is included in the Ten Commandments, the case of a rebellious son is important.

The text as a teaching tool remains intact, immutable; but its meaning is the subject of constant interpretation and reinterpretation. The bible is not a cruel club used to bludgeon people into submission; it is instead a living document that commands respect and demands interpretation and critical insight from its readers.

Critics point out that Christocrats focus almost exclusively on the verses about homosexuality while ignoring many other biblical verses that are also harshly punitive and highly problematic. They point to the New Testament verses describing women and slaves:

> Women should be silent in the churches, for they are not permitted to speak, but should be submissive, as the law also says. If there is anything they desire to know, let them ask their husbands at home. For it is shameful for a woman to speak in church. (1 Corinthians 14:34–35)
>
> Slaves, obey your human masters with fear and trembling, in the sincerity of your heart, as to Christ. (Ephesians 6:5)
>
> Slaves, obey your human masters in everything; don't work only while being watched, in

order to please men, but work wholeheartedly, fearing the Lord. (Colossians 3:22)

Slaves are to be submissive to their masters in everything, and to be well pleasing, not talking back. (Titus 2:9)

Slaves, submit yourselves to your masters with all respect, not only to the good and gentle masters, but also the cruel ones. (1 Peter 2:18)

Sampley reinterprets the harsh New Testament view of women:

It is an irony of the greatest gravity that Paul's counsel in these verses . . . has come to function for some Christians as a polity dictate that keeps modern women from being able to speak in church. . . . Paul's particular and situation counsel, written long ago to treat an unusual problem in a church in Corinth, has been reified into church law that is presumed to apply to all women . . . for all time.

Dr. David L. Bartlett of the Yale Divinity School, an American Baptist, places the biblical verses in context and reinterprets them in a manner completely at odds with the principle of biblical inerrancy. Writing in the *New Interpreters' Bible:*

for all the difference between first-century and nineteenth-century slavery, the refusal to condone any slavery is now an established Christian principle, indicating that to be a Christian in our

> time is not simply to accept the values of our honored and faithful forebears in the faith. . . . We cannot simply take 1 Peter as a clear and infallible guide to contemporary faithful behavior. Our understanding of slavery has changed.

Biblical inerrancy must not be allowed to stand as the only biblical interpretation of how homosexuals should be regarded and treated in today's America. Unfortunately, when Christocrats anchor their anti-gay positions to harsh-sounding verses and loudly preach "The bible says. . . ," the general American public receives the inaccurate message that only Christocrats truly understand and respect scriptures. It gets even worse when those who do not agree with the biblical inerrancy position are accused by Christocrats of being anti-religious or unfaithful to God because they take a different view of scriptures.

Political leaders who differ with Christocrats, but have little knowledge of the bible, frequently wilt under the strident claims that "the bible commands us to condemn and punish homosexuals." Other religious voices offering a differing perspective on the same biblical verses are either diffident or are brushed aside by Christocrats and publicly labeled modernists, liberals, or worse.

By constantly repeating only narrowly constricted readings of controversial biblical verses about homosexuals, Christocrats have successfully created the illusion that theirs is the sole legitimate religious voice on such important issues. Silencing alternate voices and duping trusting political leaders makes the Christocrats' task of baptizing America much easier.

In 2004, President Bush proposed a Constitutional

amendment on marriage. The amendment, if adopted, would limit marriage to a man and a woman, and it is clearly an attempt to override any state law that upholds the legality of same-sex marriages and provides to a homosexual couple the legal rights of marriage as a heterosexual union.

The recent overwhelming votes in various states during 2004 and 2005 rejecting same-sex marriages represent the most visible efforts to legally prohibit "deviant" sexual behavior. Following a state court ruling, Massachusetts has allowed same-sex marriages since May 2004, but only Connecticut has adopted a law that legalizes same-sex civil unions. Currently, more than eighteen states have voted to ban such unions, and the voting results came as no surprise.

Christian conservatives played a major role in the September 2004 vote in Louisiana to ban same-sex marriages and civil unions in that state. In ten of Louisiana's sixty-four parishes or counties, more than 90 percent of the voters supported the Constitutional amendment. Among the ten were six of the most heavily evangelical parishes in the state.

The amendment did slightly better among evangelical Protestants than among Catholics. The level of support in the ten most heavily evangelical parishes was 88 percent; it was 80 percent in the state's ten most heavily Catholic parishes. Statewide, 78 percent of Louisiana voters supported the measure, while over 70 percent of Missouri's voters rejected same-sex marriages in their state.

Much of the electoral strength opposing same-sex marriages in Missouri and elsewhere comes from the Assemblies of God (AG) that is headquartered in Springfield, Missouri.

In the drive to baptize America and punish homosexuals, the Assemblies of God have added a new and ominous element to the Christocrats' anti-gay rhetoric. The AG asserts that the threat posed by homosexual behavior stems not simply from "secular humanism," but also from "a growing trend in government to redefine and politicize moral issues. . . ." The government is ". . . more and more . . . defying biblical principles and interpreting sinful behavior as civil rights, i.e., abortion and homosexuality. The church . . . is obligated to respond."

The meaning of the Assemblies of God position is clear: It is not merely the individual homosexual "sinners" who are causing America to slip more and more in the wicked abyss of "secular humanism" (although that alone would provide reason enough for the AG to view gays as a threat to society); but—and this is the critical point of the AG's position—it is the American government itself that is sinful in the area of homosexuality. When the government is "defying biblical principles," the Christian church, and specifically the Assemblies of God, must respond.

I long ago discovered in my work among Christocrats and their followers that the term *biblical principles* is often employed like the political phrase *national security*. Both terms are widely used to condone any type of activity the speaker or writer intends, and both phrases transmit a power that can silence dissent, doubt, or questioning.

Biblical principles is a convenient theological construction that is frequently unexamined and undefined, but it always elicits a strong Pavlovian reaction from Christocrats. For true believers, nothing is more dangerous or wicked than a person or government who defies "biblical principles."

When a Christocratic leader accuses the government or the wicked secular society of scorning "biblical principles," it is a clear call to action for Christians who believe that the bible is the only blueprint needed to save American society from the evil forces of "secularism."

For the Assemblies of God, the government is as culpable of sin as the individual gay man or woman. The AG's threat is unmistakable and must not be minimized. God's designated Christian agents on earth, the believing Christians, must punish the sinful government. The faithful "church . . . is obligated to respond."

One way to respond is for AG members to support the proposed Constitutional amendment banning same-sex marriages. Another way is oppose the passage of any laws—federal, state, or local—that would prohibit discrimination on the basis of personal sexual orientation.

Christocrats claim that there are already sufficient laws on the books that ban discrimination based upon religion, gender, age, race, disability, marital status, or membership in any ethnic group. But gays and their religious and political allies believe that the current laws offer insufficient protection, and additional legal safeguards are needed. The Christocrats intend to win this battle by preventing the passage of any "special rights" legislation intended to protect the gay, lesbian, bisexual, and transgender communities.

While much attention has been focused on religious coercion and proselytizing within the American workplace, Christian conservatives are also applying economic pressure, including threats of consumer-based boycotts, against companies deemed "gay-friendly."

Tim Wildmon, the president of American Family

Association, a conservative group headquartered in Tupelo, Mississippi, told Religion News Service "the companies that are aggressively promoting the homosexual agenda, we are going to highlight." He added the goal of AFA's efforts is to influence and change companies' policies towards gays and lesbians. Those policies frequently include the same employee health, insurance and pension benefits that are provided for married heterosexual couples.

Wildmon also singled out firms that contribute money to gay rights parades or advertise their products on such TV programs as *Will and Grace* or *Queer Eye for the Straight Guy.* Especially drawing AFA fire was Kraft Foods because the giant company supports the 2006 Gay Games in Chicago.

Other allegedly "gay-friendly" icons of American industry have also been threatened with economic pressure by Christian conservatives including Walt Disney, Proctor and Gamble, Ford Motor Company, and Microsoft.

Leaders of the Human Rights Campaign, a gay-rights advocacy group based in Washington, D.C., believe American business will provide "equal opportunity for all" by refusing to yield to the economic threats.

Washington state is the scene of one such ongoing battle that pits Christocrats against Microsoft, a multi-billion-dollar corporation. It is another indication that Christocrats have a roster of other targets to attack, besides the government and gay individuals, in the war they are waging against America's homosexuals. Every company, large and small, is subject to threats and public criticism.

In the spring of 2005, the Reverend Ken Hutcherson, the charismatic pastor of a large evangelical church in Redmond, Washington, threatened to inaugurate a national boycott against his neighbor, the Microsoft Corporation, if the company supported a gay-rights bill that was under consideration by the state legislature.

Hutcherson had two meetings with Microsoft officials prior to the vote, and the corporation, which had backed a similar gay-rights bill the previous two years, decided to be "neutral" this time around. But officials of the world-famous software company refused to confirm that the evangelical pastor's threat had caused the firm's policy reversal.

Hutcherson, however, proudly proclaimed a victory. When asked if he thought he had played a role in the Microsoft policy change, he replied: "I don't think. I know. If I got God on my side, what's a Microsoft? It's nothing." The Washington state pastor is a close colleague of Dr. James C. Dobson, the head of Focus on the Family, the prominent Christian conservative organization based in Colorado Springs that presses for anti-gay legislation.

Fifteen days after the defeat of the anti-discrimination legislation in the state Senate by a single vote, 25–24, on April 21, Microsoft's chief executive officer, Steve Ballmer, sent a lengthy email to his employees informing them that the company had shifted its policy on the legislation. Microsoft was now in favor of any future bills that would protect homosexuals from discrimination in the workplaces of Washington state.

Ballmer wrote he did not want to "rehash the events" that caused the giant company to remain neutral as the bill was being debated. It was an obvious reference to Hutcherson and the threat of a boycott. The Microsoft executive pledged that his company will "support legislation that will promote and protect diversity in the workplace."

CHAPTER IX

THE SCHOOLROOM

The Christocrats' drive to ban abortion in the United States and punish homosexuals largely depends on developing effective legal strategies to overturn the 1973 *Roe v. Wade* Supreme Court decision and mustering the necessary political support to adopt the proposed Constitutional amendment outlawing same-sex marriages. To be successful, two-thirds of the 535 members of Congress and three-quarters of the fifty state legislatures need to adopt the amendment.

Such anti-abortion and anti-homosexual campaigns usually take place inside marble columned courthouses, the U.S. Capitol building, state legislative chambers, and county and city council meeting rooms—all physically far removed from the general public.

But the Christocrats' major effort to gain control of America's public schools is being fought out in the open at thousands of "up close and personal" encounters at local school-board meetings, the true front line in the current American Civil War. At those sessions, board members frequently argue with one another and with the audience, which is composed mostly of parents.

The school-board debates usually focus on such volatile topics as the teaching of evolution in the classrooms of America; and the removal from libraries of those textbooks, library books, CDs, videotapes, and other teaching materials Christocrats label as offensive or "antireligious." Another divisive issue is whether to abolish sex-education instruction in junior and senior high school curricula and replace it with sex-abstinence courses.

Bitter school-board battles are often about the Constitutionality of conducting holiday celebrations—usually focused on Christmas and Easter—and placing sectarian religious symbols within the classroom. Another explosive issue is the legality of inviting clergy who are Christian missionaries to speak at mandatory student assembly programs. It frequently happens that although such speakers may have been originally asked to address the dangers of teenage drug usage or questions of teenage sexuality, Christian evangelists often use the occasion to proselytize their youthful audiences, a clear breach in the wall of separation between church and state.

Public schools today are ground zero in a raging conflict over the control of curricula and teaching materials, and the choice of faculty and administrators. The title of a book written by Brad Dacus, the founder of the Pacific Justice Institute, one of the many Christian conservative organizations currently active in the U.S., and his wife Suzanne Dacus, a former public school teacher, makes clear the Christocrats' overall strategic aim in America: *Reclaim Your School! 10 Steps to Practically and Legally Evangelize Your School.*

A sympathetic reviewer praised the Dacus book because it "actually equips students for evangelism, not simply informing students of the religious rights [in public schools]." *Reclaim your School* "could potentially mobilize thousands of Christian students, their parents, and educators . . . to make a difference in one of the greatest mission [conversion] fields in our country today, our public schools." Schools with captive student audiences are a prime target for Christian missionaries.

Firmly believing that Christian conservative public-school teachers are being persecuted because of their faith, Southern Baptists, meeting in Atlanta in 1999, adopted a resolution on Christian influence in public schools. The statement paid tribute to "the only adult representation of Jesus Christ" that many "students in public schools experience in their lives." Such "public school personnel . . . maintain exemplary Christian testimonies, sometimes at great personal cost and often with very little positive results."

Testimonies in this context means a teacher's attempt to convert students to evangelical Christianity. The SBC laments the fact that such efforts "often" achieve "very little [sic] positive results"—student or faculty converts.

I am certain that my late Southern Baptist third-grade teacher who expelled Catholics and Jews from her Alexandria, Virginia classroom when she read aloud the New Testament verses to her Protestant-only students would have been pleased and religiously validated by such a resolution, especially since it comes from her own Southern Baptist denomination.

The Christocrats are pursuing a dual strategy regarding public schools. They want to destroy them and turn education over to private schools, especially those sponsored by church bodies. At the same time, as long as public schools continue to exist, Christocrats want to control every aspect of the curricula taught in such despised educational institutions.

Years ago, Falwell declared:

> I hope I live to see the day when, as in the early days of our country, there won't be any public schools. The churches will have taken them over again and Christians will be running them.

Robertson reflects this view as well. When he met with me and other American Jewish Committee leaders in 1995, he noted that while religious communities had historically provided education for young people during the last five hundred years, that role in the United States was taken over by "the state." This, Robertson said, has created a "sterile moral environment, one that must be undone."

A major goal of Christocrats is to undermine what they derisively term "government schools." Their tactics include gathering support for publicly funded vouchers for parents who want to move their children out of public schools and into private educational institutions, mainly Christian-sponsored schools.

Vouchers take money away from an American public-education system that is already short of adequate funding. Vouchers also raise serious Constitutional questions about the legality of using public funds for private and parochial education. Vouchers are similar to blood-sucking leeches that are applied to cure a medical problem, but in reality further damage an already weakened patient.

Requiring students to use textbooks that reflect "traditional biblical values," opposing sex-education courses, and supporting the teaching of Christianity in public schools are all hot-button issues for Christocrats. Added to this cauldron are unceasing demands from Christian conservatives for mandated bible-reading, usually selections from the New Testament, and organized daily prayers in America's public schools.

The National Council on bible Curriculum, headquartered in Greensboro, North Carolina, is one of many Christian conservative groups in America. The council's major goal is the inclusion of its curriculum on the bible in public schools.

It claims growing success and points to 312 school districts in thirty-seven states that have adopted the council's curriculum. The organization's efforts now reach about 175,000 students. But the bible Curriculum has created intense opposition from many educators and school parents who believe the proposed teaching material "attempts to persuade students and teachers to adopt views that are held primarily within conservative Protestant circles."

Predictably, the council denies any religious intent in its curriculum, claiming that the course of study "is concerned with education rather than indoctrination of students." However, the Texas Freedom Network has analyzed and evaluated the council's teaching material and concluded it "is a blatantly sectarian curriculum that interferes with the freedom of all families to pass on their own religious values to their children."

Other critics contend that over 80 percent of the council's suggested books and articles are linked to sectarian groups, nearly two-thirds to Protestant organizations, and just over half to Christian conservative groups. David Barton's books are part of the Council's proposed bibliography. Barton, the vice chairman of the Texas Republican party and a strong advocate in the "Christian nation" movement, is also on the council's advisory board.

The latest battleground is the Odessa, Texas public school system. In April 2005 that city's school board voted unanimously to offer a bible course in the 2006 high school curriculum. Foes of such Scriptural courses pointed out that the Council's curriculum provides "documented research through NASA" that scientifically validates the biblical claims found in the books of Joshua and Second Kings that the sun stood still to benefit the ancient Hebrews in battles following their Exodus from Egypt.

The central issue raised, however, is whether the bible can or should be taught objectively as literature and history in public schools or whether the real goal of introducing the council's curriculum is to indoctrinate students in a particular religious belief, in most cases a theologically conservative Protestant Christianity. It is an issue the Christocrats will continue to press and one that will continue to vex America for years to come.

But Christocrats have an even more ominous purpose than simply reclaiming public schools and using them to convert others to their religious faith or diverting scarce public funds away from public education. The ultimate aim in the ongoing school battles is the destruction of American public education and its replacement with publicly financed Christian academies and widespread homeschooling.

But because millions of Americans are proud products of public schools, a set of non-threatening code words is required to denigrate those familiar neighborhood educational institutions. That is why Christocrats frequently criticize "government schools" instead of calling them "public schools." It is a useful and clever strategy because *government schools* transmits negative images of a remote rigid bureaucracy regulating public education through strict centralized control. *Government schools* or the sometimes-used *state schools* creates a carefully contrived Christocratic image of atheistic educational regimentation that is saturated with the omnipresent bugaboo of "secular humanism."

In 2004, delegates to the SBC national meeting debated a resolution urging parents to withdraw their children from what were termed "Godless government schools." The statement was defeated, but the SBC did criticize "the cultural drift in our nation toward secularism."

In a sign of the times, half the members of the 2004 SBC resolutions committee educate their school-age children at home. The rejection of the anti-"government schools" resolution was not a sign of support for public education; rather, the SBC delegates believed that such a choice— pulling youngsters out of public schools—is a decision that only parents can make, not a church denomination.

But the fact that such a resolution was even debated reveals the depth of the anger many Southern Baptists and Christocrats have toward America's public schools.

At the same meeting, the SBC voted to withdraw from the Baptist World Alliance (BWA) because the international group, representing Baptists from many nations, was becoming too liberal. The BWA, SBC critics charged, was too sympathetic to homosexuals and female clergy. In addition, the BWA reflected an anti-American perspective. By cutting its longstanding international Baptist ties, the Southern Baptist Convention is increasingly a tightly controlled inward-looking institution.

As early as 1981, the Southern Baptist Convention attacked secular humanism for "playing an increasingly important role in society. . . . [It is filling] the ethical vacuum being created by the trend away from theistic teaching in the public educational system. . . ."

David Chilton, a prominent Christian Dominionist, has called for the elimination of all public schools in the United States. Chilton believes that there is no profit in attempting to improve them or strengthening the schools' educational goals. All such efforts, however well-intentioned, are doomed to failure and are counter to authentic Christian teachings and beliefs. Chilton did not hide his true intentions when he warned his fellow Christians:

> The real problem with public schools is that they exist in the first place. They are an ungodly, unlawful, collectivist institution. The many evils now spewing out of them derive from the curse of God inflicted on all institutions that defy Him. He has commanded parents to educate their children in terms of His law; that cannot be done in a public school. If we want our children to fear

Him, to grow into diligent workers for His kingdom, we cannot afford to train them in an institution which has as its fundamental presupposition that I am entitled to as much money as I can vote out of my neighbor's pocket.

Prayer doesn't belong in a public school (Proverbs 28:9). Your money doesn't belong in a public school. Most of all, your children don't belong in a public school. Institutions premised on sin must not be redeemed, but abandoned. We cannot send young maidens into brothels in the interests of "equal time for chastity." As the light of the world, we must set the standard. Our Lord never called His people to help build the tower of Babel in the hope of getting a bible study in the basement. He commanded us to build our own city on a hill.

In April 2003, U.S. Education Secretary Rodney Paige said he would prefer to have a child in a school that had a strong appreciation for the values of the Christian community. A year earlier, Tom DeLay, the Republican Majority Leader in the House of Representatives, was even clearer:

Only Christianity offers a way to live in response to the realities that we find in this world.

The evangelical pastor Tim LaHaye is the coauthor of the best-selling Left Behind novels, must-read books for millions of Christian conservatives. LaHaye, the founder of the Family Life Seminar, another evangelical organization, has also written harshly about America's public schools.

He believes Christian pastors who encourage young members of their churches to attend public schools are "philosophically out to lunch . . . because the world view of secular humanists" is being taught in those schools. Because "secular humanism" is so powerful, LaHaye warns parents that not even attendance at church Sunday Schools or once-a-week bible-study classes can overcome the philosophical and mental damage of attending public schools. "That used to be okay maybe a hundred years ago . . . *but not today.*" Dobson, the leader of Focus on the Family, believes that Christian conservative parents should withdraw their children from public schools.

Homeschooling enthusiast Kevin Cullinane, the founder of the Freedom Mountain Academy in Tennessee, has called America's public schools a "nightmare situation." Other Christocratic critics have expressed similar negative descriptions. Cullinane believes three quarters of today's homeschooled students are "believing Christians. . . . It has not always been that—in fact, some of the first people promoting . . . homeschooling were not Christians."

In a February 1995 address at the William and Mary Law School in Virginia, Robertson assailed the decisions of the U.S. Supreme Court of the 1960s that affirmed the separation of church and state and banned organized prayer in pubic schools. For Robertson, those landmark decisions—*Engel v. Vitale, Abington v. Schempp,* and *Murray v. Curlett*—were "a rape of our governing document, the United States Constitution. . . . After forty years of repeated [Supreme Court] assaults, our nation is battered and torn asunder."

In the same speech, Robertson singled out "public school teachers and administrators . . . [who] put into effect the religious cleansing in the schools that they believe has been mandated by the courts." His use of *religious cleansing* was intended to link his critical view of public schools with the brutal ethnic cleansing that was then under way in the Balkans. Robertson concluded his remarks by calling for a Constitutional amendment mandating prayer in America's public schools.

A year and a half after Robertson's Williamsburg speech, I presented prepared testimony to a U.S. House of Representatives subcommittee that was considering such an amendment. I told the subcommittee members:

> My strong opposition to the proposed amendment is not based simply upon a bitter childhood experience as a young victim of public school bigotry. There are a host of religious, legal, and historic reasons for opposing the proposed Amendment as well.
>
> Prayers and bible readings in public schools and in other public settings are bitterly divisive. The passage of the proposed amendment would cause ugly sectarian strife throughout America.
>
> The United States is a multi-religious and multi-ethnic nation. What kind of prayer or scriptural reading is appropriate when the students are not only Christian and Jewish (in all their myriad forms), but are also followers of Islam, Buddhism, Hinduism, American Indian tribal faiths, or are of no religious tradition?
>
> Public schools have problems aplenty these

days, and must not become battlegrounds in political and religious power games. Today's crop of public school students in America would become cannon fodder in the warfare that is currently being waged by some politicians and clergy. Indeed, I have the feeling that school prayer advocates have not carefully examined what the imposition of such prayers actually means in the real and complex world of public education.

Although Congress rejected the proposed amendment in 1996, it is an issue that never goes away.

But the major clash in public schools involves the teaching of evolution. Christocrats and their allies oppose such instruction and want it replaced with the so-called scientific creationism, the belief that the biblical account of creation described in the book of Genesis is scientifically accurate.

The Assemblies of God denomination asserts "that the Genesis account should be taken literally." In 1982, delegates to the Southern Baptist Convention national meeting in New Orleans declared: "The theory of evolution has never been proven to be a scientific fact. . . . Public school students are being indoctrinated in evolution-science. . . . We express our support for the teaching of Scientific Creationism in our public schools."

But creationism has run into stiff resistance in many school districts. Educators worry that if creationism, which is based on religious faith, is offered as a scientific fact, it will wreak havoc on currently taught science courses, especially biology, botany, physics, geology, and astronomy. Quality education of future scientists is important if the United States is to continue its strong programs of space exploration, medical research, and other technologically advanced disciplines.

Public schools have long been criticized for their inadequate science courses and the fact that the United States has had to rely heavily on foreign-born scientists from Asia and Europe to maintain America's status as a world-class leader in scientific research and development. The teaching of faith-based creationism, it is charged, will further weaken both the quality and quantity of science education in America.

Critics further contend that the Genesis biblical accounts of creation are just that; religious stories, not authentic science. Devoting precious class hours to creationism diverts time and attention away from the science courses required in a high-tech twenty-first century America. Despite such criticism, Christocrats continue to press for the inclusion of creationism in public schools.

While Christian conservatives push creationism in public schools, a parallel debate has also been under way among university academics. That debate has raged between "pure" scientists, including Darwinian evolutionists, and another group of professors who offer the concept of intelligent design or I.D. to explain the creation of the world and of the human family.

Until recently, that intellectual battle was fought in the lofty ivory towers of American colleges and universities. Edward Peltzer, a biochemist at the Monterrey Bay Aquarium Research Institute in California, is a former Catholic who is now a member of a conservative Protestant church. Peltzer put the complicated topic in the starkest terms for those who support I.D.: "When it comes to the origin of life on Earth, there are only two possibilities: one is that life was purposely created, the other that it arose naturally. . . . The idea that it was purposely designed is becoming ever more apparent."

Although the I.D. adherents rarely mention God, many of them are evangelicals and other theologically conservative Christians. Such academics speak of their belief in the God of the bible as the Creator. Others are more circumspect and assert that I.D. makes a Divine Creator intellectually and scientifically logical.

But the overwhelming majority of scientists attack the views of Peltzer and others like him. Typical is the response of Lawrence M. Krauss, the chairman of the physics department at Case Western Reserve University in Cleveland, who sees a not-so-hidden agenda in the I.D. position. Krauss is blunt: "The real danger is in trying to put God in the gaps [of scientific knowledge]. . . . What they're [supporters of I.D.] really attacking here is not Darwinism but science. . . . [Those who back I.D.] are not a part of science. . . . One of the most significant legacies of science in the twentieth century has been the recognition that the universe is the way it is, whether we like it or not. . . . Science has discovered absolutely nothing in the past century of remarkable activity that has any spiritual implications."

H. Allen Orr, a professor of biology at the University of Rochester, was even more direct than Krauss in his criticism. Writing in a May 2005 issue of the *New Yorker*, he called intelligent design "junk science" and said he believes I.D. "has come this far by faith."

But despite the scathing attacks from the scientific community, I.D. advocates won an important victory in their quest to make intelligent design an integral part of America's public school curricula. The No Child Left Behind proposal, a centerpiece of George W. Bush's 2000 presidential campaign, became law in January 2002. Included in the final conference report of the bill that accompanied this education legislation was the carefully crafted phrase: "Whatever topics are taught that may generate controversy (such as biological evolution), the curriculum should help students to understand the full range of scientific views that exist, why such topics may generate controversy, and how scientific discoveries can profoundly affect society."

Christocrats and their academic and political allies applauded that language and asserted that teachers throughout America had federal authority, were even legally mandated, to teach intelligent design as a science course.

Senator Rick Santorum, Republican of Pennsylvania, believed the No Child Left Behind phrase made compulsory the teaching of alternatives to evolution: "intelligent design is a legitimate scientific theory that should be taught in science classes." But Senator Edward Kennedy, Democrat of Massachusetts, disagreed and expressed his opposition to I.D.

Following passage of the No Child Left Behind bill, Representative John Boehner of Ohio, Chair of the House Education Committee, wrote in a letter: "The language is now part of law. . . . It clarifies that public school students are entitled to learn that there are differing scientific views on issues such as biological evolution." President Bush has said "the jury is still out" on the validity of evolution, while Senator James Inhofe, Republican of

Oklahoma, calls the scientific research on global climate change "a gigantic hoax."

Emboldened by statements from political leaders and the fact that more than 80 percent of Americans believe God is the literal creator of the world including all present forms of life, Christocrats have opened a "second front" in the public-school war. They are vigorously pushing school boards to make I.D. a required part of public-school science classes. As they have done on other issues, the Christocrats hope the academically sounding term intelligent design is vague enough to befuddle the general public. And they are succeeding.

In October 2004, the board responsible for the Dover, Pennsylvania area school district voted to make certain that "students will be made aware of gaps/problems in Darwin's theory and of other theories of evolution including, but not limited to, intelligent design." The language is broad enough to permit not only I.D. as science, but also creationism.

In May 2005, New York state assembly member Daniel L. Hooker, a Republican representing the 127th Assembly District, introduced legislation mandating that I.D. be taught to all public-school students in the Empire State. Hooker was the bill's sole sponsor, and his proposal was sharply criticized by Richard Firenze, a biology instructor at Broome Community College.

Firenze said:

> This bill is completely absurd. Those of us in New York who are concerned about our children's science education should sit up and take notice: It's not just in places like Georgia and

Kansas that creationists are trying to sabotage biology education.

Hooker has also introduced bills that would allow the Ten Commandments to be displayed on public buildings, remove sexual orientation from the civil-rights category, and bar same-sex marriages in New York state.

Kansas has been at the center of the evolution versus creationism/intelligent design controversy since 1999, when the state's Board of Education adopted a resolution that called into question the scientific veracity of evolution. Following an election, in 2001 a new Board of Education rescinded the 1999 action, and evolution was again placed in Kansas's school curriculum.

But in May 2005, the Board of Education conducted new hearings in Topeka that focused on whether evolution should be taught as a science and whether it should be taught alone without also putting forth intelligent design as an option for scientific study.

The board set up six days of testimony to debate evolution, but no member of the scientific community attended the hearings since three board members publicly announced in advance that their minds were made up in favor of I.D. The trio believes that evolution is merely a theory without any credible scientific evidence.

Scientists, both in Kansas and from around the country, boycotted the hearings because they considered the entire controversy a lose-lose situation since the votes against evolution were already announced and by appearing in a debate with I.D. supporters, the scientists would convey the impression that there were legitimate grounds for a serious debate. As a result of the Board of

Education's actions, Kansas' citizens have become polarized over the evolution-I.D. arguments.

More than twenty states are debating education bills that are anti-evolution. It seems clear that the Christocrats, who are often perceived as anti-science, have discovered a Trojan horse that looks and sounds scientific enough to destroy not only scientific evolution, but many other currently accepted mainstream beliefs, including geology's claim that the earth is much, much older than the biblical figure of about six thousand years and the environmentalists' ominous claims about global warming.

The most vigorous public foes of scientific evolution are evangelical Christians. But that may be changing following Pope John Paul II's death in April 2005. In 1996 the late Pope declared that evolution was "more than just a hypothesis" and his cryptic remark has been widely quoted as proof the Vatican supports the belief in and the teaching of evolution. In fact, many Catholic parochial schools and colleges in the United States teach evolution to their students.

However, just two months after John Paul II's death, Cardinal Christoph Schonborn, the Archbishop of Vienna, Austria, wrote a *New York Times* op-ed that dismissed the Pope's statement, calling it "rather vague and unimportant." Instead, Schonborn asserted that "Evolution in the sense of common ancestry might be true, but evolution in the neo-Darwinian sense—an unguided, unplanned process of random variation and natural selection—is not." Schonborn cited a 1985 comment by John Paul II that the finality of nature "obliges one to suppose a Mind which is its inventor, its creator."

Christian conservatives who endorse creationism or intelligent design, especially those associated with the Discovery Institute, were elated with the Cardinal's words, while the scientific community, including many faithful Roman Catholics were bewildered and angered by what they perceived as Schonborn's clear attempt to disassociate the Church from support of evolution.

A typical response was from Dr. Kenneth R. Miller, a professor of biology at Brown University and a Roman Catholic: "It [Schonborn's article] may have the effect of convincing Catholics that evolution is something they should reject." Francisco Ayala, a biology professor at the University of California at Irvine and a former Catholic priest, termed the Vienna's Cardinal's dismissal of John Paul II's 1996 words "an insult." Ayala also said Schonborn sees "a conflict that does not exist."

Miller and Ayala joined Krauss in a joint letter to Schonborn seeking clarification on the Church's position on scientific evolution. The three professors were concerned the Church was building "a new divide, long ago eradicated, between the scientific method and religious belief."

Whatever the outcome of the controversy, it is clear that Christocrats and their supporters will use Schonborn's article as an important piece of ammunition in their efforts first to discredit scientific evolution and then remove it entirely from public and parochial school and university curricula. It is another example of the emerging alliance between Protestant conservatives and members of the Roman Catholic hierarchy. That alliance actively opposes abortion, same-sex marriages, embryonic stem cell research, and perhaps, as a result of the

Viennese Archbishop's efforts, evolution will be added to the list of shared hostility.

The anti-evolution forces also received a significant boost when, in early August 2005, President Bush told some Texas journalists that intelligent design should be taught in America's public schools alongside of evolution. The president said, "I felt like both sides ought to be properly taught."

However, he did not express his own position on the scientific validity of intelligent design. Nevertheless, Bush's call for both sides to be presented in American classrooms drew immediate praise from Dr. Richard Land, the president of the Ethics and Public Liberties Commission of the Southern Baptist Convention. Land, who is based in Nashville, Tennessee, is an ardent and public supporter of the Republican party, and has close ties to the Bush White House.

"It's what I've been pushing, it's what a lot of us have been pushing," Land said. However, Bush's science adviser, John H. Marburger, tried to distance the president from an endorsement of intelligent design as a scientific fact: "evolution is the cornerstone of modern biology. . . . Intelligent design is not a scientific concept." The Reverend Barry Lynn, the executive director of Americans United for the Separation of Church and State and a long time opponent of Land, declared, "when it comes to evolution, there is only one school of scientific thought, and that is evolution occurred and is still occurring. . . . When it comes to . . . religion and philosophy, they can be discussed objectively in public schools, but not in biology class."

Whatever Bush's personal views on the issue, several years ago Charles Colson addressed a White House bible class that meets weekly. At that time he expressed support for intelligent design. It is unknown whether Bush was present when Colson spoke, but the weekly sessions are an indication that Christian conservatives like Colson are being heard at the highest levels of American government.

Sometimes the Christocrats' aggressive campaign against evolution even includes a city's zoo. In 2005, the Tulsa, Oklahoma zoo presented an exhibit on scientific evolution that drew the wrath of local Christian conservatives who demanded a "balancing" exhibit praising the biblical account of creation found in Genesis. In addition, the foes of evolution also expressed criticism of the zoo's statue of the elephant-headed god Ganesh at the elephant house. They claimed it was a Hindu symbol expressing an anti-Christian prejudice.

However, after the zoo directors agreed to the Christocrats' demands, there was a strong negative reaction from many Tulsa residents who were concerned their city would be viewed as a benighted backwater community opposed to science.

The zoo directors reversed themselves and, in an act of anthropological correctness, "clarified" their action by calling for "six or seven" creation stories from other religious and ethnic traditions to join the Adam and Eve biblical account at the tax-supported facility. While somewhat comical, the Tulsa zoo controversy is another indication that every institution in American life is a battleground for Christocrats and their supporters.

Florida state Representative Dennis Baxley, a Republican from Ocala, has introduced a bill that would allow university and college students to sue their instructors if they believe their views are not being respected or articulated in the classroom. It is estimated that Florida universities would need $4.2 million to cover the estimated legal costs of such litigation if the Baxley bill became state law.

In proposing the bill, Baxley described his own student experience when one of his professors "dogmatically told [the class] that evolution is a fact. There's no missing link. . . . That kind of dogmatism is what I was addressing [in his bill]." The Florida legislator believes universities are "bastions of leftist thought."

The conservative think tank, Students for Academic Freedom, has posted suggested language for such bills on its website. As a result, legislators throughout the United States, not only in Florida, can simply adapt the model wording and submit it for passage in any statehouse. It is a case of "one law fits all."

Because similar legislation has been offered in twelve other states, including California, Pennsylvania, and Georgia, it is important to analyze what is at stake in Florida. The key issues raised in the Sunshine State will surely reappear elsewhere.

Dr. Roy Weatherford, a professor of philosophy at the University of Southern Florida, slammed Baxley's bill. Weatherford, representing a broad educational coalition that included the USF faculty, the Florida Education Association, the National Education Association, the American Federation of Teachers, and the American Association of University Professors, said all those groups were unanimously against the bill.

The bill "specifies that faculty may not introduce controversial subjects when they're inappropriate, but it provides no mechanism or means for determining who gets to say what is controversial."

He added that if science professors were required to teach I.D., that "requires [them] to teach something that they do not think is scientifically legitimate or should be in the course. Would our business colleagues have to teach Marxism as a legitimate business theory? Or 'Lysenkoism' in the old Soviet Union was the orthodox form of biology; would we be required to teach that as well?"

Trofim Lysenko was a Soviet scientist who insisted that orthodox genetics was false; he also taught that agricultural productivity was directly linked to Communist ideology. He was a Stalinist who curried favor with the dictator by positing wildly inaccurate claims about genetics and agriculture. After Stalin's death, Lysenko was totally discredited.

Finally, Weatherford noted that the $4.2 million in legal fees needed if students sued their professors would only "be a real boon to the trial lawyers" of Florida.

I shudder to think where such thinking can lead if the Baxley/Students for Academic Freedom legislation becomes law. Nazi sympathizers in university classrooms could go to court and sue any professor who said that the Holocaust and the murder of 6 million Jews was a historical fact. The Nazis and their sympathizers could also demand that their fraudulent Holocaust denial position be presented to balance the professor's personal opinion about Jewish victims. In such a school or academic setting, there are no longer any facts, only opinions, and all of them must be equally honored and presented in the classroom.

A student committed to the political restoration and historical rehabilitation of the Japanese militarism of the

1930s and 1940s might sue a college classroom teacher who described the Japanese military's slaughter of Chinese civilians during the 1930s as the "Rape of Nanking." The possibilities for litigation and classroom mischief are endless, if Baxley's proposal and others like it are actually adopted. The chilling effect on professors would be enormous, making a mockery of traditional American values because the government and its agents dominated by Christocrats would dictate what is taught.

Florida State Representative Shelley Vana, a Democrat from West Palm Beach, was especially critical of Baxley's bill: "When we talk about the government stepping in, and having a stick to rein in voices it calls 'outside the mainstream,' I get worried." She added: "Should the administration call in [those] who 'insult the dignity of the country?' That's what happened to my husband in Czechoslovakia. As a student, he was called in before a people's tribunal, was sentenced to death, and had to flee the country, and he never saw his parents. . . ."

In recent years the United States Air Force Academy in Colorado Springs has been riddled with scandals. The situation is so ugly that even the school's staunchest defenders admit that something is rotten at the academy.

Established in 1955 eight years after the Air Force became a separate military service, a chief feature of the academy's beautiful campus in the Rocky Mountains is its set of magnificent chapel buildings. The Jewish chapel is an architectural gem. In 1976, women were admitted to the academy for the first time, and it seemed the Air Force Academy was a world-class institution.

But in recent years, several serious crises have rocked

the school and weakened public confidence in the academy. First there was a cheating scandal involving cadets, but the public was assured that the guilty students had been punished. That crisis was followed by a particularly nasty and widely reported sexual-abuse scandal involving female cadets who reported that their male classmates harassed them. Once again, the public was told that the problem was being solved and was under control.

The latest scandal at the Air Force Academy has involved religious bullying and intimidation of non-evangelical Christians, including Catholics and members of mainline Protestant churches, along with Jewish cadets.

There were at least 117 official complaints from people at the academy who report they have been coerced to convert to evangelical Christianity or have been victims of discrimination because of their religious beliefs. Eight of the complaints have come from Jews, including being called "Christ-killers."

The situation is so bad that the Reverend Barry Lynn, the executive director of Americans United for the Separation of Church and State, an organization based in Washington, D.C., threatened to sue the academy for its clear record of religious harassment and bias.

Lynn and his colleagues learned that the academy compelled cadets to pray at events they had to attend, and cadets were urged to proselytize their fellow cadets in dormitories and other buildings.

During official duty hours, Brig. Gen. Johnny Weida, the academy's commandant of cadets, attended an evangelical meeting that attacked secularism and pluralism, two of the Christocrats' favorite pejorative terms.

In March 2004, fliers promoting Mel Gibson's film *The Passion of the Christ* were systematically placed at every seat in the academy's cafeteria. In November 2004, football coach Fisher DeBerry hung a banner in the academy's athletic facility that read: "I am a Christian first and last. . . . I am a member of Team Jesus Christ."

In February 2005, DeBerry declared that religion is "what we're all about at the academy." By the spring of that year, the Pentagon began a task-force investigation that came after a Yale University Divinity School team in July 2004 observed the academy's week of cadet basic training. The Yale report was never made public until it was leaked to the media in March 2005. The Yale survey reported the presence of "stridently evangelical themes" that foster religious differences among the academy student body rather than building mutual respect and understanding.

In June 2005, the Air Force released its findings, indicating that there was no evidence of religious "discrimination" at the academy, but that there was a prevalent "insensitivity" directed toward cadets who were not evangelical Christians.

Critics faintly praised the report and the consensus was that the Air Force had made a good start in curing the pathology that outsiders reported was extant at the academy. As a former Air Force chaplain, I was not pleased that much of the blame for the religious tensions and abuses was directed at the immaturity of the eighteen-to-twenty-two-year-old cadets. Everyone who has served in the military knows that the leadership corps, not those down the command chain, always sets attitude and creates the atmosphere and climate at any base or post or on any ship.

All these scandals have occurred at a publicly funded educational institution that is supported by American taxpayers, a diverse population reflecting our nation's religious pluralism.

Serious questions have been raised as to whether the academy administration, faculty, and students can focus on their vital mission. Americans wonder if the nation's best interests are being served.

Chaplain MeLinda Morton, a Lutheran minister formerly stationed at the academy, has been a sharp critic of the school's toxic religious climate. She told the media that there is "systematic and pervasive" religion coercion and harassment at the academy. She also accused academy officials of lying about the religious scandal as they attempted to play down its seriousness. After going public with her complaints, Chaplain Morton was scheduled to be transferred to an Air Force base in Asia, which may or may not have been related to her public criticism of the academy. But in June 2005, Chaplain Morton resigned her Air Force commission after thirteen years of service.

Lt. Gen. John Rosa, Jr., the academy superintendent, admitted that the religious problem on his campus "keeps me up at night" and has infected "my whole organization," including the football coach and Weida, Rosa's deputy. Knowledgeable sources report that it may take six years to rid the academy of its religious pathology.

I wonder if the academy's primary goal is to produce "members of Team Jesus Christ," DeBerry's catchphrase. Is it the academy's mission to proselytize on behalf of evangelical Christianity? Or is the school's mission to educate "American airmen and women" from diverse faith communities whose goal is the defense of the Constitution, religious liberty, and freedom of conscience? Americans have a right to demand the latter, and not accept any official toleration of the former.

My Air Force chaplaincy experience differed greatly from Chaplain Morton's bitter tour of duty at the academy. On my second day at Itazuke Air Base in Japan, the base chaplain presented me to the wing commander's office, a normal procedure when chaplains arrive at a new post. I was warned that the colonel was a "tough-talking guy, a real John Wayne-type flyboy."

The commander, who had been a combat pilot in both World War II and Korea, never looked up from his large desk. I could barely see his face, but I clearly remember his unforgettable message: "Chaplain, welcome to Itazuke. Here in the Air Force, we dispense religion like toothpaste. We think everyone should have some of both, and I don't care what brand of toothpaste or kind of religion a person chooses. That's their private choice. I think it's bad for people's teeth and souls if they don't use them, but the Air Force doesn't pressure anyone. What counts is not toothpaste or religion. It's doing our mission right. That's what's important. Thanks for coming by and good luck." The meeting was over.

For many years, I thought the colonel's blunt remarks were insulting, but I now realize he was on to something important and typically American. Religion is good for the soul, but it's an individual choice. People have the right to express their beliefs, and no one has the right to coerce or harass another person because of religion.

Maybe religion is not exactly like choosing a brand of

toothpaste, but Itazuke was a lot better than the Air Force Academy where cadets are religiously harassed, badgered, and insulted. There is, after all, the freedom to be left alone when brushing one's teeth or affirming one's religious identity. Both activities must be freely chosen and fully respected.

Sadly and predictably, when the academy scandal hit the Congress, Republicans defended and condoned the religious climate at the school when Democratic Representative Steve Israel, a Democrat from New York, proposed that the Air Force provide a plan indicating how it would enhance and strengthen religious tolerance at the academy. Israel's proposal was defeated and several GOP lawmakers said that it is evangelical Christians whose constitutional free-speech rights were being repressed in the military, not Catholics, Jews, and non-evangelical Protestant cadets.

At an Armed Services Committee hearing, Rep. John Hostettler, an Indiana Republican, spoke of the "mythical wall of church-state separation" and asserted that Israel's proposal "would bring the ACLU" and "the very silliness that's been present on . . . several courts of justice over the last 50 years" into the U.S. military establishment. He was opposed to any legislation that would "quash the religious expression of millions of service personnel."

Congressional Democrats were accused of being "anti-Christian" when they expressed concern about the current state of religious life at the academy. Hostettler said:

> The long war on Christianity in America continues today on the floor of the United States House of Representatives. It continues unabated

with aid and comfort to those who would eradicate any vestige of our Christian heritage being supplied by the usual suspects, the Democrats. . . . Like moths to a flame, Democrats can't help themselves when it comes to denigrating and demonizing Christians.

His comments were so extreme that Hostettler was forced to expunge them from the official record or face official sanction.

The *Forward* newspaper quoted a Democratic Capitol Hill staffer:

There is more overt talk about various "Christian nation" ideas than I've ever heard before, and a much greater willingness to castigate opponents of the religious conservatives' agenda as anti-Christian. Frankly, I think a lot of Democrats are intimidated into not speaking out as forcefully as they'd like.

Some academy friends and critics wondered whether the school is being religiously influenced by the nearby presence of the Focus on the Family headquarters in Colorado Springs and the huge eleven-thousand-member evangelical mega-church headed by the Reverend Ted Haggard, a nationally prominent evangelical leader.

The serious problems at the Air Force Academy are not taking place in a hermetically sealed vacuum on the Colorado Springs campus. In a July 2005 *New York Times* article, Laurie Goodstein described how evangelical Christians have become a growing presence and influence not only at the academy, but also among active duty USAF chaplains.

When I served in the Air Force as a rabbi in the 1960s, I encountered evangelical ministers within the chaplaincy, but they were not the majority of Christian clergy in the military. In those years, and for decades following the 1960s, the armed forces included many Roman Catholic priests as well as a significant number of pastors and ministers from the mainline Protestant denominations—Episcopal, Presbyterian, Methodist, American [northern] Baptists, United Church of Christ, and Lutheran. During my tour of duty, the draft was in effect, and it brought a broad based multireligious population into the military.

But, clearly that situation has changed in recent years. Today the volunteer military attracts a high number of evangelicals, both white and black, and Christian conservatives currently constitute more and more of the Air Force chaplaincy. The Navy and Army report a similar situation, and the statistics graphically tell the story.

At the start of 2005 there were 611 USAF chaplains on active duty, but only 94 of them were Roman Catholics; a sharp drop of 43 percent from the figure of 167 ten years earlier. Since Catholics constitute about a quarter of the American population, they are clearly under represented.

During the same period, the number of Presbyterian Church (USA) chaplains dropped from 30 to 16, while the much smaller and theologically more conservative Presbyterian Church in America greatly increased its USAF chaplains from 4 to 15. Other mainline church bodies also suffered a sharp decline in the number of clergy in the Air Force. Indeed, the liberal United Church of Christ, the

spiritual descendant of the New England Congregationalists, have only 3 ministers in the entire USAF. There are 10
Jewish Air Force chaplains, also down from recent years.

The reasons for the radical change in the make up of the
military chaplaincy are not hard to discern. Because there
is a great shortage of Catholic clergy in the U.S., many
civilian parishes lack a priest. As a result, there are far fewer
priests than before who are available for military duty.

In addition, many of the recent graduates of mainline
Protestant seminaries are women who for a variety of reasons are reluctant to join the military. Some of their male
classmates made a mid-life career change by entering the
ministry, and they are often too old for the USAF chaplaincy since the maximum entry age is forty.

But the overriding reason for the sharp decline of non-
evangelical chaplains and the growing number of theologically conservative clergy is not age or gender
considerations. During the Vietnam War, many mainline
Protestant denominations became fierce opponents of
overseas American military involvement and that
antipathy has remained, and even grown in intensity
during the Iraq war that began in 2003. At the same time,
evangelicals, both clergy and lay, were often strong supporters of American military interventions including
Vietnam, the Persian Gulf, and Iraq.

Today there is a strong link between Christian conservatives and the U.S. military. Many Christocrats and their
supporters perceive the armed forces as a powerful
instrument of God in their battle against the perceived
enemies of Christianity, especially Islam. That worldview
reflects the religious rhetoric emanating from the Air
Force Academy.

Brig. Gen. Cecil R. Richardson, the deputy chief of chaplains, best expressed the Air Force chaplaincy's dilemma. He said, "We will not proselytize, but we reserve the right to evangelize the unchurched." It often appears that the "unchurched" are Roman Catholics, Mormons, Jews, Muslims, and members of mainline Protestant churches. At the same time Richardson recognized the historic tradition of the military chaplaincy that must serve the spiritual needs of all USAF personnel, not just evangelical Christians.

He declared, "I am an Assemblies of God, pound-the-pulpit preacher, but I'll go to the ropes for the Wicca [witches in the Air Force] if they request a religious service, liturgy or ritual."

CHAPTER X

THE HOSPITAL ROOM AND
MEDICAL LABORATORY

It's all about abortion, all day, all night, all week, all month, all year, all the time.

Abortion is the most fevered issue in American life, even surpassing national defense, the war on international terrorism, and the financial status of Social Security, drug usage, medical insurance, and education.

If I could wake up devoted Christocrats from their sleep at 3:00 A.M. and ask them: "What is the most pressing domestic issue in America today?" I am certain that their immediate answer would be: "Stop all abortions in America!" For Christocrats, the battle to ban abortions in the United States is their Gettysburg or Stalingrad, the turning point in the war they are waging to gain dominance over our society. Abortion is their overriding passion and for them, it is a fight to the finish.

If they succeed in banning legal abortion in America,

Christocratic leaders and their followers will be even more energized and empowered to press forward in the campaign to baptize America. They believe an abortion victory will so dishearten their adversaries that everything else on the Christocrats' agenda will fall into place, and the United States, by the adoption of new laws and Constitutional amendments, will become a truly Christian nation. The necessary legislation and regulations guaranteeing their brand of Christianity will control American life and will be specifically favored by all branches of the government.

Christocrats and their allies have made abortion the proverbial nine-hundred-pound gorilla sitting in the center of every American lawmaker's office—the U.S. Senate, the House of Representatives, the state houses and governors' mansions in the fifty states, and the thousands of county and city legislatures.

For Christocrats, abortion is the central question, sometimes the only question, for all political candidates and for all nominees to every judicial position in the United States, not only the Supreme Court or the federal bench. Candidates for the U.S. presidency and many other elective offices must now run the highly divisive gauntlet of groups that oppose legal abortion in the United States.

But one thing is clear: Christocrats want to make abortions permanently illegal in America, including cases of rape or incest, and even when the mother's life may be threatened. Nothing less will do. And while they may not be successful with other items on their domestic and international agenda, abortion is the one battle they absolutely, positively intend to win.

The campaign to achieve that goal has been actively under way since the U.S. Supreme Court handed down the historic *Roe v. Wade* decision on January 22, 1973. That decision made abortion legal during the first trimester of a pregnancy, and it affirmed the right of women to make choices about terminating their pregnancies. But *Roe v. Wade* also solidified fierce opposition from religious and political conservatives throughout the United States who have termed their position pro-life. Jerry Falwell has often remarked that the *Roe v. Wade* decision awakened him from his political slumber.

Today, the Christocrats are no longer sleeping. The Assemblies of God denomination urges its members to enter into the struggle by opposing abortion "in uncompromising terms" and to "hold elected officials accountable for voting records, support pro-life legislation, oppose referendums . . . challenge our physicians. . . . The real battle is being waged between the kingdom of heaven and the kingdom of this world. . . ."

The Assemblies of God, a staunchly evangelical church body, appeared to condone the use of direct action against those who perform or support abortions. In a semantically murky statement, the AG acknowledged that:

> Some professing Christians use unchristian methods to oppose abortion. But we must never forget the priority God places on His spiritual and material creation. . . . God also loves those who are pro abortion, so we must show compassion also. Yet, at the same time, we must try to halt the horrendous murder of innocents in our country.

An analysis of the Southern Baptist Convention's official positions on abortion starting in 1971 graphically reveals how the issue has been viewed by the nation's largest and most influential evangelical denomination. I believe the SBC's abortion-statement trajectory over the years is an accurate picture of how that issue became such a central concern of Christian conservatives.

The language of the 1971 resolution was benign, not rooted in a theological vocabulary, and there were no biblical references or mention of God in the text. Nearly two years before the *Roe v. Wade* decision and eight years before the ultraconservatives gained control of the Convention, Southern Baptists declared:

> we call upon Southern Baptists to work for legislation that will allow the possibility of abortion under such conditions as rape, incest, clear evidence of fetal deformity, and careful ascertained evidence of the likelihood of damage to the emotional, mental, and physical health of the mother.

Five years later, in 1976, the SBC began using sharper language in its abortion statement:

> Southern Baptists have held . . . a biblical view of the sanctity of life. . . . [We oppose abortion when it is] for selfish non-therapeutic reasons . . . [abortion terminates] . . . an innocent human being. . . .

By 1980, the conservative takeover of the SBC was well under way; that year's abortion resolution unmistakably reflected the new reality of America's second-largest church body.

> Opposition . . . toward all policies that allow "abortion on demand" . . . we abhor the use of tax money or public . . . medical facilities for selfish non-therapeutic abortion. . . . We favor appropriate legislation and/or a constitutional amendment prohibiting abortion except to save the life of the mother.

In 1982, several new elements were added to that year's SBC resolution:

> human life begins at conception. . . . Human life, both born and pre-born, . . . is not subject to personal judgments as to "quality of life" . . . we will work for legislation which will prohibit the practice of infanticide.

By 1987, the SBC was calling upon its millions of members to:

> Actively lobby for legislation to protect the lives of the unborn. . . . [We need to] make the abortion issue a priority. . . .

Four years later, the SBC yearly abortion resolution expressed optimism that

> The Supreme Court is likely to erode or overturn the Roe decision. . . . We oppose the testing,

approval, distribution and marketing in America
of new drugs and technologies which will make
the practice of abortion more convenient and
more widespread.

The Southern Baptists also reaffirmed their longstanding
plea that "unplanned or unwanted pregnancies" be carried to term and, if necessary, children of such pregnancies be offered for adoption.

The presence of Southern Baptist Bill Clinton in the
White House in 1993 drew sharp criticism from the SBC
delegates because, as president, he supported *Roe v. Wade*
and instituted several pro-choice polices:

> We oppose the inclusion of abortion in any
> health care plan which may be proposed by the
> President. . . . We oppose passage of any legisla-
> tion which would have the effect of denying
> First Amendment freedom of speech rights,
> especially as a means of responsible, non-violent
> protest at abortion clinics. . . . [We seek to initiate]
> a boycott against Roussel Uclaf [the French man-
> ufactures of the RU-486 "morning after pill"].

The 1971 abortion resolution was only thirteen lines in
length, but by 1996 the SBC statement on the subject had
grown to forty-three lines. Twenty-five years earlier, the
tone had been gentle, but in 1996 the words were edgier,
angrier, and the targets more specific: Clinton's pro-
choice policies, RU-486, partial-birth abortion, members
of Congress who did not vote to ban such abortions; but
one group received praise for the first time in an SBC

abortion statement: "American Catholic cardinals." It was a tangible sign of the new evangelical-Catholic coalition that was rapidly emerging on the American scene.

By 1999, the Southern Baptists had a new target in their yearly set of resolutions: embryonic stem-cell research. President George W. Bush addressed the 2002 SBC national meeting, and the delegates noted that Bush "reiterated his agreement with us in our historical efforts to save children from their deaths by abortion. . . ." The SBC love affair that started in 2001 with the Bush administration has only grown more fervent since then.

The 1973 Supreme Court decision also galvanized political and religious support for legal abortion. Supporters of *Roe v. Wade* called their movement "pro-choice," and since then the abortion battle has been bitterly fought in courts, executive chambers, and legislatures. But most often the issue has taken the form of public rallies, petitions, and angry one-on-one media debates between supporters and opponents of abortion.

Since *Roe v. Wade,* Christian conservative groups have consistently challenged the legality of all abortions performed in America, including those taking place during the first trimester of a pregnancy. But for more than thirty years, Christocrats have failed to overturn *Roe v. Wade.*

However, they have mounted a series of flanking attacks that chip away at the 1973 Supreme Court ruling. The targets have included abortions performed during the last three months of a pregnancy, state laws negating the requirement that minors must notify their parents in cases of abortion, and even the right to obtain an abortion in the case of rape or incest. Christocrats are strongly in favor of a Constitutional amendment banning abortion in all fifty states.

In addition, many Christocrats want to criminalize abortion by legally prosecuting physicians and other medical personnel who perform the operation. Some go further and even want to charge women who abort with the crime of murdering a fetus.

The Christian Coalition and other Religious Right groups has made the passage of Representative Chris Smith's bill called the Unborn Child Pain Awareness Act a top agenda priority. Smith, a Republican from California, introduced his legislation in the 108th Congress; it had 115 cosponsors and is similar to Kansas Republican Senator Sam Brownback's bill.

The proposed law would mandate that all abortion providers in the U.S. notify women who seek an abortion after the twentieth week of their pregnancy that medical evidence indicates that the fetus feels pain during an abortion. She must be provided with this information plus a brochure issued by the Department of Health and Human Services outlining the pain factor.

The pregnant woman must sign a government form noting whether she requests anesthesia for the fetus. Failing to comply with the law involves civil legal penalties and medical license suspension. Smith's proposed legislation would punish any of the fifty states that fail to implement these provisions with the loss of Medicaid funding.

Just as they have done with the homosexuality issue, Christocrats have developed thinly disguised phrases, encoded words, and traditional religious language to validate their anti-abortion position.

Sanctity of life, culture of life, pro-life, and the constant use of the term *baby* to describe an unborn fetus have become an integral part of the contemporary American political and religious vocabulary. Like the term *biblical principles*, the use of such anti-abortion terms evokes strong reactions from Christian conservatives.

While the Roman Catholic Church expresses a carefully nuanced position on homosexuality that differs from the all-out attacks on gays by Protestant Christocrats, the Catholic hierarchy's long-held opposition to abortion has brought the two groups together in a strong coalition.

Some American political leaders have tried to finesse and defuse the abortion question. While endorsing pro-choice public policies and supporting *Roe v. Wade*, President Clinton constantly declared that abortion should be "safe, legal, and rare." Many of Clinton's executive orders, including permitting abortions on U.S. military bases and providing birth-control information as part of America's foreign-policy programs, were immediately overturned after George W. Bush assumed the presidency in 2001.

Since condoms are a form of birth control, their distribution, even among AIDS-infected Africans, must be opposed.

Other elected public officials have advocated sexual abstinence classes in high schools as a means of decreasing the number of abortions among young unmarried women. Still others have talked of "permitting but discouraging" abortions, or they use the term *therapeutic abortions*, hoping the adjective will provide a medical justification to terminate a pregnancy. Pro-choice supporters have linked legal abortion to women's civil and human rights.

But all such efforts have never satisfied Christocrats,

whose motto about abortion might well be "illegal and never," the opposite of Clinton's mantra.

Not surprisingly, the overwhelming majority of Americans remains conflicted on the subject. Polls consistently indicate that almost three-quarters of those surveyed support abortion rights, but 77 percent believe abortion is a form of murder.

A 2005 Gallup Poll indicated that 23 percent of respondents want abortion legal under all circumstances, and 22 percent want it permanently illegal—a virtual tie. The majority of Americans, 53 percent, want abortion to remain legal but with restrictions often focused on abortions performed during the third trimester of pregnancy, the "partial-birth" procedures.

This deep ambivalence has provided fertile ground for the Christocrats' all-or-nothing strategy regarding abortion. If the murder label permanently sticks to any and all abortions, it becomes easier for Christocrats, a minority of the total population, to press for a total ban. Indeed, if abortion is, in fact, murder, then there nothing to discuss in the American public square since murder is against the law.

But it is not that simple.

I have had many intense discussions with evangelicals and Catholic leaders that centered on our religions' views of abortion. Some of the Christians I spoke with were especially hostile when they complained about the large number of Jewish organizations and individuals who support legal abortion in the United States. Unfortunately, a few Christians edged into the ugly area of anti-Semitism by charging that "secular Jews" were destroying America because of their pro-choice position.

I strongly rejected such arguments when I presented the Jewish teachings and beliefs about abortion, positions that differ greatly from the evangelical and Roman Catholic stances on the subject. It is important to remember that the Jewish perspective is not a modern creation of the twenty-first century designed to be politically correct. The opposite is true.

Judaism's teachings about abortion evolved from biblical times through the centuries of rabbinic Judaism, the Middle Ages, the Enlightenment, the Holocaust, and ultimately into today's chaotic American atmosphere. Because of that long, centuries-old process that goes back nearly three thousand years, Jewish teachings about abortion merit respectful study and careful analysis.

My Christian colleagues from all streams of Christianity were always surprised when I began my description with the words "Jewish religious law teaches that abortion is not murder." It is permitted when a pregnant woman's life is endangered or when carrying the pregnancy to full term may do grievous harm to the mother. The physical and emotional welfare of the mother takes precedence over the unborn fetus.

That is because Judaism makes a clear distinction between a potential human being still in the womb, and a full human being who has entered into the world. Rabbi Solomon ben Isaac, better known by the acronym RASHI (1040–1105), is Judaism's greatest biblical and Talmudic commentator. Rashi taught that the fetus "is not a person" until it is born (even the emerging head of the child constitutes a birth).

Judaism makes an important and necessary distinction between murder, which is strictly forbidden, and killing, which is sad but is justifiable in certain cases of self-defense and is required if a mother would die unless her pregnancy is terminated. Adding to the confusion is the fact that one of the Ten Commandments is consistently mistranslated as "You shall not kill" instead of the accurate "You shall not murder." Hebrew, the language of the bible, has different verbs to describe *murder* and *killing*. They are not the same thing.

The Mishnah, a key part of traditional Jewish teaching, declares: "If a woman has [a life-threatening difficulty] in giving birth . . . her life takes precedence of the life of the fetus or embryo. . . ."

In the Kovno, Lithuania ghetto during the Holocaust, the German occupiers ordered that every pregnant Jewish woman be killed with her fetus. In 1942, Rabbi Ephraim Oshry permitted abortions to take place in an attempt, often tragically in vain, to save the mother's life. The Germans killed the Jewish women anyway.

Rabbi David Feldman, a contemporary rabbinic expert on abortion, has written: "There may be a legal and moral sanction for abortion in certain circumstances . . . [but] abortion is to be considered only as a last resort . . ." to prevent death or injury to the mother. However, Feldman said: "political opportunists must not be allowed to equate abortion with murder. . . . Abortion can be understood in more than one way; the right to do so must be neither compromised nor stigmatized."

But Christocrats intent on banning abortion have stigmatized those who disagree with them, and they seek no room for compromise. Worst of all, when they lash out at "secular Jews" or call opponents who are Jews "baby-killers," they show contempt for Judaism's sacred religious traditions.

Abortion, although often unspoken, was at the center of the controversial 2005 Terri Schiavo case in Pinellas County, Florida, where Michael, her husband, and Mary and Bob Schindler, the forty-one-year-old woman's parents, furiously battled one another in the courts about whether her hydration, nutrition, and medical treatment should be ended. Her husband argued that he was faithfully following his wife's wishes, although she had left no written living will or medical power of attorney.

Ultimately, Terri Schiavo's husband obtained a court order to withdraw all mechanical means of life support. She was diagnosed as being in a "persistent vegetative state" for fifteen years, and in late March 2005 Schiavo's hydration and nutrition tubes were withdrawn.

But in cases where there are no specific written medical directives, Christocrats want the federal and state governments to ban any cessation of hydration, nutrition, or medication for patients, no matter the duration or severity of the patient's condition and no matter the expressed wishes of the patient, spouse, or other family members. For that reason, Christian conservatives, including members of the U.S. Congress and President Bush, saw the Schiavo case as a "culture of life" issue akin to abortion that transcended the hospice room of the comatose patient.

The Republican-controlled U.S. Congress quickly passed an emergency bill in an effort to have the feeding and hydration tubes reinserted. The law, which applied only to Terri Schiavo, called for the federal courts to revisit the case, and President Bush quickly signed the hastily drafted legislation. Republican Congressional leaders and the president both invoked the potent anti-abortion phrases "sanctity of life" and "culture of life" to justify their direct involvement in the case.

But both the Florida state and U.S. federal courts rejected any further efforts to intervene, and there was surprisingly strong public opposition to the governmental intervention in what was perceived as a personal family matter. Schiavo died on March 31, 2005.

Even though the Schiavo case was about the legal and medical status of a severely brain-damaged adult, the issue of abortion was never far from her most fervent defenders. Representative Tom DeLay, the Texas Republican and House majority leader, was ecstatic as he led the Schiavo bill through the lower house of Congress: "one thing that God has brought us is Terri Schiavo, to help elevate the visibility of what's going in America."

For DeLay and other Christian conservatives, "what's going on in America" is the specter of a large group of judges who are upholding the legal right of a woman to obtain an abortion, opting for strict separation of church and state, and ruling in favor of same-sex marriages; all major items on the Christocratic agenda.

Following Terri Schiavo's death, DeLay mounted a heated verbal attack on *activist judges,* a Christocratic term for progressive, moderate, or liberal members of the bench. DeLay's personal assault against the judiciary was so extreme that both Senator William Frist of Tennessee, the Senate majority leader, and President Bush were forced to distance themselves from the House leader's words. But DeLay's harsh public warning to the judges was clear: Do not enforce laws that Christocrats cannot support or directly oppose. If judges continue down that path, DeLay warned that the legislative branch of government would take steps to rein in such "activists."

The political fervor in the Schiavo case ebbed quickly,

once GOP leaders read the polls showing the vast majority of Americans, many of them Republicans, strongly objected to the government's intervention in a personal family medical matter. Every American could identity with the painful decisions involved in the Schiavo case, and the polls indicated that the public clearly wanted the government to stay out of such matters. In addition, the majority of those polled did not share DeLay's negative view of judges.

Months earlier, abortion was at the center of the 2004 presidential campaign. Senator John Kerry, the Democratic nominee, is a pro-choice Roman Catholic. Because of his position on abortion, he came under withering attack from several bishops, as well as from highly conservative lay Catholics.

They urged priests to deny Kerry the sacrament of communion at Mass, because his stand on abortion conflicted with church policy. Most Catholic bishops took no public stand on the issue, but Kerry was never able to shake off the charges that his fellow Catholic detractors laid upon him. It was an ironic twist of American political and religious history.

In 1960, Senator John F. Kennedy, also a Catholic from Massachusetts, was publicly criticized by some prominent Protestant ministers who feared a Catholic as president. The pastors worried that Kennedy was "too Catholic" and his religion would negatively influence his Constitutional responsibilities as president.

To rebut such charges, JFK publicly leaned over backward to assert his personal and political independence from the Catholic church in matters of public policy. In 1960, the abortion issue had not yet emerged as a divisive political issue. Interestingly, Kennedy, the first and only Catholic elected to the U.S. presidency, approved the use of federal funds for birth-control studies for the National Institute of Health, something his predecessor, the Protestant Dwight Eisenhower, refused to do.

Forty-four years later Kerry probably lost a significant number of votes because he was perceived as not being "sufficiently Catholic" on the question of abortion.

The same issue plagues other public officials who are also Roman Catholic. In May 2005, a Palm Beach, Florida, juvenile court judge, Ronald Alvarez, issued a ruling that a thirteen-year-old unmarried girl could receive an abortion.

As a result of this judicial decision, Don Kazimir, director of the Palm Beach diocese Respect Life Office, publicly criticized Alvarez and wanted the judge barred from receiving communion. The irate judge retorted: "The moment we kowtow to a religious party, we're essentially for sale . . . the day one judge does it, we're all dead."

The Alvarez-Kazimir clash raises the question of whether religious law supersedes state law. The Christocratic answer is a resounding "Yes!"

Abortion also influences our nation's international relations. In a sharp policy reversal, the Bush administration in 2001 abandoned U.S. support for family-planning programs overseas that provided condoms in AIDS-ravaged parts of the world, especially Africa.

There is an increasing number of Christian conservative pharmacists in the United States who refuse to honor prescriptions for certain medications, especially those related to birth control or contraception. In addition,

Mississippi and Illinois now permit physicians to deny patients certain medical procedures. Their refusal is based upon "religious liberty," and the right of pharmacists, doctors, and other medical personnel to exercise their religious rights guaranteed under the First Amendment. In such cases, patients either do not receive the necessary medications and treatments, or they must seek them elsewhere, a complicated and difficult activity, especially for low-income women who choose an abortion or who request birth-control information.

Abortion is also the driving force in the Christocratic opposition to embryonic stem-cell research. Christian conservatives, led by Focus on the Family, see such research as "another insidious aspect . . . fetal tissue research may actually help to 'legitimize' abortion . . . [because] some mothers . . . may be convinced that aborting their children is an altruistic act that will provide long-term benefits for society."

For Christocrats, it always comes back to abortion.

But perhaps touched by poignant calls for embryonic stem-cell research from Nancy Reagan and her son Ron, many Christian leaders, who oppose such research, have expressed "compassion for those with terminal illnesses." However, most remain strongly opposed to using embryonic stem cells as a possible weapon to combat Parkinson's disease, Alzheimer's disease, diabetes, and other crippling ailments. Such Christian conservatives make a clear distinction between embryonic and adult stem cells, since the latter do not come from aborted fetuses.

But Christina Powell, a PhD researcher at Harvard Medical School and an ordained Assemblies of God minister, admits there are "problems with the use of adult stem cells. . . . The possibility of adult stem cells containing genetic error is greater [than embryo cells]. . . . There is evidence that adult stem cells might not have the same capacity to multiply as embryonic stem cells do." But despite these problems, the Assemblies of God denomination strongly opposes the use of embryonic stem-cell research.

Conservative Christian opposition also extends to in-vitro fertilization (IVF), a procedure used by infertile couples in an effort to have a child of their own. Assemblies of God general superintendent Thomas Trask "does not support embryonic stem-cell research, IVF, or abortion as all are viewed as ways of terminating life."

There is also a disturbing element that is never far from the surface in the debate over abortion, stem-cell research, and other bioethical questions: the continuing efforts by Christocrats to link abortion and stem-cell research to the 6 million Jewish victims murdered during the Holocaust.

In a lengthy 2004 discussion of stem-cell research, an Assemblies of God writer made this abhorrent linkage:

> In World War II, the Jews were viewed by the Nazis as little more than domesticated animals. The resulting medical experiments conducted on "these pieces of property" . . . has caused the world to shudder ever since.
>
> Some may argue that the comparison to the medical experiments performed on Jews is irrelevant as the Jews experiencing those medical atrocities were "self aware"—they could feel pain—whereas an embryonic stem cell is

not self aware . . . does not have the ability to
feel pain.

However, . . . stem-cell research is similar as
it results in the dissecting and termination of life
in the name of science.

The Assemblies of God analogy is part of a growing abuse
of Holocaust imagery in contemporary America. As
World War II veterans and Holocaust survivors die natural deaths, memories grow dimmer, and language from
that period—which once meant something quite specific—
is carelessly tossed about the public square. Holocaust
parlance is currently being used in disrespectful and
wildly inaccurate ways.

During the Schiavo TV coverage outside her hospice, I
noticed signs with Holocaust terminology and symbols,
including the hated Nazi swastika. The most egregious
sign read: AUSCHWITZ U.S.A.

That reckless use of language was insulting to the
memory of the 1.5 million people—mostly Jews—who
were gassed, shot, and hanged at the Nazi death camp in
Poland. The sign was also an insult to Terri Schiavo her-
self, because it ramped up the fiery rhetoric and prevented
a cogent exploration of the complex issues of her case.

In their zeal and overblown rhetoric, Christocrats owe
the 6 million Holocaust victims the dignity and respect
they deserve. Using "Auschwitz U.S.A." and "Nazis" to
score cheap political points in today's polarized society is
shameful.

The Schiavo case was sad, but it did not involve gas
chambers, crematoria, and the mass murder of millions of
people. Whatever the issues surrounding embryonic

stem-cell research, its supporters are not Nazi storm troopers bent on killing Jews.

Focus on the Family (FOF) reflects hard-right Christian positions on many issues, including bioethical concerns. The group's official position rejects "the premise" that the use of embryonic stem cells "is defensible on the basis that it may yield scientific breakthroughs to aid the living." FOF "calls on our government, as well as the medical and scientific communities to abandon" such stem-cell research. Dobson's group opposes all embryonic stem-cell research.

But an increasing number of Christian conservatives are expressing support for embryonic stem-cell research. The experience of facing their own crippling diseases or confronting friends and family members who suffer from debilitating illnesses has changed the opinions of some people who were at first opposed to such research.

One evangelical woman, Peggy Willocks of Johnson City, Tennessee, saw a close friend suffer and die because of Parkinson's disease. Willocks told Jeffrey McDonald of Religion News Service that she studied her bible, prayed, and finally reached the conclusion that cells in a Petri dish aren't sacred because "life begins in the womb." She now supports embryonic stem-cell research.

A 2005 Gallup poll showed that 60 percent of Americans believe that such research is "morally acceptable," an increase of 8 percent from three years earlier.

Support for such research jumped sharply among Roman Catholics and members of mainline Protestant churches, but there were also significant increases among Protestant evangelicals.

In the 2005 survey, 38 percent of the latter group polled now support embryonic stem-cell research, a gain from the 2002 figure of 28 percent. Only 50 percent of Protestant evangelicals now oppose the research.

One example of a high-profile change in attitude is Representative Dana Rohrbacher, a conservative Republican from California. The Congressman remains "adamantly against abortion," but he altered his view on embryonic stem-cell research when his wife gave birth to triplets in 2004 as a result of in-vitro fertilization.

Rohrbacher said:

> *I hadn't thought it through too much before that [his childrens' birth]. I'd have to say my personal experience had a lot to do with my position. . . . To say "life begins at conception" we have to realize that science now has made that phrase obsolete.*

There are currently over four hundred thousand frozen embryos in the United States. As the personal conversions of Rohrbacher and Willocks indicate, the once solid bloc of Christian conservative opposition appears to be shifting. The battle surrounding embryonic stem-cell research is likely to intensify if the Christocrats see their support eroding.

Other bioethical battles center on proposed laws permitting assisted suicides and the withholding and withdrawal of life-support systems, particularly in long-term comatose patients.

The AG position is representative of such views:

> [We] oppose referendums in favor of assisted suicide. . . . The real battle is being waged between the kingdom of heaven and the kingdom of this world. . . .

In November 2004, California voters approved Proposition 71, which permits $3 billion for embryonic stem-cell research. Their action was criticized by two anti-abortion organizations: the Washington-based Family Research Council (FRC), and the American Life League (ALL), headquartered in northern Virginia.

Tony Perkins, the president of the FRC, reflected Christocratic thinking on such research: "As a country we cannot afford to let this type of egregious disrespect for human life become common and accepted practice."

President Bush's opposition to embryonic stem-cell research has met opposition within his own Republican party. The president's position places him in opposition to most Americans, who favor such research. A 2005 Gallup Poll found that 60 percent of those surveyed found embryonic stem-cell research "morally acceptable." An earlier Pew Foundation study indicated that 40 percent of self-identified "conservatives" approved such research, surprisingly just 5 percent less than conservatives who are against the use of embryonic stem cells for such purposes.

Bush and his supporters make a great distinction between embryonic cells and those cells taken from adult stem cells. The president is opposed to using federal dollars to "promote science which destroys life in order to save life," his definition of embryonic research.

In late July 2005, Bill Frist, the U.S. Senate's Majority Leader, broke with President Bush on the controversial question of providing federal funds for embryonic stem-cell research. The Tennessee Republican declared on the Senate floor that "It's not just a matter of faith, it's a matter of science" because such research has "the potential" to aid in the fight against Alzheimer's, Parkinson's and other dread diseases.

Frist, a physician, has generally supported the Christian conservatives' position on other issues including the Terri Schiavo case and the confirmation of "strict constructionists" as federal judges.

Frist's call to modify Bush's rejection of any federally funded embryonic stem-cell research was immediately attacked by Christocrats and their supporters. The Reverend Patrick Mahoney, the director of the Christian Defense Council, warned Frist that he "should not expect support and endorsement from the pro-life community if he votes for embryonic research funding."

But despite Bush's opposition, several states are moving forward to bypass federal restrictions and use state money for such scientific study. Republican Senators Orrin Hatch of Utah and Arlen Specter of Pennsylvania believe embryonic stem cells offer realistic hope in the medical battle against dread illnesses.

Hatch, who opposes abortion, said: "I do not believe that life begins in a Petri dish and, like many others, hope that these excess embryos can benefit mankind. . . . For me, being pro-life means helping the living." Representative Joe Schwarz, a Republican from Michigan and a physician, also opposes abortion, but he declared: "I think this is the most pro-life thing you could do."

But even if the embryos are never born, Christocrats still believe the entire procedure is morally repugnant. It is another battle that the Christocrats intend to win by defeating the seemingly inexorable movement in medical science toward the use of embryonic stem cells for research purposes.

Because Christocrats constantly press for the unconditional surrender of their perceived enemies, it is difficult, perhaps impossible for them to amicably discuss and debate with those who do not share their views on abortion and embryonic stem-cell research. As a result of the Christocrats' intransigence, the gap between them and those who support legal abortion and embryonic stem-cell research has grown wider and wider. The ultimate loser is the American people.

But it does not have to be that way.

While the battles surrounding abortion and embryonic stem research grab most of the headlines, and despite the bitter public conflict over these two issues, I can attest there has been significant progress on other key bioethical concerns, especially in New York state.

The Empire State has a highly diverse population that speaks over 120 different languages, but it is precisely there where enormous gains have been achieved on vital bioethical issues. That is because a unique interreligious, interracial, and interethnic group has been able to address those questions without the rancor and anger associated with abortion and embryonic stem-cell research. I believe the New York State Task Force on Life and the Law offers a model for other states to follow as they tackle key bioethical questions.

Since 1985, I have served as a member of the Task Force. The governor appoints the twenty-five members of the group, which includes Christian and Jewish clergy, physicians, nurses, lawyers, ethicists, social workers, and hospital administrators. Task Force members represent many diverse religious, political, and cultural opinions. The group is aided in its work by a professional staff.

Over the years, the Task Force has confronted the most difficult bioethical issues of our time and drafted specific regulations or laws for adoption by the state legislature in Albany. The record of having our proposals approved is quite high. But all that comes only at the end of a long and intensive process of public fact-finding and internal discussions within the Task Force.

At the outset, the Task Force members receive expert testimony, both oral and written, on a specific issue, and then debate the need to draft new regulatory legislation. It is invigorating work, because we must deal with a series of critical concerns including the legal definition of death, balancing patients' rights and the state's interests. This is especially true in establishing the validity of do-not-resuscitate orders issued in hospitals in cases of cardiac arrest, the creation of healthcare proxies (medical powers of attorney), drafting laws relating to surrogate parenting, the status of unwanted frozen human embryos (the result of multiple in-vitro fertilization attempts), medically assisted suicides, and determining the safety of certain popular food and dietary supplements.

My experience as a Task Force member has provided a unique vantage point to witness the rapid changes in medical technology since 1985. It has also taught me the importance of applying deeply held religious teachings to modern bioethical questions. As a result, it is clear that some long-held traditional beliefs must be updated or even abandoned in the face of twenty-first-century medical advances.

One example is the need to determine when a person is legally considered dead. It sounds simple, but in many instances it is a complex question if a patient is kept alive by mechanical means—ventilators and respirators. The definition of death is particularly important in cases of a possible organ transplant. When is it legally and medically permitted to remove a heart or other vital organs from a person for use by another human being?

In Jewish tradition, it is assumed that death has occurred when a person's breathing stops. When that happens, the body must remain untouched for an eight-minute period to guarantee that breathing, pulse, and heart have actually ceased functioning. During those eight minutes, a light feather is placed upon the lips of the presumed deceased person. If the feather does not move, the person is considered dead. Sometimes a mirror was positioned under the nostrils to see if condensation appeared on the mirror, indicating that a person was still breathing.

But what happens if a patient's heart and breathing functions continue as the result of highly complex life-support machines? Is such a person actually "alive"? Or is the patient "organically dead," even though breathing, pulse, and a heartbeat are sustained by mechanical means?

The Task Force, after a thoughtful study of religious traditions and medical technology, determined that in New York state death legally occurs when there is "irreversible brain stem damage," a condition that can only be determined by modern medical tests, and not by even sharp-eyed witnesses observing a patient or by the placement of a feather on a person's lips.

But there are two bioethical questions the Task Force did not address: abortion and embryonic stem-cell research. It is not because Task Force members are cowards or fear a public fight with Christian conservatives; it is because we had no need to offer the New York State Assembly and Senate draft legislation dealing with abortion, since that medical procedure is legal. The emerging question of embryonic stem-cell research is a new bioethical question that the Task Force may tackle at a future date.

If and when that discussion becomes necessary, the Task Force will study the question with the same intensity of purpose, mutual respect for differing opinions and beliefs, candor, and honesty with which it has approached every other bioethical issue.

It's too bad that the Christocrats, in their unrelenting power drive to ban abortion and embryonic stem-cell research, cannot do the same.

CHAPTER XI

THE COURTROOM

Controlling all branches of the judiciary is at the epi-center of the Christocratic drive to baptize America. The campaign to remove objectionable and troublesome judges from the bench and replace them with jurists who reflect Christocratic legal views is being simultaneously carried out on several fronts. The goal is to meld the judge's gavel with the bible.

Such a merger, not unknown in European history, would permanently change the entire legal system of America. In the future, court decisions affecting society and personal lives would have to pass a Christocratic religious test, including such questions as "Is the law in line with 'traditional biblical principles'?" and "Are judges faithful to 'God's law' and not 'secular humanist' legal precedents and interpretations?" Church-state separation in America would be greatly diminished, or even discarded, in the proposed linkage of American civil and criminal laws with a particular form of Christianity.

Retaining the White House and majorities in Congress is, of course, achieved by popular elections that involve fixed terms for public office-holders. In a Christocratic America, the demand for term limits, once a signature issue of conservatives, would be abandoned. This would permit preferred public officials in the legislative and executive branches, including the presidency and the U.S. Congress, to remain in office for many years. But Christocrats are fully aware that many judicial appointments, including the nine-member U.S. Supreme Court and hundreds of federal judgeships, are already lifetime positions. That is why confirmation fights over nominees to the bench are frequently so bitter.

If Christocrats can place enough like-minded judges in the nation's complex court system, the effort to impose a Christian conservative agenda upon the country will not be so dependent upon sometimes-unpredictable election results. Judges who reflect a Christocratic view of America will not stand in the way of the campaign to baptize America.

Executive and legislative branches of government dominated by Christocrats and their followers will have their new laws and regulations legally validated by a judiciary that is also sympathetic to the Christian conservative political agendas.

Because every recent poll indicates that Americans have profound respect for their courts and the system of checks and balances built into our governmental structure, Christocrats and their political allies must first wage an all-out public propaganda war aimed at weakening that traditional level of respect. Just as they have done in attacks on other major American institutions, the systematic use of a potent set of code words is necessary to break down public confidence in the American judiciary.

The widely used epithet *activist judges* is such a code word or phrase, and it is constantly hurled at many members of the bench. The primary targets of this propaganda ploy are usually judges who affirm the separation of church and state, uphold *Roe v. Wade,* restrict the placing of religious symbols in public space, and protect minority group rights, sometimes including same-sex marriages and civil unions.

Another code word, *strict constructionists*, is used to describe judges who, according to Christocratic criteria, correctly interpret the law according to the *original intent* (yet another coded phrase) of the U.S. Constitution. This approach is often called "originalism"; it translates into relentless attacks on much of Franklin Roosevelt's New Deal, Harry Truman's Fair Deal, and Lyndon Johnson's Great Society domestic programs.

Like the Christocrats, who invoke the image of an earlier tranquil, moral, and pristine America, the Constitutional originalists have their own version of the late, lamented "good old days." It was the period between 1896, with the election of William McKinley as U.S. president, and the 1920s, the decade of the Harding and Coolidge administrations.

It was an era when business interests, including trusts and monopolies, dominated economic and commercial life in the United States. In those years, the courts overwhelmingly supported unfettered free enterprise and provided little relief for the rights of workers, miners, and other members of the laboring class.

The Progressive movement of the early twentieth century, first led by Republican President Theodore Roosevelt and later by Democratic chief executive Woodrow Wilson, was a reaction to the unbridled pro-business policies and one-sided court decisions of that period. The originalists believe that the Constitution clearly went into exile with the 1932 election that placed FDR in the White House. For supporters of Constitutional original intent, the worst year in American history was 1937, the high-water year of the New Deal.

One originalist goal that would resonate with Christocrats is the legal dismantling of environmental-protection programs, minimum-wage laws, clean-water acts, endangered-species legislation, the Federal Communications Commission, and perhaps even the Social Security Act, the Federal Reserve Board, and laws regulating workplace conditions and hours of employment.

One of the chief supporters of originalism is Edwin Meese, who served as U.S. Attorney General during the Reagan administration. Meese and his colleagues, including several prominent law-school professors, believe that years of judicial intervention by "activist judges" have placed the Constitution in a frozen exile. Many Constitutional originalists have joined forces with Christocrats in their shared contempt, bordering on hatred, for the federal government (except when the power of government is useful to them in their baptizing-of-America efforts) and the many regulations and laws that are viewed as anti-business, pro-environment, and anti-Christian (i.e., church-state separation cases).

There are delicious ironies in all this. Critics charge that George W. Bush owes his successful 2000 presidential election to the five Supreme Court justices who, in an act of "legal activism," overrode the Florida Supreme Court's rulings regarding that state's election return. Christocrats desire activist judges when it benefits them in Constitutional cases involving increased religious presence in the public square, but not in church-state, abortion, gun-control, or sexual-orientation cases.

The verbal attacks on judges in the aftermath of the 2005 Terri Schiavo case in Florida was an example of the fury and rage that Christocrats and their allies have mounted against members of the bench whom they label "activist." Representative Tom DeLay said that the courts had "run amok" and that he wants to discipline judges who do not share his views.

Senator John Cornyn, Republican of Texas, made a particularly violent verbal attack on judges following Schiavo's death. He said that anger against the judicial decisions of activist judges "builds up and builds up, to the point where some people engage in violence, certainly without justification." To many observers, it appeared that Cornyn "understood" any potential future violence directed at the courts, and used the last three words as a throwaway clause or a rhetorical safety valve.

There was bitter disappointment that the federal courts did not reverse their earlier Schiavo decisions after the Congress and the president successfully enacted a special law in March 2005 that specifically called for judicial involvement. The "Schiavo law" was a direct invitation for federal judges to become actively involved by restoring her feeding and hydration tubes. They chose not to do so by upholding lower court rulings.

Tony Perkins, the head of the Family Research Council, has been especially critical of "activist judges":

> What they have done is, they have targeted people for reasons of their faith or moral position. The issue is the judiciary is really something that been veiled by this "judicial mystique" so our folks don't really understand it, but they are beginning to connect the dots. They [court decisions on church-state issues] were all brought about by the courts.

Like the elusive attribute of beauty, what constitutes an activist judge is all in the eyes of the beholder.

Not surprisingly, the same religious and political leaders who attack public education, legal abortion, the teaching of evolution, church-state separation, and other Christocratic targets are frequently the same ones who also assault the personal and professional integrity of judges who differ with them on key issues. A consistent critic of judges is Robertson.

In a June 27, 1986 *Washington Post* article, the Christian Coalition founder declared:

> I am bound by the laws of the United States and all 50 states. . . . I am not bound by any cause or any court to which I myself am not a party. . . . I don't think the Congress of the United States is subservient to the courts. . . . They can ignore a Supreme Court ruling if they so choose.

Nearly twenty years later, Robertson was even more critical

of the judiciary. The *Richmond Times-Dispatch* reported that on the May 1, 2005 ABC-TV *This Week* program, Robertson asserted that federal judges pose a more dangerous threat to America than al Qaeda terrorists. Robertson said that the judiciary is a greater threat to the country than "a few bearded terrorists who fly into buildings."

In addition to the constant verbal barrage directed against judges, legislation was offered in May 2005 in the U.S. House of Representatives that would not permit federal court judges to hold hearings or make legal rulings on the constitutionality of reciting the Pledge of Allegiance. A similar version had passed the House eight months earlier by a vote of 247–173, but the U.S. Senate had let the bill die at the end of the 108th Congress.

Republican Representative Todd Akin of Missouri reintroduced the bill, along with Senator Jon Kyl, an Arizona Republican. It is one in a series of Congressional initiatives called "court-stripping." The goal is to severely limit the legal jurisdiction of courts to rule on certain issues and controversies. The Akin bill was a reaction to a 2003 federal circuit court of appeals decision in California that ruled that the Pledge of Allegiance phrase "under God" is unconstitutional.

But in a related case, in May 2005 the Richmond, Virginia-based Fourth Circuit Court of Appeals unanimously upheld a lower court ruling that the inscription IN GOD WE TRUST on the outside of a U.S. government building in Lexington, North Carolina, does not violate the Constitution's First Amendment.

The inscription was placed on the building in 2002 and was funded by church and individual contributions. Two lawyers who work in the building brought suit, claiming the words "In God We Trust" were a violation of the First Amendment. The plaintiffs, Charles F. Lambeth, Jr. and Michael D. Lea, wanted the inscription removed.

Another example of court-stripping is a House bill that was passed in the 108th Congress but also died in the Senate. That bill would strip the courts of jurisdiction to challenge the constitutionality of the Defense of Marriage Act.

Yet another House bill, this one introduced by Alabama Republican Robert Aderholt, would reserve the legal power of displaying the Ten Commandments solely to the fifty states and not to the federal judiciary. The bill would remove the right of people to go before a federal court to challenge those cases when government and religion, church and state, appear to collide in an official way.

Aderholt's legislation was a direct reaction to the unsuccessful effort of former Alabama Chief Justice Roy Moore to permanently display a large stone monument of the Ten Commandments in the Montgomery, Alabama judicial building.

The Alabama courts thwarted Moore in his well-publicized Ten Commandments campaign and the huge stone monument was removed. He appealed that decision, but a federal court rejected his appeal, declaring that the display of the Ten Commandments in the Alabama state judicial building was unconstitutional.

In an ironic twist, an Associated Press survey in 2005 showed that although many Americans cannot accurately recite all of the Ten Commandments, 76 percent of the one thousand people surveyed approved of displaying them on government property.

But Moore remained undeterred by his judicial setbacks.

In September 2004, the former chief justice of Alabama urged a Congressional subcommittee to support a proposed law that would forbid federal judges from ruling on cases dealing with government displays of religious symbols. The result was that Aderholt, a fellow Alabaman, proposed legislation that supported Moore's position.

Moore argued that the right to place religious symbols in courtrooms is protected by the Constitution's First Amendment and is not subject to judicial review. "Acknowledgement of God is just not within the jurisdiction of the federal courts," Moore argued.

But Moore's many critics in Congress and in various law schools called upon Congress to reject the proposal as an assault on the independence of federal courts. They specifically cited a U.S. Supreme Court ruling in 1978 *(Stone v. Graham)*; in that case, the Court ruled that placing a copy of the Ten Commandments in every classroom in a state was in violation of the Constitution's First Amendment.

The High Court was clear that "the pre-eminent purpose for posting the Ten Commandments on schoolroom walls is plainly religious in nature." Although some of the Commandments represent core moral values for a just society—prohibition of murder, theft, and adultery, and the honoring of parents—the texts in the biblical books of Exodus and Deuteronomy are highly religious with their preference for monotheism, their rejection of idols, and their call for the observance of the Sabbath.

As a kind of icing on the cake, Republican Rep. John Hostettler of Indiana offered amendments to bills that would prevent the removal of the Ten Commandments monument in Alabama and block any attempt to ban the recitation of the Pledge of Allegiance in public schools.

While the courts recognized the important role that the Ten Commandments play in Judaism and Christianity, the posting of them in a courtroom, courthouse, or any other government building gives the clear message that the government—federal, state, or local—favors one religious tradition over other faith commitments held by American citizens.

One of the landmark Supreme Court decisions was in 1947 *(Everson v. Board of Education)*. Christocrats want the current High Court to overturn this decision or render it moot by emasculating its meaning and impact.

Justice Hugo Black, speaking for the Court majority, wrote a strong reaffirmation of the historic American principle of church-state separation:

> The "establishment of religion" clause of the first amendment means at least this: Neither a state nor the federal government can set up a church. Neither can pass laws that aid one religion, aid all religions, or prefer one religion over another. Neither can force nor influence a person to go to or remain away from church against his will or force him to profess a belief or disbelief in any religion. No person can be punished for entertaining or professing religious beliefs or disbeliefs, for church attendance or non-attendance.
>
> No tax in any amount, large or small, can be levied to support any religious activities or institutions, whatever they may be called, or whatever form they may adopt to teach or practice religion. Neither a state nor the federal

government can, openly or secretly, participate in the affairs of any religious organizations or groups and vice versa. In the words of Jefferson, the [Constitutional] clause against establishment of religion by law was intended to erect "a wall of separation between church and state."

A highly public linking of Republican Congressional leadership with the Christocrats took place in Louisville, Kentucky, in late April 2005. The Family Research Council organized a *Justice Sunday* telecast that was beamed to churches, the Internet, and Christian radio and television stations around the country.

Several nationally prominent Christian conservative leaders participated in the *Justice Sunday—Stopping the Filibuster Against People of Faith* telecast: Chuck Colson, a born-again Christian who served prison time for Watergate crimes founded Prison Fellowship Ministries; Dobson, the leader of Focus on the Family; and Dr. Al Mohler, president of the Southern Baptist Seminary in Louisville.

Dobson's remarks were typical of the verbal attacks on the judiciary:

There is a majority on the Supreme Court that is unelected, unaccountable, arrogant, and imperious and determined to redesign the culture according to their own values and biases, and they are out of control.

Mohler reflected the Christocrats' view that elections are not sufficient in the campaign to rid the judiciary of offending judges:

We are going to have to exercise our Christian
citizenship beyond the ballot box all the way to
the nomination and confirmation of judges.

During the telecast, Democrats were attacked for holding
up Senate votes on seven of President Bush's most conservative nominees to the federal bench, and were
accused of being "against people of faith." The potent
imagery of the bible and a judge's gavel being held in
two hands by a young man was featured, but the highlight of the program was the taped message of Senator
Bill Frist.

Frist urged Christian conservatives to pressure their
senators in an effort to end the Democrats' filibuster that
until then blocked the president's nominees:

If these senators are not prepared to fulfill their
constitutional responsibility, then why are they
here in the first place?

Criticism of Frist's appearance on the *Justice Sunday* telecast was immediate, and it came from political and religious leaders. Mark Hansen, the presiding bishop of the
Evangelical Lutheran Church of America, said:

The tragic irony of *Justice Sunday* is that it risks
perpetuating an injustice. It uses the power of an
elected political leader to polarize people of faith.

New York Senator Charles Schumer, a Democrat, said:

No party has a monopoly on faith, and for Senator

Frist to participate in this kind of telecast just
throws more oil on the partisan flames.

In another chapter, I described how a West Palm Beach,
Florida, judge named Ronald Alvarez approved an abortion for an unwed thirteen-year-old who had run away
from a state supervised group home.

Don Kazimir, a director of the Palm Beach County
Right to Life League, criticized Alvarez's decision and
said that the judge, raised a Roman Catholic, should not
be permitted to take communion at a Mass.

In addition to the abortion question, the Alvarez–Kazimir
confrontation also raises some critical issues about the
appropriate role of religion in court decisions and the role
of judges' personal religious beliefs and their legal responsibility to uphold the civil and criminal laws of the state.
The contretemps in Florida attracted media attention, but
it is not unique, as a growing number of Christocrats and
their allies are asserting that God's law trumps the civil
authority's legal system. It is one more battle in the campaign to make religious law superior to the state.

Alvarez was reared as a Catholic and was married in
the church. His children were also raised as Catholics,
although the judge no longer is an active member of the
Catholic church. Despite his noninvolvement, Alvarez
told the media that he believes in God and "My Jesus is a
nice guy and not someone to pick up the phone and . . .
punish me."

An Archdiocese of Miami spokeswoman refused to
support Kazimir's demand that Alvarez be refused communion: "The issue of someone receiving communion is
between themselves and God."

But one priest agreed with Kazimir. The Reverend John Pasquini of Tequesta, Florida would refuse Alvarez communion because the judge had permitted an abortion:

> He [Alvarez] put the law above his faith. His [civil] law is not going to save his soul, his faith is going to save his soul. . . . A public figure [like a judge] is influencing a vast majority of people by their stance, and if they were not repentant, for me I would refuse [communion] without a problem.

But John Haas, president of the National Catholic Bioethics Center in Philadelphia, disagreed and entered this view into an intra-Catholic debate that has important implications for the entire nation:

> If [a judge] is merely interpreting points of law, he should be able to proceed and go ahead and do that.

Roger Colton, a Juvenile Court judge in Palm Beach County and a church-going Presbyterian, was even more direct than Haas:

> The bottom line is that we don't make moral decisions, we make legal decisions; and I have made many decisions that were criticized by many, many others. You can't please all the people all the time. We're pledged to uphold and interpret the law.

And Circuit Judge Jorge Labarga, a Catholic, strongly supported Alvarez:

Religion is what we believe in and practice, but we have to do what we're required to do. We take an oath to uphold the law of the state of Florida. How can a judge recuse himself because he can't follow the law he took an oath to uphold? It's just not a legal possibility.

These are things a person needs to consider when making a decision to go on the bench or not. You are going to be asked to do things every day that you don't like.

Clearly, the issue is joined, as Christian conservatives step up their attacks on judges. A major part of that campaign is not only to delegitimize the legal standing of judges, but to impugn their personal religious beliefs and, in the case of Catholic judges and other public officials, to withhold the sacrament of communion, which is at the heart of the Mass.

My own sense is that religiously motivated attacks will increase upon judges who hand down decisions that conflict with the Christocratic agenda. Sadly, Alvarez was not the first target in this campaign, nor will he be the last.

During the same week that Moore was testifying before Congress about his Ten Commandments monument, the Richmond, Virginia–based Council for America's First Freedom released a commissioned survey on public attitudes on the principle of church-state separation, one of the most persistent and vexing issues that comes before judges in the United States and a prime target for Christocrats.

Fifty-two percent of those surveyed consider freedom

of religion the second most important American liberty, surpassed only by freedom of speech. But an almost identical percentage believes the separation of church and state has become too restrictive and severe or is simply not necessary.

Twenty-nine percent of the respondents said "separation is too severe and needs to be less strictly interpreted," while 20 percent of those questioned said "there is really no need to separate church and state" in America.

While Christian conservatives will be encouraged by the figures on church-state separation, the same Council for the First Amendment survey also showed that 83 percent of those polled are opposed to any legislation creating an "official religion" in America. Many fundamentalist Christians seek to legally make the United States into a Christian nation.

A more recent Associated Press–IPSOS poll conducted in May 2005 had an equally conflicting set of findings. The poll surveyed attitudes in the U.S., Mexico, Australia, Britain, Germany, France, Italy, South Korea, and Spain.

An overwhelming number of Americans believe that religion is a key factor in their lives, and almost 40 percent approve of clergy becoming involved in political issues and public-policy questions. But 61 percent believe religious leaders should not intervene in government matters.

But Americans are far more willing to mix politics and religion than most other nations, some of whom have endured internal religious warfare in their history. One of those countries is Mexico. The poll found that Mexicans are highly religious; but, because of their anticlerical history, unlike their northern neighbors, they are wary of religious leaders taking active roles in the political arena.

Professor John Green of the University of Akron, one of America's most astute observers of Christian conservative views, said: "The United States is a much more religious country than other similar countries, looks a lot like what you call developing countries like Mexico, Iran, and Indonesia."

Christocratic leaders can draw comfort from these polls. Clearly, they have been successful in publicly tarnishing the principle of church-state separation, and the AP–IPSOS survey shows that nearly two of five Americans currently believe religion has a major role to play in the shaping of national priorities and public-policy questions. If the Christocrats can attract that large base with the message that America needs to be more "religious" as a nation, they only need to convince another 10 percent of the population to move forward and transform the United States into a Christocratic theocracy. The opportunity is there.

CHAPTER XII

THE NEWSROOM

The red-brick Colonial buildings with the white
Greek-inspired columns on Regent University's
lovely campus in Virginia Beach, Virginia, appear familiar
to most visitors. They should be recognizable, because
such structures are commonplace throughout the Old
Dominion. The architectural designs stem from the classic
seventeenth-century plantation homes that wealthy English settlers built near Richmond along the James River or
erected in Williamsburg, the Virginia colony's first capital
city. In today's Virginia, thousands of government buildings, banks, schools, libraries, churches, supermarkets,
private homes, and even gas stations are modern imita-
tions of those stately houses.

But Regent's traditional architecture is much more than
a collection of "colonial-lite" buildings. The handsome
structures make a political statement about the traditional

beliefs and world view of the University's founder, the Reverend Pat Robertson.

But if visitors to the Regent campus assume that the founder of the Christian Coalition, a leading Christian conservative, was interested only in revering the Colonial history of early America, they would be mistaken.

Robertson's university is no trip down "Nostalgia Lane." It is very much a part of the twenty-first century, and among its features is a modern School of Communications and Arts whose declared mission is to place Christian conservatives in positions of authority and leadership, not only within the religious media, but especially inside the hated "secular" print, electronic, and Internet outlets.

The mission statement of the Regent School of Communications and Arts is clear: "Our . . . program provides a concentrated environment where students may sharpen their professional skills, expand their knowledge and gain a deeper understanding of how to influence the world for Jesus Christ effectively through converged mass media."

Robertson believes graduates of his Christian School of Communication will, over the years, assume important positions of authority in the media that will directly influence the kind of news and entertainment programs Americans will see, read, and hear.

Critics charge that Robertson's goal is a carefully designed campaign of covert religious infiltration that will ultimately convert the general media into Christian faith-based radio and TV stations. Since such a takeover will take years to accomplish, perhaps decades, Robertson also established the Christian Broadcasting

Network (CBN), which provides a constant stream of news programs and inspirational talk shows stressing the evangelical Christian faith. The CBN website specifically urges visitors to contact members of Congress to express support for specific legislation favorable to Christian conservatives. There are also sections on the CBN website marked "Politics" and "Rebuilding Iraq."

Robertson also set up the Family TV Channel some years ago (it was later sold to ABC-TV), but his *700 Club* is carried weekdays on the newly named ABC Family Channel.

The 700 Club is CBN's signature program, starring Robertson as a genial, highly opinionated evangelical talk-show host. The program is seen on over 135 VHF and UHF TV stations throughout the United States, in addition to the ABC Family Channel and Trinity Broadcasting, another evangelical Christian TV network. The *700 Club* is also seen on FamilyNet, the Southern Baptist Convention's TV network.

Not surprisingly, Robertson's *700 Club* projects a well-defined politically conservative agenda, but it also features a weekly "Skinny Wednesday" dieting program with advice for overweight viewers; personal, often tearful, accounts of miraculous medical cures and healing; prayer opportunities; and a constant guest list of religious and political conservatives. The CBN website also has a special section on news from Israel with a conservative political and religious perspective.

Paralleling CBN on a smaller scale is the SBC's FamilyNet, a twenty-four-hour television network that broadcasts more than fifty hours of original programming every week. Headquartered in Fort Worth, Texas,

FamilyNet officials claim a potential audience of 32 million people, but the denominational network lacks the financial resources and the coverage of CBN.

FamilyNet's president, Randy Singer, has made it clear that the Southern Baptist network's primary goal is political: "FamilyNet is a voice for evangelical Christians. It's our goal and our responsibility to help viewers navigate today's most important pro-life issues from a Christian world view." Those issues include the protection of marriage, pro-life initiatives, anti-homosexuality, and the appointment of strict constructionist federal judges.

As might be expected, FamilyNet also features accounts of prayerful recoveries from illnesses and accidents, prayer and biblical studies, Southern Baptist denominational news, a weeknight political program moderated by Janet Parshall, a well-known Christian conservative, *Family Classic Movies*, and reruns of such old TV chestnuts as *The Andy Griffith Show, Annie Oakley, The Beverly Hillbillies, Roy Rogers, I Love Lucy, My Little Margie,* and *The Loretta Young Show*.

Missing from this list are any TV shows about hospitals, police stations, lawyers, criminals, or programs containing sexually explicit situations or language. Don't tune in FamilyNet to see episodes of *Hill Street Blues, ER,* or *The Practice*.

Despite its squeaky-clean programming, FamilyNet has been a perennial money-loser for its sponsor, the Southern Baptist Convention. In September 2004, nineteen of the network's sixty-six employees were let go, and the annual budget was slashed more than half, from $8.5 million to $4 million, a modest figure for a high-tech network. FamilyNet has continued to lose money, and its parent body, the SBC's Mission Board, has made it clear that it cannot continue to subsidize FamilyNet indefinitely. The Board had authorized a $9-million grant over a three-year period.

After watching many hours of both Robertson's CBN and the SBC's FamilyNet, I felt like one of the deep-sea divers afflicted with the bends and other problems when they resurface from a voyage to the bottom of the sea.

The relentless barrage of upbeat positive medical and family news, the many personal testimonies to the healing power of prayers, the constant attacks on the secular society, especially Hollywood, the political cheerleading in support of the Bush administration's domestic and international policies, particularly the war in Iraq, and the relentless recitation of a sharply defined conservative political agenda left me numb and temporarily disoriented when I reentered a religiously pluralistic America that confronts severe challenges from a demanding and restless population that seeks tangible flesh-and-blood answers to a host of pressing problems.

But one thing is clear. A steady diet of FamilyNet and CBN transmits a strong Christocratic view of our nation and the world. A regular viewer hears constant hostility directed against "secularists," "one-worlders," "economic unification and globalization," religiously weak Democrats, the "liberal-leaning" entertainment and media industry, especially PBS and NPR, and evil "anti-capitalists" who hug trees and pose as "environmentalists."

But frequently events in the world outside the bubble of evangelical community life differ greatly from the stated goals of an institution like Regent University or the relentlessly upbeat Christian perspective seen on CBN and FamilyNet.

Mark O'Keefe's lengthy, often tumultuous encounter with the Religious Right and Robertson's Christian Coalition is a classic example of the law of unintended and unanticipated results, and it is a primer on the increasing number of clashes between sincerely held religious beliefs and the professional commitment to uphold ethical journalistic standards.

O'Keefe, a faithful Christian, is a 1987 graduate of Regent University's School of Communication, and is currently the editor of the Washington, D.C.–based Religion News Service (RNS), a subsidiary of Newhouse News Service. The religiously independent RNS, which was founded by the National Conference of Christians and Jews in 1934, is not linked or identified with any spiritual tradition or denomination. Instead, it provides daily hard news about all faith communities to both the religious and general media. I have been a weekly RNS columnist since 1991.

O'Keefe described most of his Regent Communication School classmates as "filled with faith," and convinced that God would take care of everything in their personal and vocational lives. University noon chapel services, at which Robertson would sometimes speak, were held daily.

Many students were "pea-green" and new to the communications field—unlike O'Keefe, who had previous journalistic experience at United Press International before enrolling in the Regent program.

O'Keefe felt that his personal task at the school was to "integrate biblical principles with professional journalism."

However, like many graduate students, O'Keefe found his courses theoretical but satisfying.

After O'Keefe received his Master's degree from Regent University, he became a staff member of the Norfolk *Virginian-Pilot*, a leading newspaper in the Tidewater area of the state, and it was in that capacity as a working reporter that he first encountered the Religious Right.

In 1991, the Virginia Republican party gained control of the state legislature. It was, for many people, a surprising election, and in retrospect it was a harbinger of the 1994 U.S. Congressional races and the Bush victories in the presidential elections of 2000 and 2004, in which Christian conservatives played such a major role in ensuring Republican victories.

But the Virginia election results were not a surprise to O'Keefe. As a Regent student, he had sensed the growing political power of the Religious Right and its attachment to the GOP. Following the Republican sweep, O'Keefe interviewed the new and relatively unknown Executive Director of the Christian Coalition: Ralph Reed. Robertson appointed Reed to that post in 1989, where he served until 1997.

As O'Keefe tells it, when Reed learned his interviewer was a Regent graduate, he immediately assumed O'Keefe was also a supporter of the Christian Coalition. During the interview, and in a now-famous series of remarks, he told O'Keefe:

> I want to be invisible. I do guerrilla warfare. I paint my face and travel at night. . . . You don't know it's over until you're in a body bag. You don't know until election night.

Reed's boastful remarks to O'Keefe were similar to what the Christian Coalition Director had told a *Los Angeles Times* reporter a year and a half earlier:

> What Christians have got to do is take back this country, one precinct at a time, one neighborhood at a time and one state at a time. I honestly believe that in my lifetime, we will see a country once again governed by Christians . . . and Christian values.

When Reed's comments about the 1991 election were printed on the front page of the *Virginian-Pilot*, under O'Keefe's byline, the Christian Coalition leader was furious. His stealth cover blown, Reed accused O'Keefe of using him and harming the cause of the Christian Coalition. But O'Keefe, who tape-recorded the interview, reminded Reed that Christian integrity demanded accurate reporting and maintaining high ethical standards.

In the years following the Reed interview, O'Keefe, the Regent graduate, wrote positive stories about Robertson and his growing empire, as well as hard-hitting pieces about some of Robertson's questionable financial dealings. O'Keefe reported that Robertson's Broadcasting Network not-for-profit ministry had spent $2.8 million on a commercial vitamin and cosmetics company. At the time, Robertson owned 50 percent of the stock. O'Keefe exposed the possible conflict of interest in using ministry money in a commercial profitmaking enterprise.

Robertson was forced to sell off the controversial business for one dollar and then, to make good on the huge loss, he repaid millions of dollars from his own account to offset his ethical breach of fiscal conduct. During the controversy, O'Keefe, a new husband and father, was served with a subpoena and received a series of threats as well as icy stares at the church services he and his wife attended.

Exposing Robertson's financial dealings was a stressful experience, and according to a September 20, 1993 *Washington Post* story by Howard Kurtz, an angry Robertson aide said O'Keefe had "turned from good to evil." O'Keefe said:

> People feel uncomfortable with a fellow Christian raising issues about a major Christian leader, but as a Christian journalist my biggest calling is to pursue truth.

O'Keefe told me that most of his Regent classmates did not remain in the field, and some went into religious work or similar vocations. Regent no longer offers a graduate degree in journalism, but it does offer classes in other aspects of the communications industry.

In recent years, the rapid proliferation of Christian-based radio and television stations has provided Christian conservatives a powerful means for conveying their message about the necessity of reclaiming and Christianizing America. CBN and FamilyNet may be among the best-known Christian media, but biblically centered sermons, a wide variety of church services, religious music, including Christian rock, and the full conservative political agenda are the chief components of hundreds of Christian stations.

Dobson's Focus on the Family is another Christian conservative media empire. His eighty-one-acre campus headquarters in Colorado Springs has a staff over thirteen hundred people, nearly thirty times as large as the SBC FamilyNet operation in Texas.

Dobson has a global audience of more than 200 million people, and he is heard on the radio in nearly one hundred nations. His daily TV program is aired on one hundred stations.

In early 2005, Dobson lashed out at the producers of the popular children's program *SpongeBob SquarePants*. He accused them of teaching tolerance and diversity as a part of a hidden agenda to gain public acceptance for homosexuality.

He did this in a public speech in Washington, D.C., two days before George W. Bush's inauguration. Dobson criticized a new children's video that features the TV character SpongeBob SquarePants and one hundred other popular 'toons. The video, which calls for tolerance and an acceptance of diversity, was created by Neil Rodgers, the composer of the hit song "We Are Family," the title he has given to the video that was being sent for use in sixty-one thousand schools in the United States.

Students are asked to pledge "respect for people whose abilities, beliefs, culture, race, sexual identity, or other characteristics differ from my own."

Dobson jumped on the pledge's call for "respect," and his organization labeled "We Are Family" a pro-homosexual video, even though it does not specifically mention homosexuality. Rodgers quickly responded to Dobson's attack: "Cooperation and unity are the most important values we can teach children. We believe that this is the essential first step to loving thy neighbor."

Because SpongeBob SquarePants, who lives in a

pineapple at the bottom of the ocean, is featured on the video, many of Dobson's critics mistakenly focused on the squishy soft yellow TV character.

But the Religious Right's real target is the video's call for schoolchildren to pledge themselves to tolerance and diversity. Dobson believes Rodgers is attempting to "brainwash" children to accept homosexuality. He perceives "We Are Family" as part of a campaign to indoctrinate youngsters with a "coded language that is regularly used by the homosexual community."

Dobson's attack was another chapter in the ongoing Christocratic battle with the entertainment and media industry.

The criticism of the general media becomes more than verbal when Christocrats move to block the renewal of FCC broadcast licenses for TV and radio stations considered anti-religious or anti-Christian.

The media strategy follows the same path as similar Christian conservative attacks on other major American institutions. As part of the grand Christocratic strategy, even while supporting the full panoply of parallel media outlets, Christian conservatives continue to level harsh criticism against the "secular humanist" media that they intend to either eliminate or control.

First, they constantly denounce the electronic and print media, calling them instruments of "secular humanists," "one-worlders," or "anti-Christianity." At the same time, Christocrats systematically train and develop a cadre of professional journalists, producers, writers, editors, and directors who are encouraged to work within the established media "to influence the world for Jesus Christ. . . ."

Typical of the criticism of the media is the sharply

worded resolution adopted at the 1998 SBC national meeting in Salt Lake City. The Southern Baptist delegates were irate about what they perceived as anti-Christian programming on the part of the Public Broadcasting System (PBS):

> [We] call on Congress to stop the public funding of the Public Broadcasting System for the public funding of religious bigotry. . . . We ask all of our 15.8 million Southern Baptists to contact federal legislators and urge them to stop these outrageous incidents or else to stop public funding of the national Endowment of the Arts [another popular SBC target] and the Public Broadcasting System.

The Christocratic campaign of constant religious attacks on PBS and NPR is apparently paying some important political dividends. In late 2003, Kenneth Y. Tomlinson, a staunch Republican and the former editor-in-chief of the *Reader's Digest*, was elected chairman of the Corporation for Public Broadcasting three years after he joined the CPB board. He believes the public radio and TV networks do not reflect the necessary "tone and balance" in today's America. *Tone* and *balance* are conservative code words indicating that some media personality or institution is too liberal. For Tomlinson, achieving balance means moving to a conservative political and religious position.

The CPB is a private, not-for-profit institution that receives around $400 million each year in federal money to offer a viable alternative to commercial broadcasting. Critics of Tomlinson retort that he has been pushing the public media in a conservative direction that threatens the editorial freedom of both PBS and NPR.

Tomlinson's pet dislike has been Bill Moyers, an ordained Southern Baptist minister, a former aide to President Lyndon Johnson, and the former publisher of *Newsday* on Long Island, New York. Moyers, a popular TV journalist and commentator, has hosted many programs on PBS since the 1970s.

Tomlinson hired someone to monitor three months of Moyers's most current program, *Now* (Moyers has since left the program). Tomlinson asserted that Moyers does not present "anything approaching the balance the law requires for public broadcasting."

Moyers disputed the claim and said, "Tomlinson has waged a surreptitious and relentless campaign against *Now* and me." Critics charge that monitoring Moyers is another example of Tomlinson's efforts to move public media programming to the right.

They believe that Tomlinson, by weakening the independence of public radio and television, is a political stalking horse for Christian conservatives who have historically abhorred PBS and NPR.

As CPB Chair, Tomlinson hired Fred Mann, a researcher, who tracked the political opinions expressed on Moyers's TV program. Mann's rating system included guests who were "anti-Bush," "anti-DeLay," or "liberal." Tomlinson did not notify his board members of Mann's assignment, even though the researcher was paid nearly fifteen thousand dollars by the CPB, which is supported by public funds.

In addition, Tomlinson used a White House official to check the "balance" on various other PBS and NPR programs. Tomlinson was also accused of paying for the services of two GOP lobbyists.

In June 2005, sixteen Democratic senators called on President Bush to remove Tomlinson from his CPB post, but Bush refused to do so. Christocrats have long asserted that both PBS and NPR project a liberal bias reflecting secular humanism. Not surprisingly, Christian conservatives were delighted both with Tomlinson's appointment to head the CPB and his actions since he assumed that post.

Although many observers see the Tomlinson controversy in strictly political terms, Christocrats and their political and religious followers have for years created the climate for attacks on the public media. They have been critical of the programs that air on PBS and NPR, and constantly charge that the programming is skewed toward the liberal secular perspective.

The Christocratic definition of *secular*, a major buzzword of theirs, is broad enough to include any radio or TV program that does not present abortion, gun control, gay rights, evolution, or environmentalism in a negative light either on news programs, children's programming, or talk shows.

PBS and NPR are even charged with being secular when any of their programs or guests raise doubt about the existence of God, miracles, or the world to come.

Indeed, it is easy for Christian conservatives to place the "secular" label on a myriad of issues and media personalities, when one takes into account the findings of a startling and revealing 2003 Harris Poll that surveyed what Americans believe.

Ninety percent told the pollsters that they believe in

God, an extraordinarily high figure for an industrialized society. Eighty-nine percent believe in miracles, 84 percent in the soul's survival after death, and a full 80 percent believe in the resurrection of Jesus. Scoring only three points lower is belief in the virgin birth of Jesus, and 69 percent believe in Hell, 68 percent of those surveyed believe in the devil, 51 percent in ghosts, and 31 percent, nearly one of every three Americans, believes in astrology, and a surprising 22 percent believe in physical reincarnation.

Bob Abernethy is the creator and executive producer of *Religion and Ethics Newsweekly*, the only nationally syndicated PBS religion program. Abernethy, a former NBC-TV correspondent based in Moscow, began the program in September 1997, and it has attracted a growing audience in the years since its debut. I serve as a member of the program's advisory board, and well remember my Washington, D.C., luncheon with Bob in the mid 1990s.

At the time, he was soliciting opinions from many people regarding the need and feasibility of starting a weekly PBS TV program covering religion, all religions, as authentic news stories worthy of the highest journalistic standards.

Like many other people, I encouraged Bob to pursue his proposal, and told him I was weary of seeing religion treated in the media only as a soft feature item; *sermons and songs* was the term I used. Bob agreed that religion in America was hard news and should be approached as such.

Like Religion News Service, *Religion and Ethics Newsweekly* is not linked to any specific faith community, and Abernethy told me that "Our show respects all religions and tries to cover all of them with accuracy and fairness." The program has received major funding from the Lilly Foundation based in Indianapolis. Recently, the show has also received some CPB funding as well.

Abernethy lamented that not one of the major commercial broadcast networks—ABC, CBS, FOX, and NBC—or the cable news outlets—CNN, FOX, and MSNBC—has a full-time religion reporter. "Religion is a good story and it is growing in importance, but it is not being adequately covered by the general media."

Abernethy acknowledges that the media, including his own program, "has become a little more sensitive" to the growing importance of evangelical Christians in both the religious and political life of America. He points out that Christian conservatives believe the "national media, not the local media," is attacking them. As a result, they are "hostile" to the national networks.

Abernethy's distinction is an important one. Evangelicals constantly assert that they are ridiculed and marginalized by the national networks, but they have greater respect for the local radio and TV stations where, they believe, they are better able to make their conservative case and press their agenda.

The founder of the *Religion and Ethics Newsweekly* program is proud of the four-part series he and his staff presented on evangelical Christianity in the spring of 2004. Abernethy feels this group has gained "enormous new influence" in recent years, and he, like every other journalist, sees evangelicals and other Christian conservatives pressing their hot-button issues of posting the Ten Commandments in public buildings, mandating school prayer and bible-reading in public schools, and retaining the words *under God* in the Pledge of Allegiance.

He sees the "slow degradation of public affairs in broadcasting news. Many foreign news bureaus have been closed." But he does not think the Internet and the many blogs will replace the kind of general TV news program he produces each week on *Religion and Ethics Newsweekly.*

Abernethy is keenly aware of the growing influence of Christian conservatives and their demand to shape the media to their theological and political goals. But, like O'Keefe, Abernethy believes the solid "tradition of journalism is still here. . . . It is a noble, ethical thing to do with one's life."

The Christocratic thrust for power in America comes at a time when broadcasting must compete with narrowcasting for viewers and listeners. With well over 150 cable channels to choose from and a seemingly limitless number of blogs or personal commentaries on the Internet, the impact of the traditional broadcast networks is diminishing as their audiences shrink in size.

In their place are radio stations, TV channels, and Internet blogs that are aimed at a specific audience niche: sports of all kinds, pets, cooking, science, comedy, history, rock music, politics, classic movies, opera, dance and symphonic music, programs in languages other than English, and, of course, religion.

Clearly, Christian broadcasters and the televangelists have found their niches, and they intend to increase their audiences from the currently announced number of 141 million potential listeners and viewers.

CHAPTER XIII

THE LIBRARY ROOM

A long with every other major institution in American life, Christocrats have targeted public libraries. The anti–public library campaign is similar to their attacks on public schools.

First, it is necessary to discredit the detested institutions and at the same time demand alternatives to replace them with publicly funded private schools and private libraries that reflect Christocratic "family values" and "mainstream morality."

Second, because Christocrats recognize that there will always be public schools and public libraries in America, their parallel goal is to gain control of these institutions after a continuing campaign of defamation and criticism that includes charges that American schools and libraries foster secular humanism, universalism, and "anti-Christian teaching and reading environments."

Controlling public schools means that local school boards must adopt curricula and teaching materials that meet Christocratic approval. Controlling libraries means gaining operational control of the various groups that authorize the purchase of new acquisitions. The hiring and supervision of library staff is also a key component of library control.

It is a brilliant win-win strategy: Christocrats acquire control of the institutions they have publicly vilified and weakened, while they also gain public funding for their own alternative schools and libraries.

Correctly believing that libraries profoundly influence millions of young people, Christian conservatives first aim to neutralize the libraries' impact on students through a series of carefully planned assault campaigns. They frequently soften their calls for the removal of offending materials by employing a kinder, gentler word: *challenge*.

A *challenge* questions the content or message of a book or other library item. The next step is the call for the removal of "challenged" items that are deemed too "objectionable" to remain in a public library. Offensive material may include printed and audio books, CDs, videos, tapes, newspapers, and magazines.

Especially vulnerable are library materials that present "clear non-conservative positions on the environment, nuclear disarmament, AIDS testing, homosexual rights, and other political issues."

Also under attack are items dealing with human sexuality, abortion, and religions that Christocrats label as anti-Christian like witchcraft and sorcery. Books with an "ultraliberal bias" are also on the Christocrats' removal list.

In addition to demands that certain books be removed or kept from young readers, Christocratic attackers usually demand that they or their supporters screen in advance all planned library acquisitions. This will ensure that new library materials meet the strict requirements of Christian conservative critics.

In today's war, the battle for control of America's public libraries has moved to the U.S. House of Representatives, where conservative Republicans have a working majority.

Representative Walter B. Jones, a GOP House member from North Carolina, has introduced the Parental Empowerment Act, which would require every school district in the United States to establish a committee giving parents the power to select books for public-school libraries.

The American Library Association (ALA) has asserted that Jones's proposed law is not needed. Emily Sheketoff, an ALA official, said: "Libraries . . . are very tied to the community because they're run by the public. They serve the public. You have a librarian who goes to graduate school in library science, and they learn how to choose materials that will reflect the desires of the community. The entire community."

But Jones and other Christian conservatives believe that young readers are being exposed, "brainwashed," to homosexual reading materials and library exhibits on gay themes. Jones said: "I just think this is an effort by the extreme Left to desensitize or brainwash the elementary school children of America. If we're going to maintain the Judeo-Christian principles that this nation was founded on, then we've got to help the parents protect their children."

The ALA sees Jones's bill as a thinly disguised attempt to censor library books. The association is fearful that the bill would cede control to a small group of parents who are strongly committed to a specific religious and political agenda. Sheketoff added: "A small number of parents could hijack the entire process."

In a time of shrinking library budgets across the country, the requirement that future book, CD, video, tape, and magazine purchases must initially pass a Christocratic moral and religious litmus test has had a chilling effect. In some localities, the Christocrats have secured de facto veto power over public libraries' new acquisitions.

Because there are so many libraries in the United States, Christocrats have mounted a series of both wholesale and retail attacks. The former include assaults upon the Chicago-based American Library Association and its policies, while the latter include criticisms of local libraries' choices of books, displays, and exhibits. A key tactic is to force elected officials to withhold or curtail public funding from community libraries that do not reflect or represent Christian conservative values.

Once public library leaders and their staffs have been successfully cowed into submission, the next move is to gain control of these important institutions through majority Christocratic membership on the various boards that exercise authority over acquisitions and the hiring and retaining of personnel.

Of course, useful benign-sounding code words are always necessary to conceal the Christocrats' true intentions and avoid the charge they are engaged in library censorship, something most Americans strongly oppose.

In 1995 in Fairfax County, Virginia, a local organization,

Family Friendly Libraries(FFL), was established. The group's chief adversary was "the American Library Association guidelines and requirements" which, the FFL charged, reflect "a very liberal agenda . . . [that is] deeply involved in politics . . . has considerable influence over the kind of training librarians receive and encourages disrespect for patrons who criticize and provides methods for intimidating them."

FFL asserted that:

> tax-paid librarians must give preferred collection development to LOCAL legal and moral standards rather than those of a private national group [the American Library Association]. . . . Librarians should NOT shirk their responsibilities to the community to protect its children and preserve community standards. . . .

What began as a local northern Virginian citizens group has recently come under the direction of Citizens Concerned for Values (CCV), a group based in Cincinnati. CCV has a broad-based conservative agenda and, on its website, the organization notes that it is "officially associated with Focus on Family as a Family Policy Council in Ohio."

Focus on the Family is one of the nation's largest Christian conservative organizations. The pattern is that FFL, which began as a local group, is now part of a much larger operation, the kind of mergers and acquisitions tactic that is a feature of contemporary corporate America.

At the heart of the ALA's "very liberal agenda" is its

Library Bill of Rights, which was first issued in 1939 to commemorate the 150th anniversary of the Bill of Rights. The current ALA statement has been amended several times since then, the latest in 1996, but the strong original wording has never been weakened.

The Library Bill of Rights, written during the decade of Nazi book-burnings in Germany and Austria, has recently been criticized, as more and more American public libraries come under attack.

It includes these provisions:

> In no case should any book be excluded because of the race or nationality, or the political or religious views of the writer. There should be the fullest practicable provision of materials presenting all points of view concerning the problems and issues of our times. . . . [These materials] should not be proscribed or removed from library shelves because of partisan or doctrinal disapproval. Libraries should challenge censorship in the fulfillment of their responsibility to provide information and enlightenment. . . . Libraries should cooperate with all persons and groups concerned with resisting abridgment of free expression and free access to ideas. . . . A person's right to use a library should not be denied or abridged because of origin, age, background or views.

While the FFL "remain basically opposed to removal of existing library collection materials," that has not been the case with other individuals and groups.

When my two daughters were growing up, they loved to read Judy Blume's books. Her novels were aimed at youngsters, especially girls, who were first confronting their sexuality, and bodily and hormonal changes. In her stories, Blume showed the normality of such changes and the authentic feelings that young people experience.

But in 1984, some Christian conservatives in Peoria, Illinois, were successful in banning Blume's volumes from that city's public library. Her writings were considered indecent and filled with explicit sexual material. Five of Blume's works are on the ALA's list of the "100 Most Frequently Challenged Books."

The ALA defines a "challenge" as "an attempt to remove or restrict materials, based upon the objections of a person or group . . . thereby restricting the access of others." Such challenges are directed to both public school and community libraries. Between 1990 and 2003, the ALA said that there were 581 challenges to remove books from libraries based upon their homosexual content. The Library Association also reported an additional 1508 challenges of books that were perceived as inappropriate for young readers.

The ALA notes that "for each challenge reported there are as many as four or five that go unreported." The number of challenges is increasing each year.

Objections resulting in challenges usually focus, the ALA says, on perceived "sexually explicit material," "offensive language," "violence," "racism," "homosexuality," "occultism," "nudity," or "promoting a religious viewpoint." Of course, Christocrats do not challenge books and other library materials that promote their own religious beliefs.

Joining Blume on the most-challenged list are some well-known books and prize-winning authors, including Mark Twain's *The Adventures of Huckleberry Finn* and *The Adventures of Tom Sawyer*, John Steinbeck's *Of Mice and Men*, Maya Angelou's *I Know Why the Caged Bird Sings*, all of J. K. Rowling's Harry Potter books, J. D. Salinger's *The Catcher in the Rye*, Alice Walker's *The Color Purple*, Madeleine L'Engle's *A Wrinkle in Time*, Stephen King's trio of *Cujo, Carrie*, and *The Dead Zone*, Maurice Sendak's *In the Night Kitchen*, Toni Morrison's *The Bluest Eye*, Aldous Huxley's *Brave New World*, Daniel Keyes's *Flowers for Algernon*, Isabel Allende's *The House of the Spirits*, Kurt Vonnegut's *Slaughterhouse Five*, William Golding's *The Lord of the Flies*, Roald Dahl's *James and the Giant Peach*, Richard Wright's *Native Son*, and Ken Follet's *Pillars of the Earth*.

The American Library Association has also published a list of the "Top Ten Challenged Authors of 2004." Heading that list is Phyllis Reynolds Naylor, author of the Alice series. Close behind are Robert Cormier, who wrote *The Chocolate War*, Blume, and Morrison.

The books currently under the strongest attacks are J. K. Rowling's Harry Potter series. Christian conservative critics charge that her books foster and encourage witchcraft. Pat Robertson, speaking on his *700 Club* TV program, blasted Rowling's hugely successful books and ominously predicted that God will abandon those societies that do not condemn witchcraft:

> what we're doing is asking for the wrath of God to come on this country. . . . We don't need to be bringing in heathen, pagan practices [the Potter series] to the United States of America.

A York, Pennsylvania mother, Deb DiEugenio, was joined
by Pastor Tony Leanza of the New Wine Christian Center
in her appeal to the local school district that the Potter
books be taken out of the local schools. Ms. DiEugenio said:

> [Harry Potter books are] . . . against my daughter's
> constitution, it's evil, it's witchcraft. I'm not
> paying taxes to teach my child witchcraft.

Other anti–Harry Potter attacks took place in Connecticut,
Florida, Kansas, North Dakota, Ohio, Maine, and California. On December 30, 2001, the Reverend Jack Brock of
Alamogordo, New Mexico's Christ Community Church
actually led hundreds of people in what he termed a "holy
bonfire." Copies of the Potter books, and offending CDs,
records, and videotapes were destroyed. Brock called the
Rowling series "a masterpiece of satanic deception."

Brock's actions reminded me of the 1933 bonfire in
Berlin, when the Nazis happily burned books by "degen-
erate" Jewish authors. Heinrich Heine's words from his
1823 tragedy *Almansor* still haunt me: "Wherever they
burn books, they will also, in the end, burn human
beings."

In 1994, *The Adventures of Tom Sawyer* was removed
from the seventh-grade curriculum in West Chester,
Pennsylvania, because parents complained that the
classic is filled with racially explicit language.

The Diary of Anne Frank was challenged in Wise County,
Virginia, in 1982 for sexually offensive passages. A year
later, members of the Alabama State Textbook Committee
rejected the *Diary*, written during the Holocaust, calling it
a "real downer."

The book has also drawn criticism because Anne's teenage writings reflect "religious relativism," especially these famous quotations:

> We all live with the objective of being happy, our lives are all different and yet the same.
>
> It's really a wonder that I haven't dropped all my ideals, because they seem so absurd and impossible to carry out. Yet I keep them, because in spite of everything I still believe that people are really good at heart.
>
> I simply can't build my hopes on a foundation of confusion, misery and death. . . . I think . . . peace and tranquility will return again.
>
> Parents can only give good advice or put them on the right paths, but the final forming of a person's character lies in their own hands.

Not to be outdone by the "ultraliberal" ALA's list of challenged books and authors, another conservative Fairfax County, Virginia, organization Parents Against Bad Books In Schools (PABBIS), created its own website where it listed hundreds of "bad books." Many of the same authors who appear on the ALA's most-challenged list also appeared on the PABBIS lists: Angelou, Walker, Morrison, Blume, and Cormier.

Unlike Family Friendly Libraries, which does not use specific religious language to buttress its positions, PABBIS is quite clear about the source of its agenda and criticism of public libraries. PABBIS accused the Fairfax County School Board of "embracing all religions . . . except for the Christian Faith. . . . Many of these books have anti Christian themes and are blasphemous of Jesus the Lord."

The PABBIS list of objectionable books is a long one, but one title, as a rabbi, especially attracted my attention: *Exodus,* the famous 1958 novel by Leon Uris.

At first, I thought the book's strong pro-Israel perspective might be the cause of the PABBIS discomfort. But I was wrong. Aside from some curse words and sexually explicit paragraphs, the bulk of the *Exodus* criticism was directed at Uris's detailed description of the Nazi death camps during the Holocaust.

The Fairfax Schools had suggested *Exodus* for summer reading by ninth- and tenth-grade students, but PABBIS found the novel highly objectionable. I list only some of the many offending sentences:

> 30,000 dead in Camp 1 . . . 15,000 corpses just littered around. . . . Fathers holding their hands over the eyes of their sons as German pistols went off in the backs of their heads . . . his hobby was throwing infants into the air and seeing how many bullets he could fire into the body before it reached the ground. . . . His wife . . . was also an excellent shot . . . merely clubbed and kicked people to death . . . warehouse of human hair for the manufacture of mattresses! . . . especially finely shaped skull would be preserved as a paperweight! . . . forced them to dig their own graves . . . they stripped them and forced them to kneel beside their own graves and shot them in the head. . . . 33,000 Jews were rounded up and shot over immense pits in a period of 2 days. . . .

> Every morning the streets . . . were strewn with
> new corpses . . . and every known atrocity con-
> ceived by man was committed. . . . Kill the Jew!

Those who challenge Anne Frank's *Diary* and Leon Uris's *Exodus* want to have it both ways. They object to one Holocaust-era book, a real-life diary written by a fright-ened young Jewish girl hiding from the Nazis in Ams-terdam with her family, who still believes "people are really good at heart," an uplifting message. Indeed, Anne Frank offers a strong "pro-family, moral message" urging her readers to retain hope and courage even as she suffers during one of humanity's darkest periods in history.

As every reader of the *Diary* knows, a Dutch Nazi sym-pathizer betrayed the Frank family, and the hiding place was discovered. Anne and her mother and sister were murdered at a Nazi death camp in early 1945, just a few months before World War II ended. Only Otto Frank, Anne's father, survived the Holocaust.

But for some Christian conservatives the words of the Jewish teenager are too relativistic, which I take as a thinly veiled criticism that her strong faith in humanity's goodness was not rooted in Christianity. As a result, Anne's extraordinary optimism in the face of radical evil is objectionable and deemed not appropriate for high-school students. Yet many of the high-school students I have known and taught are frequently searching for a moral model of their own age to emulate. Who better than the youthful and remarkably hopeful author of the *Diary*?

The attack on the Uris novel is the mirror image of the Anne Frank criticism. The late Pope John Paul II termed the past century the "Century of the Shoah" (Hebrew for "Holocaust"). He urged Catholics to undertake intensive educational programs to learn about the horrific Nazi era between 1933 and 1945.

Central to any understanding of the Holocaust is knowledge, an awareness of the radical evil that took place in what the same Pope called "Christian Europe." This is especially critical for the generations of students born after the Holocaust.

Exodus, even with the flaws that are present in any historical novel, is one way students can gain some insight into the Holocaust period. Of course, Uris also tells a love story and describes the sexual encounters of people who are living under extraordinary stress because of the Holocaust or because of Israel's 1948–49 War of Independence.

By reading both Anne Frank and Leon Uris, students will face the moral questions of the dilemma human beings encounter every day of their lives. Are people really good at heart, or is the Holocaust not an aberration, but tragically the way the world really is?

But the *Exodus* example is not unique: on the contrary. PABBIS offers a detailed analysis of many other books that the organization deems objectionable.

In many locations, the attempt to remove challenged and objectionable books from library shelves has failed, but sometimes it is a near miss. In 1991, a Christian conservative group was able to remove five books from the Fort Vancouver, Washington, public libraries. The volumes, not surprisingly, included books dealing with gays and lesbians.

A year later, the same group, Residents Enthusiastic for Quality Education, demanded that the town's public libraries prevent minors from reading Madonna's book *Sex.*

The Fort Vancouver library officials refused, and they reaffirmed their commitment to free access to library materials.

In 1994, the angry opponents of the library's policy inaugurated a campaign to defeat a proposal to build a new library branch. The anti-library forces were narrowly defeated by only four percentage points, 52–48.

In 1993, a Spokane, Washington, group, the Coalition for Better Community Standards, unsuccessfully attempted to have *Sex* removed from that city's libraries. The local library board strongly endorsed the ALA's longstanding policy of open shelves for all library readers and visitors.

In addition to books on library shelves, there has been a long, bitter fight over which textbooks are suitable for use in America's classrooms. The basic issues raised by Christocrats and their supporters are familiar ones: placing intelligent design/creationism texts in science classes, opposing strong pro-environmental textbooks that criticize capitalism, and employing the always-present, always-useful epithets that charge that a textbook is anti-Christian or anti-religious.

As far back as the 1960s, Mel and Norma Gabler of Texas were among the first to recognize the political importance of public school textbook selections:

> Textbooks mold nations because they determine
> how a nation votes, what it becomes, and where
> it goes.

And textbook purchases are a big-ticket item for boards of education in America. The states of Texas and California are America's largest purchasers of classroom texts. As a result, textbook publishers and authors are increasingly under economic and Christocratic pressure to produce acceptable products that will not offend the religious, political, and cultural sensibilities of Christian conservatives.

Some authors and publishers in search of increased sales make preemptive concessions in their textbooks on the Christocratic hot button issues.

Watchdog groups who oppose evolution and "green environmentalism" especially attack school science books. In 2001 a bitter fight in Texas focused on a text that, according to a Christian conservative group, made "discriminatory comments about Christianity and property ownership."

The publisher of *How the World Works* made changes in the text that editorially softened the description of industrial corporations. The Texas board that authorizes textbook purchases accepted the revised version and bought the books.

A few years ago, a high-school economics text had its cover photo of the New York Stock Exchange altered. The male sculptures that are iconic symbols of the NYSE were given a few strips of protective clothing to hide their private parts.

But the challenges to textbook writers and publishers are much more than skin-deep. It is a struggle over the kind of political, scientific, social, cultural, and religious values America's students will receive.

And Christocrats know that if they gain domination of public libraries along with the libraries of public schools, they will decisively control the future education of America's student population. It is one of the major battles that will determine our nation's future for generations to come.

CHAPTER XIV

THE PUBLIC ROOM

Following his decisive military triumph over Napoleon in 1815, the Duke of Wellington said: "The battle of Waterloo was won on the playing fields of Eton."

If he were living in America today, the English Duke would say: "The battle raging in the United States will ultimately be won or lost in the public rooms and on the public squares of America."

Christocrats and their supporters have mounted a series of strong attacks on all significant sectors of our national life. For them, the outcome of the major battle currently under way for control of public space, public buildings, and public rooms will determine victory or defeat.

Today, 82 percent of Americans identify themselves as Christians. While that percentage is slowly dropping, no one doubts that in the decades ahead the overwhelming majority of Americans will continue to call themselves Christians.

However, a Christocratic victory would be a visible sign that America is indeed a Christian nation, not because of the large number of Christians among its citizens, but because of newly adopted state and federal laws. Legislation, not demography, would be the key in converting the United States into a theocratic republic.

There is general agreement that at least fifty of the fifty-five white men who drafted the U.S. Constitution in 1787 were professing or believing Christians. In eleven of the original thirteen states, candidates for public office were required to affirm that they were Christians. Some of those restrictive laws remained in effect until well into the 19th century. Indeed, Maryland did not rescind its infamous "Jew law" until 1826. That law required all public officials to take oaths of office while holding a copy of the New Testament; a statute effectively barring Jews from elective positions within the state.

But that is about all the various groups in the current war agree upon. Everything else about the role of religion in early American history is a matter of heated debate.

Those committed to the principle of church-state separation make the indisputable point that neither Christianity nor Jesus is mentioned in either the Declaration of Independence of 1776 or the Constitution of 1787. They assert that this was no mere oversight or historical accident, but rather that it was a conscious decision to keep specific Christological references and all religious language out of both "creation" documents of the United States.

The spiritual language of "enlightened" men of the Western world living in the Age of Reason during the late eighteenth century was steeped in deism, with a remote God and the belief in the power of rationalism. The Founding Fathers frowned on, and perhaps feared, what they termed the dangers of religious "enthusiasms." Such "enthusiasms," and the collective memory of the Anglican church's persecutions of minority religions in Britain, were a constant warning to prevent similar events in the new nation.

The Founders were also aware of the earlier religious intolerance that was present in the Massachusetts Bay Colony and in other colonies. By 1787, 180 years after the establishment of the Jamestown, Virginia, colony, there were many Christian groups in the United States, along with a small Jewish community. No single church body was dominant in the new republic.

Richard Brookhiser is a politically conservative author and editor who wrote a recent biography of George Washington. Brookhiser told the *New York Times* in February 2005:

> The temperature of a lot of 18th century religion was just a lot lower [than today]. . . . People care passionately about the founders because they want the founders to be like them. . . . Christians and secularists say the founders are like them. . . . They [the founders] couldn't conceive that the country could ever change so much. But, look, if they wanted a Christian state they could have done it. They were writing the rules. They could have put God in the rules.

It is not only God who does not appear "in the rules," but Jesus and Christianity as well. Was it an accident, or a conscious choice, to omit references to Christianity from the founding documents of the new nation? Many American historians believe it was a conscious decision, not an oversight.

But today's Christocrats, led primarily by David Barton, the vice chairman of the Texas Republican party, have a different reading of America's early history than Brookshier and others. Barton has written "the transcendent values of biblical natural law were the foundation of the American Republic. . . ."

To prove his point, Barton provides visitors to the nation's capital specially designed personally guided tours of Washington, D.C.'s public buildings, including the Capitol, that emphasize the Christian origins of the nation. He draws attention to various paintings, sculptures, and writings that have a Christian motif or theme. He calls his efforts "spiritual heritage" tours.

Barton searches for every clue about early American leaders that can bolster his contention that America's Founders were professing Christians and that Christianity and/or "the Judeo-Christian tradition" is the bedrock foundation of the United States, and that it must be legally reclaimed.

Any early historical reference to the bible, God, Divine Providence (Washington's favorite religious term), the Ten Commandments, Almighty Being, Christianity, the Gospel, Supreme Being, and Savior becomes evidence in Barton's ongoing campaign to prove his central assertion.

But even Brookshier and other conservatives remain

unconvinced by Barton. They charge that he is using twenty-first-century religious ideology, vocabulary, and belief to describe and explain the men who gathered in Philadelphia in 1776, and then again in 1787, to draft the Declaration of Independence and the Constitution. Historians also charge that it is necessary to probe more deeply into what certain specific religious terms meant back then, rather than employing the definitions currently in vogue in our religiously saturated society.

But Barton goes further than simply searching for overt or covert Christian references in the writings of Washington, Jefferson, Franklin, Madison, and the other founders. He has written that America is a republic founded upon Christian principles, and is not a democracy. Barton has amassed an array of quotations of early American political leaders that specifically refer to biblical/ religious precepts as foundation stones of the new republic.

Barton's supporters frequently cite these words from Washington's first Inaugural Address:

> The propitious smiles of heaven cannot be expected in a nation that disregards the eternal rules of order and right, when heaven itself has ordained.

Patrick Henry, Jefferson's arch political foe in Virginia, is also quoted:

> It cannot be emphasized too strongly or too often that this great nation was founded not by religionists, but by Christians, not on religions, but on the gospel of Jesus Christ.

Emma Willard (1787–1870), a champion of women's education in the United States, was the most explicit:

> We [the U.S.] were born a Protestant Christian nation, and, as such, baptized in blood. Our position ought to be defined as that.

But others challenge Barton's assertions. Forrest McDonald, a conservative historian at the University of Alabama, said:

> Just because the founders were a Christian nation and just because they expected it to be a Christian nation doesn't tell us anything about what we should do today.

Susan Jacoby, author of *Freethinkers: A History of Secularism,* has also collected an equally impressive number of facts and quotations from the nation's early leaders indicating their antipathy to the establishment of any state religion in America. She also shows that the omission of Christological/religious language from the Constitution was clearly noted and vigorously debated as the thirteen states voted up or down on the newly written document.

One particular provision of the Constitution was a source of concern for a North Carolina Protestant minister. Article Six, Section Three reads:

> The Senators and Representatives before mentioned, and the Members of the several State Legislatures, and all executive and judicial Officers, both of the United States and of the several States,

shall be bound by Oath or Affirmation, to support this Constitution; but no religious test shall ever be required as a Qualification to any Office or public Trust under the United States.

The North Carolina clergyman was certain that this Constitutional provision—"no religious test"—was "an invitation for Jews and pagans of every kind to come among us."

Further north in Massachusetts, the same Article caused one prominent Bay State leader to warn:

A Turk [Muslim], a Jew, a Roman Catholic, and what is worse than all, a Universalist, may be President of the United States.

But as Jacoby notes "the omission of God elicited the most inflamed rhetoric." A New York minister, John M. Mason, said that not mentioning God in the Constitution was

An omission which no pretext whatever can palliate. . . . We have every reason to tremble, lest the Governor of the universe . . . overturn from its foundation the fabric we have been rearing, and crush us to atoms in the wreck.

It is clear that the omission of religious language, and especially the lack of any Christian references, was widely noticed and hotly debated during the Constitution's ratification process. The absence of such terminology was neither an oversight nor an accident.

However, after reading both Barton and Jacoby, there is little doubt that the argument will continue unabated, with the Christocrats pressing the case that the United States was founded as a Christian nation.

The issue flared up in 1992 when Mississippi Governor Kirk Fordice declared that the United States is a "Christian nation." He made his remarks during a meeting of Republican leaders following Bill Clinton's victory over George H. W. Bush in that year's presidential election. Fordice created a firestorm of criticism, as well as eliciting support from Christian conservatives.

In 2004, the Texas Republican party's state convention adopted a platform plank affirming the position of Barton, the party's vice chairman:

> That the United States of America is a Christian nation, and the public acknowledgement of God is undeniable in our history. Our nation was founded on fundamental Judeo-Christian principles based on the Holy bible.

The Texas GOP platform also spoke of "the myth of the separation of church and state."

Despite public protests from Christians, Jews, and Muslims, no one in the national Republican party, including President Bush, repudiated the action of the Texas Republicans.

However, the core questions in the current war remain: Will the United States become a Christian nation, as Christocrats demand, because most of its founders in the late eighteenth century were Christians? Or will America continue as it has and remain a nation guaranteeing full religious freedom for all faith communities, even though more than four of five of today's Americans identify as Christians?

Christocrats are aware that they cannot yet place the cross, the crown of Jesus, or other specific Christian symbols in America's public rooms. However, as a first step, they have focused their energies on the Ten Commandments as an opening wedge in the battle to baptize America.

Many Christocrats believe that the Ten Commandments, as found in the biblical books of Exodus and Deuteronomy, constitute the legal and moral foundation of a Christian nation. Because of the Commandments' importance among Christian conservatives, they have actively engaged in a campaign to display the Scriptural passages in many public spaces throughout the country, especially courtrooms and public-school classrooms.

In addition to the current campaign of displaying the Ten Commandments in high-profile public rooms, in 1956 the famed film director Cecil B. deMille cooperated with the Fraternal Order of Eagles in providing thousands of Ten Commandments monuments and markers, which were placed in parks and other public property throughout the United States. It was part of a publicity campaign to promote deMille's cinematic epic of the same name. As a result, the Ten Commandments today appear in many public spaces.

One of deMille's granite monuments, on the grounds of the Texas state capitol in Austin, was the centerpiece of a legal case that eventually reached the Supreme Court. It was charged that the presence of the Ten Commandments on state property was a violation of the principle of church-state separation. At the same time, there was a similar legal challenge to the posting of framed copies of the Decalogue in two Kentucky courthouses.

The Supreme Court handed down two five to four decisions on the same day in late June 2005. The High Court
ruled that the recent posting of the Ten Commandments in
the Kentucky case was unconstitutional, while the decades-
old monument in Texas was permitted. The murky opinions indicated that the Court would allow religious
symbols to remain if they have been in existence for many
years and if those symbols are part of a larger display of
public monuments, as was the case in Austin. (The display
of the Ten Commandments in Texas is one of thirty-eight
markers and monuments on the capitol grounds.)

However, newly placed or mounted religious symbols
are illegal, especially if they were installed for clearly religious purposes and stand alone. That was the view of the
five Justices in the Kentucky case.

Two dissents reveal the deep feelings such cases engender
among the Supreme Court Justices. John Paul Stevens was
opposed to both displays of the Ten Commandments and
wrote that the Decalogue is clearly religious in content and
its presence on public property signals that the "state
endorses the divine code of the Judeo-Christian God."

Not surprisingly, Antonin Scalia was in favor of the two
displays, and in his dissent in the Kentucky case wrote:

> Nothing stands behind the court's assertion that
> governmental affirmation of the society's belief
> in God is unconstitutional except the court's
> own say-so.

But Justice Sandra Day O'Connor, in rendering her last
Supreme Court opinion, put the questions in the sharpest
possible terms:

Those who would renegotiate the boundaries
between church and state must therefore answer
a difficult question: why we would we trade a
system that has served us so well for one that
has served others so poorly?

Why indeed?

The Court's split decision did not satisfy either those
who support church-state separation or Christian conservatives. The Reverend Barry Lynn, executive director of
Americans United for the Separation of Church and State,
felt "our hand was strengthened [by the Supreme Court
decisions], but we are not planning to go and launch a
vast new set of lawsuits." Lynn wants to concentrate on
the battles within the U.S. Congress.

But angry Christocrats vowed to place a hundred more
monuments in cities throughout America, while most
public officials recognize that such efforts will not be
legally permitted as a result of the Kentucky decision.

Dobson, the head of Focus on the Family, lashed out at
the Court's decisions:

People in churches across America had better get
busy and demand the right kind of appointments to this court. There is no bigger issue on
the Christian agenda.

Predictably, Ernest Istook, a Republican representative
from Oklahoma, reintroduced his proposed Constitutional amendment that would permit displays of the Ten
Commandments in public spaces and areas, as well as
mandating prayer in public schools and also guaranteeing

that the words "under God" continue to be part of the Pledge of Allegiance. Previous efforts by Istook to move his amendment forward have been unsuccessful.

Over 70 percent of Americans polled in 2004 by the Pew Forum on Religion and Public Life are in favor of displaying the Ten Commandments in public places, but at the same time a 2005 Associated Press-IPSOS poll revealed that 61 percent of Americans do not believe religious leaders should influence public policy questions or governmental decisions.

A day after the two decisions on the Ten Commandments, the Supreme Court let stand a lower court's ruling that the Great Falls, South Carolina city council could not keep the name Jesus Christ in the prayers that open its meetings.

The decision ended a four-year battle between a local Wicca witch and a Great Falls lawyer who represented the city council. Great Falls has a population of twenty-two hundred people, but the case has national implications because the Fourth Circuit Court struck down the Christological reference, calling it unconstitutional since such government-sponsored prayers are an official affirmation, a clear favoring of one specific religion, in this case Christianity. The circuit court ruling applies to South and North Carolina, Maryland, Virginia, and West Virginia. While governmental officials or agencies in other areas of the country were not directly involved in the Great Falls case, the decision has created a legal precedent to ban such overt religious language from official meetings, hearings, sessions, and other governmental functions.

Texas figured prominently in another example of the Christian conservatives' campaign to eat away at and ultimately eliminate the separation of church and state. In early June 2005, Rick Perry, the Republican governor of the Lone Star State, signed two bills in a Fort Worth evangelical school that would ban same-sex marriages and weaken abortion rights.

One bill requires women who seek an abortion and are less than eighteen years of age to gain parental permission before the procedure can take place. Previously, it was only necessary for a minor to inform her parents. The second bill called for a statewide vote on same-sex marriages.

The governor signed both pieces of legislation in the gymnasium of the Calvary Christian Academy, and not in the school's chapel where religious services are held. But Perry's actions drew protestors who demonstrated outside the academy as well as cheering supporters inside the building.

Robin Lovin, a Methodist minister and a professor at nearby Southern Methodist University in Dallas, denounced Perry's action. He said:

> There are lots of reasons to go to church on Sunday, but making laws isn't one of them. . . . [Perry's action] is a pretty clear symbol that the church is at the service of the state or the state is at the service of the church, and either way we've crossed an important line that has a long history in both politics and theology.

Christocrats consistently link their religious tenets with their belief that God has ordained the United States for a sacred destiny among the family of nations. Put another way, they believe the Christian Cross and the American

Eagle are both instruments of God, linked together for a special unique task.

The merging or conflation of church and state is particularly evident on the Fourth of July in a growing number of Southern Baptist churches.

One SBC church in Euless, Texas, actually spends more money on its Independence Day services, a national holiday, than it does for Christmas or Easter, Christian religious holy days. The services, called "God and Country Day," attract more people than the usual worship services.

In 2004, a group of U.S. soldiers rappelled into the Euless Baptist sanctuary while uniformed church members appeared with rifles and military helmets. There was also a fireworks show inside the church. The congregation's music director said "It's just a big patriotic, feel-good moment."

But critics, including Christian scholars and leaders, condemned such church-state linkages within a sanctuary. Brent Walker, the executive director of the Baptist Joint Committee in Washington, D.C., said:

> We have obligations to Christ and Caesar. They're both appropriate and good things, but they're not the same things.

John Green, of the Pew Forum on Religion and Public Life, said:

> Many conservative Americans believe America has a special role . . . a product of providence. . . . [They] honor America with effusive celebrations that do identify American foreign policy with

doing the sorts of things that God would like accomplished.

In Ashland, Kentucky, members of the First Methodist Church perform *America: A Pilgrim's Prayer, A Patriot's Dream*, a musical that celebrates religion's role in early American history. The annual performance, including an explosion of confetti inside the sanctuary, takes place on the Sunday nearest to the Fourth of July, and the attendance is four times the normal service.

The church's music director, Margaret Vance, said:

> I'm a real flag waver. I think the proper people need to be thanked for our freedoms . . . [the principle of church-state separation is] a bunch of hooey.

CHAPTER XV

THE WORKROOM

David C. Gibbs, Jr., the president of the Christian Law Association, has written that the workrooms of America "provide an obvious venue for sharing the Gospel."

The statistics are indeed "obvious" and inviting for Christocrats, because millions of full-time employees in the United States work 8.3 hours each day, more time than they devote to sleeping or to another any other daily activity. Well over 90 percent of Americans consistently tell pollsters that they believe in God, and 48 percent told the Gallup Poll that they talk about their religious faith nearly every workday. Clearly, the workforce is a ready-made "congregation" ripe for Christian activists.

Employees are similar to public-school students, because both groups are required to be present in either a workplace or a required assembly program. Workers must earn a living for themselves and their families, and state laws require youngsters to attend school. Both captive audiences are attractive targets for Christian missionaries.

As in the other rooms of the American national mansion, Christian conservatives are conducting multiple campaigns as they seek to convert America into a Christian nation.

The first public campaign is an effort to make certain that the civil rights of Christian workers are fully respected in the workplace. In this endeavor, Christocrats have been joined by a host of other religious communities—Catholic, mainline Protestant, Jewish, Islamic, and Hindu—in guaranteeing the religious rights of employees.

Such protection is provided in Title VII of the 1964 Civil Rights legislation and President Bill Clinton's 1997 "Guidelines on Religious Exercise and Religious Expression in the Federal Workplace." The eleven pages of single spaced Guidelines go into minute detail describing what is and what is not permitted within U.S. Government workrooms.

Employees "may keep a bible or Koran" on their desks and "read it during breaks." But all religious posters "must be displayed facing the employee." These are usually pictures of Jesus, various saints, rabbis, gurus, and other spiritual figures. Workers are "permitted to engage in religious expression . . . that is reasonable and . . . does not interfere with workplace efficiency."

The Guidelines cover coffee breaks, behavior at parking lots and "areas accessible to the public," including courtrooms. While there can be no "impression that the government is sponsoring, endorsing, or inhibiting religion. . . . Employees may wear religious jewelry."

Questions centering on the free expression of religion, including the wearing of distinctive clothing—skullcaps, turbans, and other religious garb—permitting government employees to have beards, the complex question of proselytizing, providing for holiday observances and prohibiting religious bigotry within the government were all addressed in the Guidelines.

Supervisors cannot require or coerce employees to attend prayer sessions or bible classes. And, of course, religious discrimination is not permitted in the hiring or promotion of federal employees. While religious speech and "proselytizing" are "entitled to the same constitutional protection as any other form of speech," there are limits, safeguards, and protection built into the federal Guidelines to protect workers from aggressive conversion efforts.

One of President Clinton's goals in 1997 was to prevent a religious war breaking out among federal employees within government workplaces that include post offices, national parks, airport security areas, and many other locations.

Rabbi David Saperstein, the director of the Religious Action Center of Reform Judaism in Washington, D.C., spoke for many faith communities when he praised the president's efforts:

> These guidelines provide vital protections for
> the religious freedom of federal employees
> in a manner that is fair and equitable to everyone

in the workplace: the religious worker, his or her co-workers, and his or her supervisor. This is vitally important particularly for those employees of minority religious groups whose rights are often restricted within the culture of the workplace.

Since 1997, the courts have interpreted both Title VII and the Guidelines in a narrow way, especially the provision in the 1964 law that there must be a reasonable accommodation of workers' religious practices, unless doing so would create undue hardship. Courts have defined *undue hardship* as even a slight or *de minimus* expense or inconvenience to the government.

Religious groups have objected to this grudging judicial reading of the law. In March 2005, the Workplace Religious Freedom Act was reintroduced in the U.S. Senate and the House with bipartisan support. The Act is an attempt to provide relief for employees who are religiously observant while making sure such observances do not impinge upon the rights of other workers.

But there is a second campaign currently under way, focused on the workplace, led by Gibbs and other Christocratic leaders who share his views. Certainly there can be no objection to encouraging workers in both the public and private sectors who are Christian to exhibit the highest form of "Christ-like" ethics on the job, including honesty, integrity, fairness, and compassion. That kind of behavior is expected from members of all religious groups.

But in today's America those ideals are not sufficient for Christocrats and their supporters. They want to use the workplace to convert people to evangelical Christianity and to move America's economy away from any traces of either socialism or capitalism. Their aim is to convert both people to a strict form of Christianity and the economic system to a system called "Kingdom economics."

One Christian leader who advocates both types of conversion is the Reverend Dennis Peacocke who heads Strategic Christian Services in Santa Rosa, California. He goes even further than Gibbs in sensing fertile ground for Christianizing the nation's workplace and economy:

> We are now standing at the foundation-laying stage of one of the most significant Christian movements of church history, the advocacy of a Christian values-based economy. . . . It has the clear potential of radically redefining historic economic theory. . . . Believers must do more than simply legitimize personal ministry [a term frequently used to describe conversion efforts aimed at fellow workers] in the marketplace. . . . The marketplace and Christian economics will lead to the world's largest evangelistic harvest in the 21st century.

Peacocke wants to cast aside both capitalism and socialism and replace them with Kingdom economics. Socialism and "Satan . . . offer man a false and unattainable security," while capitalism is "destructive" with its "driving concepts of 'opportunity,' 'gain' . . . [that] have produced some highly undesirable systemic results."

Peacocke's description of a Christian-based economy contains many "feel-good" words, but is short on specifics:

> Gift discovery and development; character for-
> mation; power and resource sharing . . . relation-
> ally driven organizations; investment banking . . .
> rather than usurious interest-driven banking;
> resource-backed currencies. . . .

However, in such a Christian economy, the bible, Old Testament law, must be the ultimate source of authority.
Peacocke is clear on this point:

> Kingdom economics . . . is driven by obedience
> to God. . . . Technology and globalization are
> filled with a myriad of evil potentialities, they
> can be used . . . to spread God's Kingdom to the
> marketplace and Kingdom economic practices
> and policies.

For Peacocke, workers must do much more than

> simply legitimize personal ministry [conversion
> efforts] in the marketplace. Only doing that will
> serve to "baptize" either capitalism or socialism
> . . . because we have failed to confront either
> alternative from a biblical point of view [Old
> Testament law].

There is more than a whiff of Christian Reconstructionism
and Dominionism in Peacocke's economic scheme. By
demolishing both capitalism and socialism, he is following
the game plans laid out by earlier Christocratic leaders,
including Reconstructionism's founder, John Rushdoony.
He demanded the dismantling of the American republic and

its replacement by a United States that is governed solely by Old Testament law. Transforming the workplace to a Christocratic model is an imperative if the new Christian America is to succeed.

Many observers of the current American scene miss a critical point. Christian conservatives, especially those committed to Dominionism and Rushdoony's Recon, are interested in both individual conversions and a total societal change that includes the imposition of Kingdom economics. It is a mistake to assume that Christocrats will be content with controlling American society while the economy remains firmly in the capitalist camp; a Christocratic America requires the abolition of capitalism.

Peacocke's organization, Strategic Christian Services (SCS), is one of many Christian conservative organizations that focus on transforming America into a faith-based nation driven by Kingdom economics. SCS's special mission is to help "leaders apply biblical truth to businesses, churches, and culture."

In addition to SCS, there are forty-nine other Christian workplace ministries in the U.S. and Canada. Some of them are Christian professional affinity groups of evangelical physicians, dentists, nurses, engineers, and professors.

Many of the organizations simply urge Christian employees in the workplace to follow an ethical code and act as a role model that will attract others to the evangelical faith. That is a passive form of witnessing to the Christian faith.

However, several of the forty-nine organizations are like the International Coalition of Workplace Ministries (ICWM) in that they specifically focus on transforming "your workplace for Jesus Christ" and offer "resources, information and networking . . . that will help you fulfill your calling in the workplace."

The Reverend Jon Cook, one of the leaders of another group, the Fellowship of Companies for Christ International (FCCI), has described the workplace in vivid bellicose terms:

> The secular vocations of Christians are a war zone. There are spiritual adversaries to be defeated (that is, evil spirits and sins, not people). . . . Now is the time to be encouraging and equipping our workplace leaders to fight the spiritual battle in the workplace. . . . Secular work is not a waste when we make much of Christ from 8 to 5. . . .

The federal guidelines addressed the religious issues within the government workplace, but there are no such rules, regulations, or policies that apply to the private sector. Each company or firm is fair game for zealous religionists, most of whom are Christian conservatives.

Many of the forty-nine organizations described above offer Corporate America spiritual conferences, prayer breakfasts and lunches, bible-study classes, employee retreats, books, CDs, videos, and motivational speakers (a.k.a. missionaries), all dealing with such themes as "Getting Your Bottom Line Right with Christ," "What Would Jesus Do?," "The Executives' Inner Quest for Self," and "Believers in Business."

A 1999 *Business Week* article reported that there were ten thousand bible and prayer groups in U.S. workplaces, and at least thirty conferences on spirituality. The magazine noted there was only one such conference in 1994. There are many more today.

Some top officers of well-known corporations participate regularly in "Vision Quests" and "Marketplace Ministries." In addition, an increasing number of companies are hiring "corporate chaplains" to address the religious and emotional needs of their employees.

Of course, this being America, there is an organization specializing in this unique kind of evangelization. Corporate Chaplains of America, which:

> Provides genuine "Caring in the Workplace" through its workforce of "certified Workplace chaplains . . . [who] build relationships with employees through chaplains with the hope of gaining permission to share the good news of Jesus Christ in a non-threatening manner.

In almost every case, corporate chaplains are evangelical Christians who visit assembly lines, offices, shops, malls, and stores. While they bring personal spiritual balm to Christian conservative employees, many corporate chaplains also conduct prayer sessions and bible classes that are approved, and often sponsored, by management. A *Fortune* magazine study in 2001 reported that at least 230 American companies have staff chaplains for their employees.

David Roth, who directs an organization called WorkMatters, admits his visits to various workrooms are "very explicitly Christian." Roth senses a greater spiritual hunger among workers since the 9/11 terrorist attacks and the gross ethical violations of Enron, Tyco, Adelphia, WorldCom, and other such companies. "My market is unlimited," Roth said.

But Harold Burke-Sivers, a Benedictine oblate and a member of the Catholic Society of Evangelists, has written:

> It's not easy being a Christian in the workplace. Secular ideology is so pervasive in the professional environment that we often have a difficult time fitting into the culture of the office. Many of us simply "go with the flow."

He wants committed Christians in the workplace to actively and vigorously defend "the absolute truth of Christianity and the moral certitude of the distinctly Christian vision."

MSNBC has reported that a few large companies are overtly religious. These include ServiceMaster Co. and its subsidiaries Terminix and TruGreen ChemLawn. CFA Properties closes its Chick-Fil-A restaurants on Sundays even though it loses business each week to McDonald's, Burger King, and other fast-food chains.

By bringing God and especially Jesus into the workplace, Christocrats face the serious risk of first angering Catholics, Jews, Muslims, Hindus, American Indians, Buddhists, Wiccans, and others, and then encouraging them to also demand their own particular "ministries" for workers.

Will the marketplace, the workrooms, offices, and factories of America become a competitive missionary war zone, filled with tracts, pamphlets, CDs, and one-on-one conversion assaults on "non-believers"? Despite the claims that spirituality on the job increases efficiency, a religious combat zone will result in a large number of emotional and spiritual casualties. Productivity will decrease and there will be a plethora of lawsuits charging harassment and the violation of workers' civil rights.

Up to now, evangelicals have been the most aggressive religious group in bringing their specific message to the nation's workrooms. But they do not have a monopoly on either faith or spirited men and women of other religions who will also proselytize.

And in addition to adherents of traditional religions, there is little doubt that representatives of dangerous religious cults and Satanism will also be inspired to seek converts in the workplace.

The Federal Equal Employment Opportunity Commission reports that it is receiving an increasing number of religious-bias and harassment cases. The 2004 figures indicate that complaints have jumped 27 percent in five years and 40 percent during the decade from 1994 to 2004.

Once, the "American public square" was more than a figure of speech. Historically, it was the physical area in a community where opinions, ideas, debates, alliances, and conflicts were played out for all to see and hear. Today, the true "public square" has moved indoors to the proverbial water cooler, copying machine, company cafeteria, and executive dining room.

America has not yet set mutually agreed-upon limits and parameters for religious discussions on the job. Until and unless that happens, Christocrats will continue to exploit the workshop; and we already see the tensions they have created.

Working in today's America with the profound fear of corporate mergers, takeovers, and bankruptcies places great strain on workers. The recent corporate scandals have shaken public confidence in corporate America.

Religious solace is desperately needed by executives and secretaries alike; but in a religiously diverse nation, there are ample—indeed, abundant—resources, both human and physical, to meet such pressing needs. Those resources are called churches, synagogues, temples, mosques, and meeting houses.

But making the private sector workplace a missionary and proselytizing free zone is not happening in America. Pam Carlson, president of ROC Carbon Company in Houston, Texas, has said:

> Thinking that Christ should not be brought into the workplace is heresy, heresy of the worst kind.

The announced purpose of Christian workplace programs is to provide for the religious needs of a company's employees. But I have observed many workplace prayer sessions and bible-study classes, and it is clear that the true goals are something else: gaining converts to evangelical Christianity and "Christianizing" America's businesses so they become commercial extensions of theologically conservative churches.

Louis Maltby is president of the National Workrights Institute. The Institute, based in Princeton, New Jersey, was established in 1988 and is an offshoot of the American Civil Liberties Union (ACLU). Maltby is concerned that companies frequently hide their religious programming from the general public. Maltby notes that "The law in this area [religion in the workplace] is not very good. The law doesn't generally recognize the subtle coercion that goes on" in corporate America.

Maltby adds:

If your boss held a prayer breakfast and you were fired for refusing to go, you've got a case under Title VII [of the 1964 Civil Rights Act]. If your boss holds a prayer breakfast and you go because you're afraid to stay away, you probably don't have a case.

Unlike the federal guidelines, there is no standard religious regulation or oversight in private industry. Everyone agrees that there is no possibility Congress or President Bush will push for any legislation that would limit the "free exercise of religion"—that is, missionizing in the workplace. It remains a chaotic situation filled with ambiguity, tension, and confusion.

Cardone Automotive Manufacturing in Philadelphia has Paul Spuler, Jr. on its payroll as a "vice president for spiritual life." "My passion is to see as much prayer as possible get integrated into this business," said Spuler, a former Assemblies of God pastor.

Larry Ihle of Dexterity Dental Arts in Farmington, Minnesota, said many non-Christian employees have converted to fundamentalist Christianity. Ihle said vendors and suppliers are receptive to prayers for their well-being.

Employers frequently cross the line. In 2004, a federal court jury in Indianapolis awarded $270,000 in damages to six Catholics and a Unitarian who charged that they were victims of religious discrimination. They successfully claimed that their employer, Preferred Management Corporation, required them to conform to the evangelical owner's beliefs. They also said that under-performing employees had to pray with managers as a means of improving their on-the-job efficiency. The judge in the case issued a stay on the judgment pending an appeal.

The pressure on employees to accept their bosses' invitations to attend such "voluntary" events can be intense, especially in times of high unemployment, layoffs, and fear of losing one's job. As a result, many civil-rights organizations and religious communities regularly receive complaints from employees who feel unduly pressured to attend corporate-sponsored religious meetings.

Anxiety and stress are likely to increase in the workplace as the Christocratic campaign intensifies. The already-blurry lines between the legitimate religious concerns of employees in a fiercely competitive economic environment and the aggressive Christian conversion campaigns aimed at workers make it harder for company executives to sort out what is actually happening in their workrooms.

The *Fortune* article described why much of the business world remains ambivalent to the growing inroads of religion into the workplace:

> As much as Americans say they believe in God, most also believe in religious freedom, and hence in the separation of church and the boardroom. And considering all the crimes committed in the name of one god or another, it's only natural to imagine zealous executives doing more harm than good. So while the business world has found ways to talk about race, gender equity, sexuality, disability, and even mental illness, religion has remained the last taboo.

Taboo or no, the Christocrats have targeted the workplace in their escalating campaign to baptize America.

INDEX

Mahoney, Patrick, 227
mainline Protestants and Protestantism
  biblical interpretation, 155–56
  Christian conservatives among, 7
  Christocrats among, 11
  church-state separation support, 115
  criticism of Israeli policies, 113–14, 120
  dominance, 1900s–1970s, 150
  embryonic stem-cell research support, 224–25
  on evangelical support of Israel, 117–18
  evangelicals and, 87–88, 92–93
  Jews and, 107, 114
  Palestinians and, 117
  as threat to core evangelical beliefs, 4
  as "unchurched" in U.S. military, 203
Maltby, Louis, 312–13
Mann, Fred, 263
Mao Tse-tung, 54–55
Marburger, John H., 190
Marty, Martin E., 92
Maryland, 286
Mason, John M., 291
McDonald, Forrest, 290
McGurn, William, 29
McVeigh, Timothy, 52
media
  Abernethy's unbiased PBS program, 265–67
  Associated Press–IPSOS poll, 248, 296
  Christocratic agenda for, 14–15, 252–53, 255, 259–62, 267
  Christocratic attack on public broadcasting services, 262–64
  lack of "hard" reporting on religion, 265, 266
Meese, Edwin, 236
Mexico, 248
Microsoft, 168–69
military academies in Christocracy, 16–17
military interreligious cooperation, 129
Miller, Kenneth R., 189
Mishnah, 216
Mississippi, 221
Missouri politics, 165
Mohler, Al, 243
Moore, Roy, 240–41
Moral Majority, 66–69, 115, 116–17
Mormons, as "unchurched" in U.S. military, 203
Morton, MeLinda, 197
Mosner, Bob, 58

motion picture censorship in Christocracy, 15
Moyers, Bill, 90, 263
MSNBC, 310
Muslim fundamentalists, 5

National Association of Evangelicals (NAE), 111–12
National Council of Churches (NCC), 89, 91, 96, 115, 116–17
National Council on Bible Curriculum, 175–76
national identification card in Christocracy, 18–19
National Public Radio (NPR), 262–64
national security and biblical principles equated, 166
National Workrights Institute, 312–13
Nazis. See Holocaust
NCC (National Council of Churches), 89, 91, 96, 115, 116–17
new American Civil War. See also Christocratic agenda
  battle against libraries, 272
  Christocratic politics and, 72–73
  Christocratic war against government, 65–67
  Dominionists against secular humanists, 59–60
  Parsley's righteous war, 12–13
  same-sex marriage issue, 158 (See also homosexuality)
  in the workplace, 308, 310–11
New Deal policies as anathema to Christocrats, 236
New Interpreters' Bible, 156, 163–64
The New Millennium (Robertson), 44
New Testament, 151–53
New York, Christocratic agenda in, 186–87
New York State Task Force on Life and The Law, 228–31
New York Times, 60–61, 147, 200–201
news media. See media
Niebuhr, Reinhold, 87
Nixon, Richard, 57
No Child Left Behind and I.D. in schools, 185
Nostra Aetate declaration, 107
Now (Moyers's PBS program), 263
NPR (National Public Radio), 262–64

O'Connor, Sandra Day, 294–95
Odessa, Texas, 176
O'Keefe, Mark, 256–59
Oklahoma City bombing, 43–44, 52
Olasky, Marvin, 51
Old Testament. See Hebrew Bible
On Public Discourse and the Free Exercise of Religion (SBC resolution), 97